May read[...]
richly bless you
you courage and hope.

It All Comes Out in the Wash

A Squeaky Clean Memoir

MAY DILLES

WESTBOW®
PRESS
A DIVISION OF THOMAS NELSON
& ZONDERVAN

Introduction

FOR MANY YEARS I KNEW that someday I would write a book about my husband Caleb's and my mishaps and adventures together. We are just not "normal" people. That is, if there truly is a "normal." It's all a matter of perspective, really, and it's all relative. A Theory of Relativity is not just for science nerds. It's for *all* of us.

I think I might finally understand it. *All* of us are related. Not just us humans, but everything. Every single thing. Every person, plant, animal, rock, bug, water. Even man-made stuff, because it didn't start out that way. First, it started out as God, who is all things, and is in all things. God is pure energy; the glue that holds everything together. As my old psychology professor put it, "the ghost in the machine." He is also the everything that the glue is holding together! No matter how small energy can be broken down, God is still there, because He *is* everything! No matter how huge man can build something, it cannot surpass the bigness of God. When man rearranges matter and comes up with something "new", it's not *really* new. It's just a rearrangement ... ***of God!***

Sometimes man does not know how to handle what he has rearranged. It could be a new and powerful drug, a fertilizer, a weed killer, a weapon of mass destruction, or a power plant that could inexpensively heat and cool thousands of homes and offices and shops. Sometimes what man has rearranged works brilliantly, other times it's deadly. When man is practicing creating, much like a son emulates what he sees his Daddy doing, sometimes he goofs. Or the earth burps or wretches, and what man has made gets broken. Then man goes, ***"oops."***

It's like little children making sandcastles by the sea; they labor hard and long, and stand back to admire their creation. Then … in comes a wave. In one swift second, all the child's work is destroyed. Destroyed? No. It just changed form.

In my little world, my human family and my animal family are *related*. First, because we are all a part of God. Second, my husband and I are related by marriage. Third, our kids are related to my husband and I because we helped God create them. Our horses and our dogs and our cats are related to us because they came to live with us and be a part of our family.

We live on a farm. That piece of ground connects us and contains our house, our barn, our pasture, our forest. The humans and animals go from house to barn to pasture and back. (If the other humans would let me, I'd let the horses come in the house. They would probably like that.) It is God's farm. It *is* God. He's the dirt, the grass, the buildings, the streams, the animals, the people.

What we do, or don't do, affects everyone and everything. And not just in our immediate family. It's like when someone throws a pebble into a pond. The ripples caused by the plunk of the stone going into the water go ever outward. Whatever our actions, they eventually go around the globe.

On our farm there are lots of chores that need to be done every single day. Way too much for one person to deal with. Whoever it is would collapse of exhaustion if they tried to do it all. If everyone who lives here pitches in the chores get done easily. The hard part is trying to get everyone to work together. It requires each person to look outside of their own wants, needs, rules and regulations.

Here's our family's little example. In our house, there are always meals to cook, dishes to be washed, laundry to be done, bills to be paid, papers to look through, bathrooms to be cleaned, floors to be swept and mopped. Down at the barn, there are always stalls to clean, buckets to fill, animals to feed and look after, horses to groom and exercise. The list is long.

It makes sense for some things to be done by one particular person in the family, because they know the most about it, are better at doing it, and it fits with their schedule. Other things could be done by any family member, especially with a little training by the person who knows how to do it best.

This is where things can get messy. The person who is really good at something needs to have time to do it. If somebody else did it without being trained it could cause serious problems. If the expert at that thing gets stuck doing all or most of the other stuff, too, because everybody else in the family is doing what *they* want to do, then that person gets overwhelmed.

If we live unto ourselves, separate from the desires and needs of others, it doesn't work so well. It makes life hard not only for the overwhelmed person who is trying to do too much, but also for the person living unto themselves. Separation is lonely. Sometimes we need help. The person who feels overwhelmed feels resentful. Usually that resentment is directed toward the person who won't help. Then *that* person feels hurt, angry and lonely!

This example is just our little postage stamp corner of the world, but as you have probably already figured out, it grows ever outward like ripples on a pond, until it engulfs the entire universe.

There you have it.

The Theory of Relativity.

* * *

Five years ago I suffered a near fatal horse-back riding accident. The doctors and my MRI said I had a Traumatic Brain Injury. I swiftly, miraculously recovered. I sat down to write the account of that experience as emails to my sisters and closest friends. As I wrote, I knew somehow those emails would become a book. It started out as a chronological detailing of my recovery, but it soon took a life of its own.

I am embarrassed to admit it, but I had to get my husband to show me how to use the word processor. I *could* use it, a little, but I tried to avoid the computer like the plague. Computers don't like me in much the same way horses don't like my husband! Computers don't buck, bite, or kick, but they do other nasty things, and they enjoy doing them to *me*. I needed my husband, Caleb, to show me how to *computer-whisper*.

I've written the book myself, but Caleb is in these pages so much that he should receive credit for co-authoring it, as I envisioned both of us writing a book together years ago. Along with giving him credit, I would also like to give him a huge punch in the nose. Talk abound *yin-yang*. The two of us are polar opposites. True to that old adage, we were attracted to each other, all right. The attraction sparked a romance, which led to a marriage, which led to children (both two *and* four-legged), which led Caleb to find a steady income, which led to college, which led us to Washington, which led us to today. *Talk about the theory of relativity!* If I hadn't met and married Caleb, I would not have had all the life experiences that were worth writing a book. Or "I would have done something else", as Caleb calmly says, and I would write about that. Who knows? *Only God.*

The spark that lit from our attraction turned into such a roaring fire it nearly melted both of us. I'm not talking about the *Johnny Cash* song kind of fire. I wish! I'm talking about the fire of misunderstanding that almost devoured us. Caleb and I are so opposite that one spewed flames, smoke and ashes while the other went into a deep freeze. Could be that it's a good thing. I kept Caleb from freezing to death and he kept me from incinerating.

Now, after thirty-five years of both ignition and thaw, we are two lukewarm old duffers. Kind of comfy to be around, like an old horse. Or an old dog. Or an old cat.

I hope this book is a comfort for you to read.

Chapter One

ON AUGUST 7TH, 2010, I hauled my beautiful, wonderful 4 year old gelding, Memphis (his show name is Blue Suede Shoes) up Interstate 5 to Blaine, Washington, to a little horse show at Sunset Park. It was a newer County park built by horse people for horse people. They had built a dandy introductory cross-country jumping course and were hosting an Event Derby (where you ride a dressage test and then jump a combination of stadium and cross-country jumps) as a fund raiser. Memphis, a Percheron-Thoroughbred cross, was young and very green (meaning unskilled), but such a good boy. He seemed ready to go.

It was a bit rainy that August in the Puget Sound area. August around here is usually a picture-postcard-perfect summer month. I saddled up Memphis in a drizzle and headed to the dressage warm-up area, a grassy knoll beside the outdoor sand arena. All was well until I asked Memphis to canter. His unshod hooves slipped on the wet grass, and he fell. It wasn't a big deal; Memphis did not fall and squash me. He leaped back on his feet with a bewildered look on his lovely face. I should have rolled clear, got up, brushed off my breeches and remounted, just as I've always done. At least that is what everybody that saw it happen has told me. I don't remember a thing.

I didn't get up. I lay still and quiet. I was out like a light. The E.M.T.s stationed at the show hauled me off to the Intensive Care unit at Saint Joseph's Hospital in nearby Bellingham. Folks at the show caught and settled Memphis safely in a paddock. My husband Caleb was called. The E.M.T.s called my mom in North Carolina, for they saw "Mom" on my cell phone, which was in my pocket. Caleb called the kids. He called *everyone.*

The docs in the E.R. determined I had suffered a substantial Traumatic Brain Injury (TBI). They weren't sure if I would live. I was in a hard coma for three days, and on life support. For another seven days, I stayed unconscious, but made little stirrings and signs that I was coming around. During that time everyone that Caleb contacted told others, and soon a huge prayer network was actively praying for my recovery. Praying took form in many different ways. People cried out to God on my behalf, sent me healing energy, and caring thoughts.

And then ...

THIS happened. I was still in a coma. I don't know exactly what you would call it, a Near Death Experience I suppose, but it was real as real can be. It has changed my life and has set the tone for everything that has taken place since. Here it is:

I was on an old-fashioned steam train bound for heaven. Jonathan Edwards has a song on one of his CD's called *People Get Ready (by Curtis Mayfield)* that I really love, about a train picking up people on the way to heaven---it was *that* train.

People get ready, there's a train a comin,'
It's picking up passengers coast to coast.
All you need is faith to hear the diesels humming,
You don't need no ticket, you just thank the Lord

It seemed like I was in the dining car, but there was no one else in there except this cute, *cute,* older couple at a table. They were so incredibly happy that they got to go to heaven *together.* No words were exchanged. I guess we didn't really need to talk.

THEN ... in comes **God.** I didn't have to ask Him who He was! He looked about 60, was a little bit fleshy, and was wearing a nice, slightly fussy pleated muslin gown and tire-tread sandals. He had long salt and pepper hair that was a little curly at the ends, and bangs, like Captain Kangaroo used to wear! His arms and face were shiny, and I wondered if he had been shoveling coal into the engine. He looked like He could use a shower and a better haircut! How funny of God to wear such a get up. Remember the Christopher Reeves *Superman* movies? There was one scene where a guy spotted Superman in his tights and cape and exclaimed, "*BAD OUTFIT*!!!"

I remember being aware of God's incredible strength. You wouldn't know it just by looking at Him, but you just *knew.*

He walked right up to me, looked me in the eyes and asked, "What about your horses?" And he started chuckling, *heh, heh, heh.* I said, "Oh no! I need to get off. Please stop the train." God was chuckling to himself the whole time, standing there in His Bad Outfit. He was enjoying himself in His Bad Outfit enormously. He knew I would react like that. In fact, in His presence I felt so *known.* Known past, present, and future. And loved! *So* loved. God had one of his angels stop the train. Then He, with incredible gentleness and tenderness, took my elbow to steady me. He helped me walk down the steps of the train car. Then he was gone. So was the train.

Judging by the light, it was dawn or dusk. I didn't recognize where I was. I thought maybe it was a desert, because it was a tan color like sand and you could see far off. But there were a few trees and clumps of bushes which didn't quite go with a desert. And water ... maybe a small lake? A big hill was in the distance. I didn't know where to go, so I started walking. I just kept *gettin' it.* The next thing I knew I was lying in a hospital bed wondering where I was and *why* was I in a hospital bed? Boy, that was the best nap *ever,* but I really do need to ride ... pretty soon a most overjoyed Caleb came in ... and soon the kids along with my beagle, Hallie. It was such a joyful, happy time! Even though I really *did* need to get on with riding all my horses ...

I have heard that chuckle many, many times since then and I can chuckle it, too. *Heh, heh, heh* ... Abba, you are such a comedian.

About six or seven weeks out of the hospital, I walked down to the barn at dawn to feed and water my horses. As I was dipping buckets of water out of our big pasture trough to fill the buckets in the stalls, I looked up and gasped. I suddenly realized *that* was the view I saw when

I got off the train! It's the beautiful valley across the highway from where we lived for sixteen years. The hill was *Lord* Hill, a 1,300 hundred acre trail system I had ridden on many, many times. It was late October, and all the tall pasture grass had turned a lovely shade of tan. There were groups of bare-branched cottonwood trees---just like I saw in my NDE---and the clumps of vegetation were blackberry bushes. There was enough standing water in the pastures from the recent heavy rains to form a small pond. The train had dropped me off ... at *home.*

Chapter Two

I WAS EMOTIONALLY AND PHYSICALLY fragile after I awoke from the coma. While conscious between many moments of cat-napping, I was always moved to tears at *something*. Caleb and the kids gave me a new nickname: "Bubble and Squeak." I cried about my train ride and seeing God in his "bad outfit." I cried about the love shown me by my family and friends who came to visit. I was grateful and cried about the compassionate care of the staff in intensive care at Providence Hospital in Everett, where I had been transferred after I woke up. My daughter Maeve said that I wouldn't stop talking, even though my voice was hoarse and raspy from the breathing tubes that had been down my throat. She tells me I said, "I have a lot to say and I just want to say my piece!" I talked and bubbled and squeaked so much I drove Caleb and the kids a little crazy. Caleb came up with a very blunt, off-color phrase to get me to shut up. I tried to get him use just the first letter for each word so it wouldn't sound so crude. Since I wasn't allowed to talk as much as I wanted, as soon as I was home from the hospital I started pounding on the keyboard in front of my son Ryan's computer.

So ... here is my "piece." If you get tired of my story, you, don't need to be as rude as my husband. You can just close the book.

Chapter Three

WITHIN A FEW DAYS I was transferred to the second floor rehabilitation unit of Providence Hospital. That's when the fun and games began. I was kept really busy by the speech, occupational, and physical therapists. I liked *them,* but not so much all the exercises. Most nights I was wakeful and slept in fits and starts. About the time I was ready for a real snooze, the day would begin and I would have a full day of therapies. I loved it when the therapists had days off and I could catch up on my sleep!

Sometimes, late at night, I felt afraid. A few of the nurses' aides that came in on their rounds were abrupt and in a hurry. One aide especially frightened me. She always seemed stressed and highly annoyed when I needed anything. Later I learned that the second floor was really short staffed. That might explain why some of the aides were lacking in their bedside manner. Maybe they had a lot of personal problems plaguing them that carried over into their work. Maybe *I* was a difficult and annoying patient! Maeve says I was. I was always trying to get out of bed to go to the barn.

There was one night in particular when someone different came in to check on me. It must have been two or three in the morning. I was usually awake at that time. I was overwhelmed at the love and tender concern she showed for me. She was extraordinarily gentle and tender in the way she adjusted my bedclothes, tucked me in and asked me if I needed anything. I never saw her face; the room was very dark. I never learned her name or found out who she was. I think she was an angel.

There was another angel in the form of a Korean doctor that came to visit me on a daily basis. He quickly and efficiently checked me over and asked me how I was doing, and then always asked if he could pray for me. I always answered *"YES!"* His prayers were just like his bedside manner; quick, efficient, simple. And simply *wonderful*. I had the privilege of visiting him as an outpatient after I was discharged. It was a joyful reunion. Through tears of joy and gratitude I thanked him for all those wonderful prayers.

One thing stands out in the memories of those early days on the second floor. So many of the patients were in a desperate condition; much worse off than me. There were stroke victims, the head-injured, and one young mom who had contracted H1N1. She had been transferred to Providence after a misdiagnosis at a different hospital. I had great compassion for her. I felt compassion for *all* of them. I wondered how the aides and nurses were treating them. I wondered if their families cared about them like mine did. All I could think of was that these people needed other people to take their hands tenderly in their own, make gentle eye contact with them, listen to them, and speak tenderly with them. ***Let them know that they mattered.***

Everyone needs to know that they "matter," not that they are just *matter*. When I say everyone, I am talking about every *one*, not just humans. Every thing, from the biggest mountain down to the smallest microbe. It all matters. We all matter. We are all *matter*, and we are ONE. I didn't know I mattered much to anyone but Abba, my horses, dog, and cats until *The Great Head Bonk*. Then I realized I how much I mattered to my husband, my family, and my friends. *For every action, there is an equal and opposite reaction.* I think about those little metal balls hanging in a row that demonstrate this principle. You pick up the first one, drop it, and it whacks into the next one and sets off a chain reaction down the line. The last ball gets the whole thing going in the opposite direction, and it keeps going for a while until the energy runs out. I may be the one who got physically whacked on the side of my head, but that moment set off a chain reaction through a whole community of people who cared about me. I'm glad I got to live and to experience all the love and support that poured out of the cracks in everyone as a result from that whack!

I thought often about the young woman who was stricken with H1N1 that was on my floor. Her mishandled treatment had left her incapacitated. She had contracted MRSA and had to be kept in isolation. She couldn't speak, but she could moan. And moan she did, at the top of her lungs, day and night. The hospital staff seemed to find it highly irritating; it probably was, but it broke my heart. She had a husband and some kids, but I don't know if they ever came to see her. If they did, it wasn't often. She seemed very alone. When she contracted MRSA she was *really* alone, in quarantine. Looking back, I think she symbolizes what we are feeling; what the earth and *all* its' creatures are feeling. *"Help! I need help. People have almost killed me out of ignorance. Look what they've done to me! Help! Please help me."* I knew her anguished cries were her attempt to express her loneliness and utter despair. Maybe I knew that because I have spent years learning to speak horse, dog, and cat. They don't speak English, but they are always talking. You just need to tune in and learn their language.

Chapter Four

I KNEW THAT MY DAILY round of therapies were probably important and helpful, but all I could think of was how I really needed to get to the barn and eventually get back on a horse. That would be *real* therapy.

The recreation therapist who took patients out of the hospital for little excursions asked me where I wanted to go. To town? To the waterfront? Um … no. *I wanted to go to the barn!* I talked her into taking me out there one day. I went in a special van with a wheelchair ramp. Such pomp and ceremony! You'd have thought Cleopatra had arrived.

It was a big day. The horses seemed genuinely happy to see me. Hallie was overjoyed that I was back in our "normal" environment. Caleb and the kids were thrilled I had progressed far enough to handle a trip like that. I don't know what the therapist thought. Most people aren't "horsey". Sometimes they look at horse people like we are from another planet. I'll never forget a freezing cold winter evening years ago. I took my kids, then still pretty young, to Fred Meyer to pick up a few items. We had come straight from a day at the barn and we looked pretty ragged. A child tugged at her mom's sleeve and pointed at us and said, "Mom! Mom, *look!* Homeless people!" The mom shushed her child in embarrassment, but I laughed. It's still funny when I think about it.

I was unloaded out of the special van in my wheelchair and pushed to the barn aisle. I proceeded to give all the horses lots of carrots. That's about all I *could* do. A couple of them chewed on my fingers in gratitude. Ticket, a horse recently given to me, chomped on my fingers kind of hard, as if *they* were carrots. He nibbled in a very friendly but very greedy way! I couldn't get them out of his mouth. The results:

bloody fingers with a couple nails that died and eventually fell off. Sheepishly, I smiled through the pain and hid my mangled fingers. I was so overjoyed to see my horses I didn't care about my injuries, but I think the poor therapist was horrified. Our second and last outing was a very safe one, down to the Everett waterfront for lunch before I was discharged. *Truly* boring.

Chapter Five

I HAD A DELIGHTFUL OCCUPATIONAL Therapist. She was young and pretty and had lots of energy. Her job was to help me relearn to go potty, shower, dress and eat; you know, *functional* stuff. That girl saw me buck naked *a lot,* and I am a modest person! I couldn't even fasten my bra when we first started. She used to say to me "Gotta get those *girls* zipped up!" We joked a lot about my "girls". She made occupational therapy fun.

I had two terrific Physical Therapists who worked me hard. Later I found out one of them was the aunt of one of my favorite students!

There was another Physical Therapist that I saw only once, but she made such an impression on me! When I first tried getting out of bed she was there. She helped me try to stand up straight and use a walker.

I don't remember her name. I thought for sure she was from the coastal area of North Carolina. She had that *look* and that "language", but not the accent. She was really cool; not from N.C. though. *Land sakes*, I could have sworn she was born and raised in Oriental!

I have been back to the hospital to visit staff. I gave my O.T. a hug, but I didn't see anyone else. Maybe they were visiting angels too.

Chapter Six

I GOT SPRUNG FROM THE hospital September 9th, 2010, one month and two days after my "internment", Of course we stopped at the barn on the way home, and I went daily after that. Usually Caleb or one of the kids took me, as I couldn't yet drive my truck. We stayed long enough to clean their stalls, fill their water buckets and pasture troughs, check the horses over and distribute lots of carrots. I couldn't ride, and my kids weren't into riding any more. Instead of spending 12 hours a day there, I spent about an hour, then home to lie down and rest. Gradually I helped more and rested less. I started brushing and handling the horses. I made much faster progress in my recovery once I was out of the hospital and back at the barn. It was the best therapy in the world.

Caleb paid a couple of my instructor friends to teach my lessons for me in case I was able to get back to it, and things were looking good that I would. They kept the horses worked, too, including the babies. I looked on with a twinge of envy.

Soon the owner of the horse barn asked me to take my horse Ticket home. She needed room for another boarder to come in, and Ticket was just taking up space. I had care-leased Ticket in the spring before my accident when I met his owner at a cross-country camp. His owner and I got to talking and realized we had evented together in the same divisions when Ticket and my Appaloosa Sport Horse *All That Jazz* were just starting to compete. How well I remembered Ticket. He was a beautiful chestnut Thoroughbred with chrome (white markings) and an unusual roan splash cascading down his left hindquarter, a gift from one of his ancestors. Ticket usually won our division. Jazz was such a handful I was thrilled to even finish. When I saw Ticket was entered in our division, I knew he would come in first or second.

At the camp we both attended, his owner was riding a new horse. She said Ticket was just hanging out in a pasture on Vashon Island. His owner had tried to sell him as a hunter for big bucks. He flunked the pre-sale veterinary inspection; his hocks flunked the flexion test. Therapeutic hock injections would have been *his* quick ticket back to riding and competing, but instead Ticket got turned out to see if rest would help.

As we talked, she asked if I would be interested in care-leasing Ticket and trying to sell him for her. I thought about it a lot. I needed a lesson horse plus I had a student in mind to possibly buy him. His owner thought he would love the attention my riders would give him. I told her I would pick him up on Vashon when I brought Memphis and Jazz to the Pony Club Horse Trials in June.

After the competition I loaded up my horses and followed Ticket's owner to where she had him boarded. The mom had Ticket ready to load. He was the same pretty chestnut I remembered … but with cracks in both front hooves from coronet band to sole. He was wearing shoes that looked a little overdue. I knew the cracks were bad news. I mentioned them to Ticket's owner and she blew it off with a wave of her hand. I was too chicken to tell her I wouldn't take him. We loaded him in the trailer and I headed for the ferry.

He rode home nicely with Memphis and Jazz. He settled in to his new digs without a hitch. I called my two farriers, a married couple, and told them about his feet. They said I should give him back to his owner because those kinds of cracks couldn't be fixed and that I would end up dealing with one abscess after another. They said they wouldn't touch him with a ten foot pole.

While I was mulling over what to do with him, I got a call from my sisters back in North Carolina. My 89-year-old mom had experienced kidney failure and was in the hospital. They kept me posted on her recovery and before too long it was time for her to go home. My sisters and sister-in-law were doing an excellent job looking after her, but I wanted to see Mom and help my sisters. My sister and brother in-law got me a plane ticket with their Frequent Flyer Miles. I made arrangement for my horses' care with the barn owner, husband Caleb and son Ryan, and flew east to North Carolina.

As if on cue, shortly after I arrived in Raleigh Ticket's left front foot abscessed. The barn owner called my vet, who came out and treated it. The barn owner, who was caring for Ticket and his foot, called to let me know. I told her I was going to call Ticket's owner to come get him. She pleaded, "Oh don't do that! He's such a nice horse. I really like him." I told her I didn't need a horse with such big problems. She suggested having her farrier work on him, but I didn't know him well at all. I called Ticket's owner and made arrangements for her to come for him when I returned.

While at my mom's house, I took daily walks down the street for physical and spiritual exercise. The road past her house dipped down steeply to a dead-end. The day after I called Ticket's owner I was chugging back up the hill talking to God and thinking about stuff. Ticket popped into my head, along with the distinct impression that I should keep him. I said, "*Abba,* is that you? Are you sure? I need Ticket like a hole in the head!" The idea stayed with me as I trudged up the hill. I said, "Okay, Abba. I'm putting out a fleece. I'm gonna call Caleb and ask if I can keep Ticket. If he says no, which I think he'll do, I won't keep him. If he says yes, which won't be like Caleb at all, I'll know I heard right and I'll keep him."

I called Caleb and asked if I could keep Ticket. He said *yes,* which was about 180 degrees opposite of what I thought he'd say.

I left messages for Ticket's owner saying I changed my mind and he could stay. When my visit with my mom was over I flew back to Washington. Soon I was back at the barn tending to my horses. One afternoon Ticket's owner pulled up with her trailer. I guess she hadn't got my messages. When I told her I would keep leasing him, she said I could have him. She got in her truck and drove away. He was staying, all right.

My vet came for a follow-up visit. His foot was better, but I had her do flex tests on all four legs. Three flunked. *Oh boy.* With those feet and those flexions my vet recommended euthanasia. At least he walked, trotted and cantered sound on the longe line. I went ahead and made arrangements with the barn owner's farrier to start working on Ticket. At least *he* was optimistic!

Then came the Great Head Bonk, then my recovery, then a request from the barn owner to bring Ticket home as she needed room for a new boarder to come in. We did just that and he fit right in. In fact, he became fast friends with Ryan's old curmudgeon warm blood, *What About Bob*, and an "aide" to my 30 year old, most beloved, totally blind Appaloosa, *Sump*. He was truly a healing balm to that situation, as Bob and Sump both missed 33 year old Pete whom we had lost in late spring. It was amazing to watch the three of them. I had been so worried that Bob would bully Sump with Pete gone. He never did, and I am grateful. When Ticket came, he made the world right for them.

Chapter Seven

THE DAYS STARTED TO DRAG and be a little boring. I missed spending my days with the horses. They had all lost some weight and Shadow, the "old Dragon Lady" pony had a bad case of diarrhea. That wasn't too unusual. My horses had been too fat anyway, so nothing was truly amiss. We got Shadow's diarrhea cleared up, but I was a bit anxious. I had always cared for my ponies myself; it felt really weird to only be there a couple hours daily instead of ten.

The barn owner had asked Caleb to start paying full board on the horses when I was in the hospital. Before the *Great Head Bonk* I traded most of my board for training the owner's horses and giving her lessons. Caleb had paid a month's board just before I was released from the hospital. I was angry when I found out about it. Before I moved my horses to that woman's place Caleb and I had spent quite a few bucks and lots of hours putting up electric fencing and bringing in gravel and sand to make things safer and more functional. She didn't have the money or the desire to make any improvements, so we agreed that these would be "banked" in case I ever got sick or hurt and couldn't work. I wrote all our expenses and all the hours we worked in her log book and also on my calendar at home. Later, when I brought it up she didn't remember agreeing to that plan. She seemed very offended, like I was making it all up. I had been constantly working and spending money on improvements that benefited both of us and doing extra stuff around the farm *and* training her horses. I brought her some boarders. I looked in the log book that stayed in her barn aisle and couldn't find the agreement. It looked like there were some pages missing. I still had it written down on my calendar at home, so I knew I wasn't crazy or my head injury was affecting me.

I started to think I should move the horses. The thought of yet another barn and yet more drama made me nauseated. Friends would call with leads and tips but I didn't have the heart to pursue any of them. I thought about bringing them home to the farm we rented, but there was nowhere to teach or ride. Uneasy days passed by.

In bed one morning, somewhere between sleep and waking, I clearly heard Abba's voice telling me, "Get them out, *NOW*". When I told Caleb we should bring them home right away, he thought I was nuts; head injured. He didn't want to do it. Bringing four more horses home meant we would have to ask our landlord's permission. It meant extra work and expenses to bring more horses to the property, not to mention it would be ending the income that paid for *all* the horses! It also meant I would lose the ability to try riding again. There wasn't a safe place to ride where we lived, only slippery mud and grass. There was always lots of heavy equipment rumbling around. Our landlord ran a heavy construction business and kept all his work vehicles there; really big dump trucks and front end loaders. Not a great setup for riding or teaching.

I felt so strongly I had heard from Abba that I kept bugging Caleb until he finally said OKAY. We got them out. Packed up everything and left. The barn owner was furious. Family and most folks I knew thought I was making a bad, brain-damaged decision, but it turned out to be exactly the right thing to do. With the money from the charitable fund our dear friend Teagan set up, Caleb fortified the existing stabling and built two extra stalls that were amazing and beautiful. We brought in lots of gravel to the muddy paddock area. For a while, our landlords did not complain about the extra horses being there. They charged us a reasonable fee for the additions to our home herd. They were friendly and fairly supportive until we adopted another dog. Then our relationship went down the toilet.

Chapter Eight

My youngest daughter Maeve had gotten a job at a local espresso stand after it became apparent I was going to be just fine and dandy instead of an invalid. The doctors just weren't sure what my recovery would look like, so Maeve moved back home to look after me. She had been living in Kirkland with her best friend from high school and managing a coffee shop. The owner of the coffee shop decided to do something else, and Maeve was out of a job.

A very nice woman, Brenna Sawyer, would come by Maeve's coffee stand in her SUV with her dog buddies. Usually they were heading off for a little run. George was one of her buddies. George is a dog. That's God spelled backwards. He's a senior citizen Kelpie/Black Lab cross, maybe. He hails from Georgia. George, from Georgia. Brenna rescues dogs on the side when she is not being a busy accountant. She found George on the internet. She had him treated for a load of heartworms and flew him out to the Pacific Northwest. Brenna was trying to find him a family to call his own.

Maeve came home from work one day and told me about George. As she talked I suddenly knew he should be our dog. I didn't know just *why* we were supposed to take George, but I felt he would teach Caleb and I something. What that something was, I wasn't sure. I called Brenna after Maeve got her phone number for me. We arranged for a meeting, and I asked God for another sign. I wasn't at all sure that Hallie would tolerate another dog in her little beagle kingdom at all, at all. If she made room in her heart for George, then so would we.

We used to have two dogs. Hank, our wonderful coonhound had passed a few years ago. Hallie, our little "Amazon Princess" beagle was currently enjoying being front and center dog. We had gotten her when Hank was four or five, and she very quickly wiggled her little way into our hearts. Hank was somewhat reserved and couldn't always handle Hallie's *joie de vivre*. We tried hard to reassure Hank, but soon Hallie's nickname became "Little Usurper". Now that Hank was no longer with us she was thoroughly enjoying being The One and Only.

Brenna brought George over on a Saturday. They walked in and George said, "Hello, I'm pleased to meet you. I'm George, and you are my new family." It was very much the way our ancient orange tabby cat Mead showed up at our doorstep several years ago. He had heard we took in cats.

Hallie got off her throne (our old couch) and came to check out George. She very politely introduced herself, then went back to the couch and proceeded to fall back asleep. Brenna and I exchanged wide-eyed looks. If I had been wearing dentures they would have fallen out. Usually Hallie is quite vocal and very cheeky about *any* canine visitors, be it visitors' pups or a neighbor dog.

A few days later Brenna brought George to stay with his collar, leash, heartworm medicine and a crate. He slept in the crate a couple of nights, then progressed to our other couch. In a couple weeks when Hallie let George sleep on her throne, I knew I had heard right about taking him in. They even ate side by side without squabbles.

About two weeks after George came to stay, Hallie started sleeping. She slept and slept and slept. At first I was worried about her, but then I realized she was sleeping because she *could,* because George had come to help her look after us. Hallie was exhausted from looking after me and everyone else in the family after my accident. Even though she was just a little beagle, she took her job very seriously. She had been so worried about me and everyone else as well. When George came, Hallie knew she could finally get some rest. After about a week of sleeping seemingly non-stop, she perked right back up.

George was still an intact male and had a bit of wanderlust, so we kept him on a very long rope. He enjoyed trotting down to the barn and going on walks around the farm with the kids. George was totally fascinated by the horses and the cows. Being a herding dog, that is what he wanted to do with them. He would bark and nip at their heels. After Sump stepped on George's paw, he learned to chill out a little bit.

Our landlord's daughter-in-law, who lived in the other half of the house, had a flock of free-range chickens. George loved to dive into the middle of the flock to get them flapping and squawking. They quickly learned to stay just beyond the length of his rope. One morning I was taking Sump for a walk around the farm and decided to take George along. Everything was going fine until we rounded a corner down by our landlord's tool sheds. We surprised the chickens, who were just inside the door, and they surprised us. George lunged through the door and came out with a chicken in his mouth. I made him drop it right away. The chicken flapped its' wings wildly and took off. I couldn't find any blood or skin, just lots and lots of feathers. I cleaned those up, put Sump away, and went to tell our landlord's daughter-in-law what happened, but no one was home. All day I kept my eyes out for an injured or expired chicken, but they all seemed okay.

The next morning I ran into our landlord's daughter-in-law down in the barn. She asked me if I had seen what happened to the chicken. I told her about George grabbing it. She was very upset that I hadn't told her. She said the chicken had a gash that she had to clean. I said I was sorry and that I would have told them if they had been home.

The chicken recovered just fine, but not the girl. She wanted George gone immediately. She said she was afraid for her children; that George might attack them next. I tried to reason with her, but to no avail. George is totally gentle and sweet. The *idea* of him attacking her kids was utterly ridiculous. Her chickens or cows would attack those girls before George would.

She would not budge. I called Brenna and told her my dilemma. She thought the whole situation stunk, but agreed to take him back and came to pick him up. She and I were both angry and sad. I hated giving George up. I hoped that somehow that girl would have a change of heart. Brenna agreed to hang on to George just in case she did.

Shortly after that the landlord's daughter-in-law's brother was over with his black lab. As I drove my truck and trailer into the drive down to the barn to unload horses, he came trotting triumphantly by with a chicken in his mouth. I rolled down my truck window and yelled, "*drop it!!*" He did. The chicken died. This time I told the girl right away. I am sure that lab was a very nice dog. I noticed he was still allowed to come, but he had to stay on a rope. I wonder if the landlord's daughter was afraid that dog would attack her kids.

I was left wondering why George was meant to become our dog, and then suddenly he wasn't allowed to be our dog. What was it we were supposed to learn? One thing, I think, was about teamwork. I saw how George took over so Hallie could rest. When Hallie was rested and refreshed, they seemed to take turns looking after me, even though George pushed Hallie out of the way sometimes. The amazing thing was that she *let* him! It seemed there was still more to learn, but now George was gone.

Chapter Nine

THAT NOVEMBER RAIN POURED DOWN for days on end. Flooding was forecast along many rivers, including the one which runs through the town and right past where I used to teach and board most of my horses. Abba sent me down to look at the swollen river and pray for mercy. He had me pray for the river not to jump its' banks and bring disaster. It didn't. He had me pray earnestly for the barn owner, her husband, her horses and her land. I even e-mailed her that if she needed help getting horses hauled out of there, I would come. She never answered my email, but she called me one day all undone. She told some very disturbing things that happened to her. The poor woman was scared to death.

I had been so angry and hurt at the way she treated Caleb and I following my accident I never wanted to see or speak to her again. I was also very sad, because before I got hurt I *thought* we were pretty good friends.

Abba told me quite clearly to go to her house the next day. I normally would not be that bold or brave, but I went on request. I knocked on her door to see if I could come in and pray with her. She was quite taken aback when she opened the door to see who it was, but she let me in. I held her hands as we prayed. She seemed very uncomfortable, but there we were. I prayed for God to protect her and have mercy upon her and all her animals.

I have seen her only once since then. A few months later we found ourselves pumping gas at the same gas station, at the same pump. I looked up and there she was. She saw me too, but looked away. We didn't speak. We pumped gas into our trucks and then drove away. I heard she sold two of her incredible horses I was training. Her place went up for sale.

Chapter Ten

NOW THAT ALL MY HORSES were in one place a good part of each day was spent shoveling their poop. Caleb, Ryan and Maeve went to work and my oldest daughter Enya, who has Down Syndrome, went to her various programs for disabled adults. It was just me, the animals, and horse poop. It took me a long time to shovel all the poop from seven horses. I was a lot slower and weaker than I used to be. Shoveling poop was my physical therapy. Poop and I got intimately acquainted. I thought I had gotten to know it pretty well over the years, but I discovered there was lots more to poop than meets the eye. God began to speak to my heart as I picked up piles and piles of it.

In fact, I was so busy listening to God one morning as I was cleaning the paddock I didn't notice my young thoroughbred Gus sneaking up behind me. Suddenly I was swooped off my feet and deposited, neat as a pin, in my Rubbermaid cart. I didn't even bang a knee or an elbow going in. I sat there in shock for a moment, rubbing my throat where my gray hoodie had suddenly tightened against it. I looked around, and there was Gus. I swear he was laughing. He had picked me up by the hood of my sweatshirt and deposited me in the wheelbarrow; on nice, juicy wet poo. If it hadn't been so amazing I would have been really angry. I sat there in the poo cart laughing along with Gus.

We had just spent a big pile of money having gravel hauled in and graded for the paddock and walkway out to the pasture. We put gravel in every fall, otherwise it turned into a deep sea of mud over the winter. That is bad news for horses' legs and feet. If you give a rip about your horses and live in the Pacific Northwest, you mud-proof their living areas. If you don't clean up their manure on a daily basis, it ruins the gravel that cost a pretty penny. It makes a difference even if you miss a day. The horses poop, poop, poop all day and grind it into the gravel. Soon you can't pick up the poop without picking up a bunch of gravel; the same gravel you paid a lot of money for and worked hard to put down for the horses.

But … you *want* horses to poop profusely, because if they can't, they will *die*. Horses can't throw up. If they can't throw up and they don't poop, their guts more or less explode. It's called colic, and it ranges from slight cramping to complete blockage and twisting of the intestines. Sadly, I have lost a couple of horses that way. It seems they get tummy aches from just breathing! They are big creatures, but their stomachs are small and delicate. You really have to be knowledgeable and careful with their feeding program.

So, I am thankful for lots of poop. No poop puts me in a panic!

When poop is allowed to compost, it becomes wonderful fertilizer. It is from the stuff we ingest, just turned into a different molecular form. If all we ever ingest is garbage, it's still garbage when it comes out. If we take in stuff that's healthy, we still poop it out, but it's not garbage. It's great stuff! But here's excellent news: God can transform garbage into wonderful fertilizer! He is **THE GREAT COMPOSTER**. He makes fertilizer for our *souls*. The very trash that we took in can be composted to enrich our souls! Nothing is wasted by God. Think about it. Herbivores were made to eat grass. Grass needs fertilizer to stay rich and green, and not get choked out by weeds. Herbivores poop fertilizer for the grass they eat. What a seamless operation it is meant to be! Grazing animals eat grass and then the grass becomes poop inside the animal. The animals poop on the grass. As it breaks down it becomes food for the soil, which is food for the grass, which is food for the grazer. Then the whole cycle starts over.

When man breaks that cycle, nothing prospers. It suffers, including man. I think that is why Jesus ate a last supper with His disciples before he was crucified. He said *He* was food and drink. We should eat Him, drink Him, release Him as fertilizer for another soul. If we don't do that,

24

our soil becomes weak and barren, and only produces weeds. If you *know* you are full of poo, ask God to compost it and make it really great stuff. Have you ever felt "under the pile"? Maybe you are composting! Ditto if you are moldering, steaming, or being tossed about with a sharp pitchfork. It's not comfortable, but the end results are *rich*. When you really stink, thank God for it!

As I was shoveling day by day, God told me that people need to clean the dung out of their *heads* on a daily basis, too. So much garbage gets in there from the world. It could be stress in your relationships to your husband, wife, your kids, your parents, your boss, your employees or friends; on, and on, and on. If we turn to drinking or drugs, TV, computer, or *anything* besides sitting quietly with God, that's just more dung we dump on top of our manure pile, and it gets piled really high!

But, there is more good news! There is hope for all of us garbage eaters.

If we turn consistently and constantly to God, the expert manure picker, He is happy to clean the garbage out of our heads. Just being still before God gets his shovel going. The time you spend with Him will be unique because you are unique. There is so much material out there on how to meditate and how to pray which can be very helpful in getting you started and keeping you going. The main deal is … just do it! If you have a lot of dung, a.k.a. stress in your life, better do it lots.

It is not hard at all, and practice makes better. I think the most difficult thing is just *getting started*. God showed me how to curl up with Him the way Baxter, our very shy Coon kitty, liked to curl up with me on our comfy old chair in the quiet of the early morning. No one else was around so he felt safe. I was not distracted by the million other things I do all day and my lap was available for him to snuggle in---for as long as he could stand it. He began to like to come by and be petted. He liked my comfy lap and my fingers gently scratching his ears. Sometimes it was just for a few moments, sometimes he lingered. He *liked* my company. That made me so happy that he liked my company because he was a very chicken kitty when it came to people.

Baxter was a young Maine Coon Cat. He was adopted from a cat rescue from another state by the owner of the barn where I recently had kept my horses. Len and I love Maine Coon Cats, so she gave him to us. He was a gorgeous silver tabby complete with toe and ear tuffs and a great plume of a tail that he liked to curl around his feet. He was extremely shy and wary. It took nearly two years for Baxter to let us hold him. He finally stopped diving under the freezer whenever we acted like we might pet him or pick him up.

Two weeks after I was home from the hospital I started waking up very early in the morning. I would go to bed between eight and nine and wake up around four. Since it was so very early, I started sitting in Caleb's overstuffed leather chair, a.k.a. Caleb's *Throne,* to drink coffee and try to spend time with Abba. That was one of many gifts of *The Great Head-Bonk.* I had struggled for so many years both to rise early and spend time with the Lord. I had always been a miserable failure at both. My head-bonk turned that around.

I started my days "on the Throne," coffee in hand. I have always found spending time with Abba extremely difficult. My mind would wander endlessly. Praying was laboriously hard and boring. I was rotten at being still, and to top it off I often would fall back asleep. Caleb and I used to joke that *"we were going off to seek the Lord."* What that really meant was we were going off to take a nap! A week or so after I began to try to sit quietly with Abba, Baxter tentatively approached the *Throne.* He eventually crawled up and tentatively sat on my lap. It was a breathless, wondrous moment.

He started coming every morning. If I moved, he'd launch away. Sometimes he would only stay for a couple minutes, sometimes for a half-hour. It was thrilling to have him relax and purr on my lap as I scratched his ears; a huge milestone.

That's when Abba began to speak to me. He told me that Baxter was a lot like me when it came to spending time with *Him.* I was way too worried about how it should be done and how long I should do it. He said, *Relax.* Just enjoy Him. Sit on His lap. Let Him scratch *my* ears.

That changed everything. Now it is nearly effortless. I learned about some breathing exercises and meditative practices that were very helpful, but what really got me going was what Baxter taught me. We are all God's little kitties. We are all hurting and scared. Don't be afraid to curl up with God, and don't think you have to do it a certain way, for a long time, or have a big agenda. Your time with God will be as unique as you are, and unique as your own walk with God.

Chapter Eleven

After we brought all the horses home, we settled in to see if we had done the right thing. I was pretty sure we had, but Caleb, the kids and my friends had pretty big doubts about my decision making abilities. I felt I had heard from the Lord quite clearly, "**Get them out,**" so we did.

Any time you add a horse to an existing "herd" you have to be very careful. It's like a high school girl transferring to a new school in the middle of her senior year----it can be stressful, tough, and pretty scary. You try to manage the herd and minimize the dangers to the best of your abilities. It takes time, lots of time. It takes lots of observing and monitoring personalities and their behaviors. You must diligently stay on standby, ready to rescue a horse in danger.

Bob, Ticket and Sump were already here and getting along swimmingly. Then we brought home macho man "All That Jazzy", the two "Punk Boys" Gus and Memphis, and Shadow, our 25 year old matriarch. She was the only female in the bunch. She affectionately "tolerated" the big dumb guys. They were *her* guys, nonetheless.

I wasn't sure how long it would take to socialize them. Sump would be 30 in the spring. He was totally blind. That made things way more complex. I didn't want anyone to get injured. I was especially concerned about Sump. He got along amazingly well, but if you changed his routine it threw him for a loop and he panicked. When he panicked he tended to run headlong into things like fences or stall walls.

I kept the groups separated for awhile. They met through the stall walls and through the paddock fences with lots of posturing and squealing. It was really interesting to see them relate and observe their different personalities.

When I finally decided it was time to try turning all the horses out together, I didn't put Sump out with them. Bob the Bully turned out to be *Bob the Coward* in the new social setting. Jazz promptly put him in his place, as did Shadow (girls don't mess around). Bob had finally met his matches, even though they were both two hands shorter than he was. He completely lost face---and his place in the herd---the one he had achieved by preying on the smaller, older, weaker horses that had lived with him.

After a couple months the horses all went out together and got along fine with only occasional squabbles. Finally I put Sump out with the rest of the herd. He looked like he was going to be okay in the mix.

One afternoon some people drove up the driveway as I was hitching my trailer and said there was a horse lying down in our pasture, and it didn't look right. I ran around the back of the house and found Sump down and tangled in the fence. I ran in the house to grab Maeve, who happened to be home. We were able to keep him still, cut the wires, and extract him from under the fence. He got back on his feet. Aside from minor wounds and getting shaken up, he was okay, thank God!

We found out that Gus, our youngest, was *"doin' a Bob"*. He was trying to assert himself to a higher place in the herd by picking on the old blind guy. We took extra care not to have Sump and Gus in close proximity to each other any more. Gus is so much like Bob; goofy and eccentric, which could have been really bad if Bob hadn't taught us so much from handling him.

I have learned a ton about people from watching the horses. I am sure that is the main reason God had me bring them all home. I watched them a lot. God has taught me so much about people and how important it is to treat each other with respect and love, and how most of our problems are caused by misunderstandings. How easy it is to misunderstand one another! How easy it is to jump to conclusions! How often the conclusions are *wrong*. We are misunderstood by others.

We misunderstand *them*. No wonder society has major problems. No wonder there are wars and rumors of wars.

The funny thing is people call animals dumb. Excuse me. Who's dumb? We think we're the most highly evolved species on the planet. Our brains may be more complex, but that fact just serves to make us more complicated. *Not* better.

Chapter Twelve

PART ONE IN THIS EPIC adventure came to a close. Part Two began. I was home. So were my ponies, living where we lived. Maeve, no longer needing to be home as my caregiver, got a new job. Caleb returned to work. Deep breaths taken all around. What was next? Ride a horse, of course! But there was a round of jumps to clear first.

Fence one: I needed to find a place to ride. I couldn't ride at home. There was no arena, and the rain had returned for the winter. Actually, make that fall, winter, spring, and occasionally summer, too. We were having one of those rainy all the time years, which is why my "incident" occurred in the first place. We usually don't have *any* rain in August!

I didn't want to chance riding on wet grass outside of a proper arena when nobody (except God, of course) knew whether I would stay on or lose my balance and slide right off, or how my mount of choice would act in new digs, separated from the other horses. The kids and I had ridden at home in the pastures and around the farm many times in the past and we knew how slippery it could be. The horses could be a bit spooky, too.

Along with the internal whistle signaling me to begin my jump round came an email from Zoë Heston. She had been the show secretary up at Sunset Park in Blaine and had faithfully monitored my recovery as well as sending up boatloads of prayers on my behalf. Zoe had contacted a fellow instructor who was showing her horse on that fateful day. She lived about 10 minutes from us. She had a beautiful outdoor arena, and had said *"YES"* when Zoë asked if I could try riding again at her farm. I gave her a call, and we set a date.

Fence two: Who to ride? My lesson pony Shadow was really quiet and dependable, but a little small for me. The *Punk Boys* were young, squirrelly and hadn't been ridden for a few months. Ticket was still on hoof rehabilitation and rest. Sump was 29 years old, blind, and hadn't been ridden for years. Bob was well, *Bob*. That left All That Jazz. Even though he was 8 years old, Jazz could be excited and spooky at times, and had a big buck to go with it. He had dumped me many times. We had been through so much together in five years; best friends and worst enemies. In the end, my heart chose Jazz.

Fence Three: I needed warm bodies. No one knew if I could get on by myself. No one knew if I could sit on Jazz without support. No one knew if I could stay on Jazz in motion, or if I could control him. I needed a leader and side walker. I asked my friend Sonya if she would come supervise this event. She was a Master certified N.A.R.A.H. riding instructor. Our relationship began when I started to teach her daughter. She also worked for the mother of two of my other students. Sonya ended up being my trainer as well, being extremely helpful in working on dressage with Jazz.

Maeve came along to lead Jazz; Caleb to walk beside and catch me should I slip off.

On that wondrous warm, sunny day, we loaded up Jazz in the trailer. Caleb drove with Maeve riding shotgun, and me in the back. When Maeve was little she often played with Playmobil® figures. One Christmas we had an old fashioned electric train set that went around under our tree. She had a frontier-era set of Playmobil® characters that she put on the train. One was a girl dressed in buckskins, who stood on the top of the caboose with a shotgun aimed and ready to blast off any perpetrators that threatened the little train. To this day we still call Maeve the *"girl with the shotgun"*. It suits her.

We drove to the barn and parked the trailer. Soon we were joined by Sonya.

Fence Four: could I even mount up? I stood on the mounting block, put my foot in the stirrup and swung my leg over Jazz with as much grace as I could muster. It wasn't too hard. When I was settled in the saddle, I had a "moment" where the tears came, tears of joy and gratitude toward God, Jazz, and all the people who had made this moment possible. Len snapped a picture with his cell phone. Then, with Maeve leading Jazz, Caleb side-walking, and Sonya keeping an eagle eye on everything, we proceeded.

Fence Five: would Jazz be a good boy? Jazz was incredible. He *knew* he had to be a very good boy and take good care of me. We walked; I didn't lose my balance. We stopped; same thing. We turned to the left and turned to the right. I actually felt pretty stable up on his back (no pun intended). After about 20 minutes my body got a little tired and started listing to the right. But there was one last fence before we went through the finish flags.

Fence Six: trotting. Jazz, Maeve, Caleb, and I did a short little jog. Then we wound things up. I was jubilant. The future looked bright, even though I slept for three hours when I got home.

Chapter Thirteen

AFTER THAT FIRST RIDE AT the gracious trainer's place, I wanted another one! This time it was an Eventing Derby jumping course I had to face in order to make that happen. A Derby course is a mixture of both stadium and cross country fences. Getting on Jazz and seeing if I could stay on proved to be a very quick and easy stadium round. This is the course I had to jump in order to ride again:

Fence One: I wasn't driving yet. Caleb wasn't around much to drive my truck and trailer. He was working long hours for Arby's® all the time. When he wasn't on the road slaving away at his job, he was slaving away at his job at home on his computer. In his spare moments he was still trying to finish the stalls for the added horses! Ryan and Maeve couldn't drive it either. They had gotten out of the horse scene before they learned to drive, let alone learn to drive a horse trailer.

That first fence seemed huge and imposing. I sat at the start box as time passed by. Too much time. I was afraid to get going.

Fence Two: I didn't know where to go ride Jazz next. The woman who loaned me her arena for that first ride was a busy trainer and I figured she didn't need some fragile lady and her crew teetering around and taking up space. I didn't want to impose on her. Sonya suggested asking Trinity Farrier School if I could go up there and ride. It was a nice place and very close to my house; only four minutes away. I dragged my feet about asking them because:

Fence Three: I am a chicken.

Fence Four: Their place looked expensive.

Fence Five: Rumor had it the owners were *those* kind of uptight Christians.

Fence Six: It looked primarily like a Western-riding barn.

As time went by, I felt like God was poking me in the back to go ask them. I drew myself up to my full 5'5" and sent them an email, which was less intimidating than calling. I got a quick reply from the owner, Lisa Roderman. It sounded guarded but somewhat encouraging. We made arrangements to meet up at the farm. On the appointed day I drew myself up to my full 5'5" and had Ryan drive me up there.

The first thing Lisa asked me was if I was a Christian. She had seen the quote on my email, *"When God is about to do something great, he starts with a difficulty. When he is about to do something truly magnificent, he starts with an impossibility."* — *Armin Gesswein*. As soon as I said I was, she relaxed and we had a wonderful chat. I told Lisa my train story. She loved it. "Of *course* I could come ride," she said.

The start bell rang, and off I went. When Ryan drove me home, I jumped out of his car, into my truck and drove a mile to Roosevelt Store. A couple of days later I drove four miles to the end of Roosevelt Road to get gas at the Shell station.

Fences one, two and three completed in fine form.

About a week later I drove my truck and trailer and Jazzy-boy up to Trinity. I missed the main driveway and had to back the trailer in a tight place and turn around. I *did* it!

Sonya met me there to keep an eye on things. I mostly rode all by myself. It was *GREAT!* A few days later I went by myself and *cantered*.

Within a few more rides I was ready to take my dressage lessons with Sonya again.

Before long Lisa told me I could teach there if I wanted to, and I *wanted* to. We worked out the costs of hauling in and a plan. I repurchased liability insurance. Being there *was* expensive, but not unreasonable. My students started to return, and I raised my fees a little to cover the expense of being there.

I did not find the Rodermans to be the uptight Christians I had imagined. They were passionate about their faith, but did not lord it over anyone or beat anyone over the head with their bibles. John and Lisa were upright and honest, not uptight and neurotic. They ran their barn and farrier school with integrity and principle. It was refreshing and healing.

Fences Four and Five completed in fine form. It *was* primarily a western barn, but there were a couple of people who rode English. Everyone was friendly and nice. One of our neighbors on Roosevelt Road, whose older daughters I had taught years previously, brought her younger daughters to work and ride there. Lots of kids were in 4-H, one of whom owned a gorgeous older white thoroughbred, an event horse who had been given to John because he was having chronic hoof problems. The owner of the horse's vet was recommending euthanasia. He had saved the horse's feet *and* his life through corrective shoeing. John then sold him to Augusta Hoffman, who then proceeded to win big in 4-H jumping and dressage. I felt right at home. The people who rode Western were super friendly too. One gal, after I introduced myself and we chatted a little, suddenly gasped and said, "Wow---*incredible!* You're the woman on the *Caring Bridge* page!" Then she proceeded to tell me that somehow she got on the page while randomly searching the internet one day. She was drawn into my story and her heart went out to me and my family. She couldn't believe I was standing before her now! It was total confirmation that I was right where I was supposed to be.

Fence Six conquered and we sailed through the finish flags. These courses were shorter and easier than I thought!

I was totally elated. Now I had a nice place to ride and teach. It was a four minute drive from my house. The people were totally cool. God is so gracious! He let me work that out; get *my* priorities taken care of first. Then He went to work on **HIS**.

Chapter Fourteen

I WOKE UP REALLY EARLY one morning thinking about all the wonderful ways God had worked out my riding and teaching challenges. I made coffee, fed Hallie and the kitties, then settled down with a cup in "*The Throne*". That was the name of Caleb's and my favorite beat-up, cat-scratched, overstuffed leather armchair, bought at a second hand store down by Fort Lewis where military families shed their possessions before shipping out overseas. The Throne is where I was having the most incredible visits with Abba. Shortly after sitting down, I got up to get a wooden Captain's chair. I put a pillow on it for a footrest. There in the chair, all curled up and cozy, lay Maeve's young orange tabby cat, Pippin, adopted from the barn I had just left. He stayed in the chair as I moved it in front of the *Throne*. I put my feet in it and settled down to hang out with Abba. A few seconds later, Hallie hopped off the couch and came to investigate. Since she is my number one gal, *and she sure knows it,* she wanted to make sure that Pippin wasn't honing in on her territory. That would be me.

Hallie was incredibly gentle about it. She walked around the chair a few times, eyes bright and body all recruited, wagging her little Beagle tail in a most enthusiastic, friendly way. Pippin wasn't sure *what* she was going to do. Hallie put her front paws up on the seat and stuck her head through the chair rails, vigorously wagging her tail. Pippin eventually jumped off the chair and hurriedly walked off a few feet. Hallie pursued in her usual high-energy way, but stopped about a foot and a half from Pippin's nose. This happened twice; Hallie's tail wagging furiously the whole time. Exasperated, Pippin finally jumped up on the back of our couch to be with Baxter, his best bud.

Hallie then jumped up on the chair *quite* pleased and satisfied. I put my feet back up on the chair. She walked on them, like a bridge, over to my lap. Then God suddenly opened my eyes and ears to see what I hadn't been able to see or hear for a really long time.

*S*even years ago Caleb said I could buy a horse. I hadn't ever bought a horse for myself. When I was a kid my parents bought me horses. When I was a very young woman I was given an Arabian stallion and purchased an inexpensive half-interest in a Half-Arabian gelding with a student. I had to part with them and enter into a l-o-n-g stretch without horses. When that time was over, God began to send horses to me. I was given a gorgeous thoroughbred mare from a therapeutic riding program. We leased a fabulous pony I knew from there for the kids, and ending up buying him later for $750.00. Caleb and I did buy a couple of inexpensive ponies for the kids and my riding school, but not a horse for me.

The story of the events leading up to the purchase of my dream horse *Noble Valentine* is my story; the story of my life.

Chapter Fifteen

I WAS BORN A CENTAUR in 1955. That's right; half horse, half girl. My astrological sign is Sagittarius. My mom says I was horse crazy even as a toddler. Whenever she would take me to the grocery store, I would insist on getting whatever little bags of plastic horses were on display in the toy section. I collected hundreds of them and played with them endlessly. I sat on my first horse when I was four. A neighbor girl rode by our house and offered me the chance to sit on her horse. I was terrified. It seemed huge! But I was determined to do it, so I did. For a couple minutes, anyway.

When I was five we moved from Ohio to New Castle, Pennsylvania. An Amish man would drive his horse and buggy down our road delivering fresh eggs and milk. There was a pond across the street from our house, and he would stop to get his horse a bucket of water. I always watched and waited for him. When I saw them coming down the street I would be out there, waiting. I would watch the horse take big gulps of water, look into his big brown eyes and fall into a dream. The Amish man didn't say a whole lot, but he always took time for me to visit with his horse.

Our neighbors up the street kept a little pony and a big horse. I got to ride the pony by myself. They would bring the horses down to our house and share them with us. We had a sloping back yard, and up and down on that pony I would go. He was a pinto pony named Scout. He must have been a pretty good little pony. I still have pictures. I remember it as though it was yesterday. How happy I felt!

We ended up moving to North Carolina a year later, and that was the end of that. Little did I know, being very young, that we settled 20 minutes from Southern Pines, a very well-heeled "horsy" community. I think my parents didn't really want me to know about Southern Pines, as that community seemed way over the top wealthy for my family to even consider mingling with *those* people.

We lived very close to my maternal grandparents in Pine Bluff. They had an amazing home with a large yard in which to pretend *I* was a horse. I spent hours cantering sandy paths on their property. I dreamed of the horse that used to live in the old stable/carriage house, now converted into a charming guest cottage. I was too busy *being* a horse to pine away for those nearby rolling green sand hills where real horses galloped and grazed. These days, Southern Pines is a winter home to many top eventing trainers, with a huge endowed property that has been turned into an equestrian park. It features a beautiful cross-country course, home of some prestigious events. How ironic.

We lived in little Pine Bluff a couple of years, then moved to Cary, North Carolina. It was closer to my Dad's work in nearby Raleigh. Cary was pretty rural back then, which was totally fine by me. We bought a house on Rose Street, a dead-end. It was quite a stretch for my parents; a whopping $17,500.00. That won't buy you an experienced, high-quality show horse these days, even in the recession! It was fairly spacious, had a downstairs recreation room with a brick floor, a nice, big backyard, and no front door. That was how we gave directions to folks who were coming over. "Come to the house on the dead-end street with no front door." My dad built a brick bar downstairs, and I used the barstools as jump standards, with broom sticks as poles. I would jump higher and higher on that brick floor. I crashed hard a few times but didn't tell my mom, as I figured she would forbid any further jumping activity. When spring and summer came I would make a jumping course out in the back yard. It was a perfect cross-country course; up and down the sloping yard and in and out of the trees. I was never lacking for exercise, that's for sure.

I coerced every friend I made into playing horse with me. I always had rope reins tied around my waist. Usually I could talk them into being the rider, but sometimes I had to take turns and let them be the horse. We cantered and trotted around the yard and up and down our street. There was a short, paved dead-end street waiting for further development just down the hill from my house, and that became our riding arena. I'm surprised we didn't wear grooves in the pavement. We wore out our sneakers, though!

I also built elaborate miniature horse farms in our grassy back yard. Stables were cardboard boxes; string was fencing with Tinker Toy® fence posts. I modeled them after the elaborate thoroughbred farms I saw in pictures and read about in my fiction and non-fiction horse books. I had pastures for all my Breyer® mares and foals and sturdy paddocks for the stallions. There were weanling, yearling, and two-year-old pastures, just like in Lexington, Kentucky. The boxes were run-in sheds complete with water buckets, feed buckets, and hay mangers, overflowing with freshly mown hay (mowed lawn clippings). How I hated it when I had to pack up everything so my dad could mow the lawn again!

The neighbors in back of us had several fenced acres with an old barn. They had an old, wooly black Shetland pony that they would tether out in their front yard. Somehow I wrangled an open invitation to come ride him anytime. I would hike over there, haul the reluctant fellow up the steep slope of their front yard, then jump on him bareback. He would high-tail it to the bottom, slam on the brakes, slam his head down, and start eating like a house on fire. We would repeat that process over and over 'til I had to go home. Maybe my mom called, or maybe his owners took pity on the poor little beast! One day that old pony took matters into his own teeth. 'Round about the fifth time dragging him up the hill, he took those teeth and raked them firmly down my back as I was head down, pulling that poor fellow up the hill with all my eight-year-old might. *OW.* That hurt. I let the pony rest and went home. I don't remember if I told my mom; probably not. I didn't want her to tell me I couldn't ride anymore!

"No one can teach riding better than a horse."
(C.S. Lewis, from *The Horse and His Boy;*
The Chronicles of Narnia series).

I have that quote on a plaque. I found it at a tack store years ago, and it has followed me and kept an honored place in many tack rooms.

For a little while some guy kept a Quarter Horse mare in the neighbor's old barn. She was young and I certainly wasn't allowed to ride her, but I would walk over to the barn every day and feed her bits of grass and hay and just hang out, watching and trying to commune with her. She was lonely and would whinny, *"Is anybody equine out there?"* I would hear her from my backyard. I would whinny back. I practiced whinnying so much that eventually I would whinny and she would answer! I suppose that is the closest I ever got to becoming a horse.

In elementary school I organized my classmates into large herds of wild mustangs during recess. Even the boys got into it, especially since they got to be wild stallions! The herds galloped around, found water holes and grass to eat, fought off cougars, and had foals. Frequently one stallion would challenge another for possession of his band of mares, and fighting would erupt. There were squabbles amongst the mares and foals. Sometimes it was really hard to tell when the playing stopped and became real. The teachers eventually put a stop to the whole game and made us play dumb stuff like kickball.

All this time I begged my parents for a horse and for riding lessons. I begged God to give me a horse or better yet, turn me into one. I prayed that I would transform into a horse in my sleep. Every morning it was such a disappointment to wake up human. Then I figured it out. Our limbs are put on different! I couldn't go to sleep lying like a human---when I woke up a horse, my knees and hocks would be backwards! So then I made sure I went to sleep very stiff-armed and legged---boy was I determined. But it didn't work..*sigh.*

Chapter Sixteen

When I was nine my parents gave in and sent me to a summer day camp at a stable not too far from home. I got to ride a huge old red horse named Topper. He was fabulous. When the instructor asked if anyone knew how to post, I showed them so hard I almost posted myself right out of the saddle! I only knew how from watching Walt Disney's *The Horsemasters: Follow Your Heart*, but I did pretty well.

Camp was over way too soon. I kept pestering my Mom about more riding lessons so she found a lesson program about a half-hour from home, owned by the local T.V. station magnate. I took a few heavenly lessons there; the instructor was terrific, and we were gonna learn to jump! But soon the property was sold and the stable shut down. I was in such despair my mom put her search for a new barn in high gear. She found one not too far from our house. It was owned by Roland and Gillian Lyons. They had five sons. It was just a little hole in the wall, a makeshift stable in the woods. Gillian was expanding her business a little after doing some Girl Scout camps. The first thing I asked was, "Will you teach me to JUMP?" and Gillian said "sure." What my mom and I didn't know was that she didn't know beans about teaching riding, period, let alone jumping! She was lying through her teeth, but we bought it.

I did learn how to ride. Pretty badly! I rode Gillian's motley crew of horses and I loved every one of them. She had a big fenced oval in the trees that she called an arena. It was on a slope. We would chug up one side and zoom down the other. It was kind of like riding my neighbors' Shetland pony.

I became a fixture at Gillian's barn. I would hurry home from school, throw on some jeans, and head for the barn. I was there for hours every weekend too. I rode and rode, and helped with all the chores. They weren't chores to me. It was *heaven.*

When I was eleven my parents finally got me my first horse. She was a little gray mare, and her name was Gray Lady. She was one of the better lesson horses, older and quiet. I rode her everywhere. I even rode her home. I would tie her to a tree in the yard, get a snack, then go on my way. She was a perfect first horse for a young girl; very safe and sensible, but game for adventure.

I guess Gillian thought I needed a show horse. I had tried a couple of little shows on her school horses. I don't remember winning any ribbons, but I was hooked.

Gillian was a real horse trader in those days. A walk-trot pony came to the barn. A walk-trot pony is one of Saddlebred type, very flashy with high knee action. This one looked like he had lots of Hackney Pony blood. They canter, too; Walk-Trot is just the name of the show division. Apparently I was learning to ride Saddle Seat. I didn't know; I kept waiting for someone to teach me to jump! My parents bought me this pony, and Gray Lady went back to Gillian. We named him Hy-Flyte. At our first show he ran off with me and my trainer had to come rescue me. He was quite the handful. I never showed him anymore after that, but I did ride the snot out of him. I would jump on him bareback in a halter and go lickety-split up the driveway to the barn. I just wanted to ride; it didn't matter how. I had my first serious fall off of him, resulting in a mild concussion. I couldn't remember anything I did that day. Of course we never wore helmets back then! I just remember tacking him up on a cold day and jumping on. I guess he was a little cold backed and bucked me right off, and I bonked my head. I got right back on and rode the pants off of him; at least that's what everybody said.

Somehow I got to be a pretty good Saddle Seat Equitation Rider. Gillian was going through phases with horses and trainers. She had Tennessee Walkers and Morgans and finally settled on Arabians. She bought several, got a good trainer, and started breeding them as well.

I showed some of Gillian's horses and some of the horses they took in
for training in the Junior and Amateur divisions. Sometimes there were
equitation classes. I did pretty well, except sometimes I was nervous and
stiff as a board. Gillian's oldest two sons started functioning as trainers.
The rest of them all rode to a certain degree and they all worked in the
barn. They were an interesting bunch, the Lyon's. They were probably
the poster family for dysfunctional, but what did we know back then?
My mom was busy working. She was also plotting and planning very
quietly but very determinedly to leave my dad. She was thankful to
have me in a place where I was busy and happy all day. I guess it was a
trade-off for never being home to help clean house.

The summer of my 14th year Gillian took me on a buying trip
to Will Jamison's place in Lumberton, N.C.. He owned a bunch of
Arabian mares and a National Champion Arabian stallion. He was a
good breeder of fine stock. Will had a bunch of foals for sale and Gillian
was going to get some. She said she took me along to help her decide
which ones to buy. What she was *really* doing was letting me pick out
a foal that my parents were going to give me for Christmas! I had no
idea. I was flattered that Gillian asked for my advice. I picked out a rose
gray colt that floated across the pasture to check us out. Gillian said *yes*
to that one. She also bought his sister. It was a fun trip!

Gillian brought them home after they were weaned that fall. She
told me the little colt was to be sold, and would I please handle him a
lot so that he would be gentle for his new owners? Of course I jumped
all over that! Her middle son handled the filly. We had lots of good
times gentling those babies. We nick-named them Gomer and Patty,
aka *Gomer's pile* and *Patty's duke!!*

Right before Christmas that year, Gillian informed me that Gomer
had been sold to a family for their young daughter. She asked me if
I would spend extra time making him pretty, as he was going to be
delivered on Christmas Eve. I was heartbroken, as I had become very
attached to the little fellow. But it was business, so I said, "Of *course.*"
I spent a long time on Christmas Eve grooming him and crying into
his mane. Then it was time to go home to my family, as we always

opened our presents the night before Christmas. I tearfully bade Gomer farewell, envious of the young girl who was going to get him, and thinking I would probably never see him again.

My family did their annual Christmas Eve ritual of carefully opening one present at a time, after "Santa" carefully examined the name tags on each package, then handed out presents one at a time in careful and just-so order to each person. Relatives with cameras took lots of pictures. It *just-so* happened that one of my packages was the very last one. Looking back, I remember the sense of anticipation in the air. As I carefully unwrapped the present with all eyes glued, I opened the slim box. Inside was a photograph. Of *Gomer*. I drew a quick breath and looked at my mom in wonder. "*He's yours now*," my Mom said with a smile. "*You* were that young girl." I broke down sobbing, this time with joy. I don't think there was a dry eye in that room! My dad and brothers took me out to the barn that very night, so I could cry *happy* tears into Gomer's mane.

I had to wait a few years for Gomer to get big enough to ride. I handled him a *lot*. I showed him in halter at the North Carolina State Fair. He won! He was a beautiful boy. About the time he was old enough to ride I hit puberty. Hmmmm … an adolescent horse and an adolescent girl. We both thought we were *all that*.

I trained him to carry me with the help of the resident trainer. I wanted to do it all by myself, but after about the third or fourth major wreck, Gillian and my mom insisted that I hand him over to the trainer to put some miles on him. I was *annoyed*. I wanted to do it all by myself. Looking back I am sure Gillian and my folks were fearful for my life! Now *I* am the lady that tones down the headstrong 15 year old girls. I was back on Gomer in no time. I rode him all over the place.

I started to show that spirited young boy. He would put in brilliant performances in the English Pleasure classes, only to blow it at the end by refusing to stand still; freaking out at the clapping and cheering of the audience. Once at the fair some well meaning dude tried to rescue me by grabbing Gomer's bridle, but that just made him rear sky high and broke my bridle to boot. Gomer got a reputation as a bad actor.

The summer before I became a high school senior, I decided I had had enough of the Lyons. Gillian thought I was her adopted daughter, but it had become oppressive. The boys were a little scary; so was the dad. The Lyons had become major players on the Arabian show circuit and their oldest son Derek was training all the horses. I went to almost all the shows and sometimes got to ride a horse or two in the junior and amateur classes to help bring in more points. In exchange I worked hard as a roadie and groom. But I was at that age where independence was calling; I wanted new adventures, and I wanted to jump! I started looking around and found a beautiful barn on the other side of Raleigh. A Hunter-Jumper barn. It was expensive and a long ways to drive. My mom had a hissy-fit, but I was determined. The only way I could leave the Lyon's was to lie and sneak out under the radar. There was a big out-of-state show I was supposed to go to, but I said I couldn't; I had to go visit my dad. That made Gillian happy; for some reason she liked my dad but not my mom. I secretly made arrangements to borrow a truck and horse-trailer and high-tail it out of there after they left for the show. Gillian's middle son drove the truck. He was sad to see me go, but completely understood.

I got Gomer settled in his new digs. There I was, a poor, hick saddle-seat girl in the midst of moneyed folks who jumped their fancy, expensive thoroughbreds. I loved it. The people were nice enough. I made friends with the young trainer, who has since then become famous enough to appear on the cover of *Practical Horseman*. He even gave me a jump lesson or two on Gomer. The hunter-jumper people thought it was a little odd when I tied tin cans to Gomer's tail, but I explained that's what you do to cure horses of being frightened by loud noises. Spectators didn't carry on for the hunter rounds the way they did for saddle-seat classes; it just wasn't part of their culture. It wouldn't do to cheer crazily and stomp one's feet and clap when a person is jumping big fences! The whole idea of Hunters Over Fences is calm, quiet, and fluid.

An Arabian breeder showed up one day at the barn to board several of her horses. We hit it off right away, and I ended up riding for her. My friend Sissy got to ride one of her horses too, and we hit the trails and had a blast. It was my last year of high school, and Sissy was my best friend. I only needed four classes to graduate, and I wasn't a slave at Gillian's anymore. I had a lot of freedom. Sissy was a kindred spirit; we were emerging artists and loved nature and animals.

The lady with the Arabians hauled Gomer to a show in Winston-Salem for me, which was very kind of her. Gomer was his usual amazing, beautiful self until the line-up, of course. This time I was ready with a plan. When he started to dance around, I smacked him with a whip. Really hard. He was stunned. He tried it a couple more times. **Blammo.** He stood still for the rest of the class. *Mission Accompli.* The hardest thing for me was to spank him like that in front of a crowd of people, because I am *so* not like that. But it was totally what he needed, and it did the trick. From there on after, all I had to do in the line-up was hold the whip at the ready, and he was a good boy.

I took him to a large recognized Arabian show in Richmond, Virginia. I hitched a ride with a girl who used to ride at Gillian's, but who now was training on her own and was working with her parents out of a barn they had bought. My friend Sissy came along. Little did I know, she brought a secret weapon; *Teacher's Scotch.* She decided that uptight Gomer and uptight May Dilles needed a little help loosening up. It sure worked. Even though I don't really remember much of the ride or how on earth I stayed on, it must have been pretty good, because we won the English Pleasure Championship! To this day, if I am feeling a little nervous before a morning dressage test, I'll have a little Bailey's Irish Cream in my coffee. Thanks for the enlightenment, Sissy.

Sissy and I partied our way through our senior year of High School and somehow graduated. We were going to go to Appalachian State University and study art together. As our equally wild and wooly summer came to a close, I started having grave doubts about leaving my horse behind. I felt sure I would flunk out of college. I got out my *Arabian Horse World* magazine and wrote to about twenty farms looking for an apprentice position. Sissy went off to college without me.

A couple of places answered. One was in Utah, which might as well have been Siberia. One was a little closer; Lilyville, Alabama. I flew down there for a visit. It was a big, beautiful, old southern ante-bellum type of an estate. It looked like something out of *Gone With the Wind*. It was a big breeding farm. I didn't know the trainer, but I had seen her around at some of the shows I went to with the Lyons.

After I met and interviewed with the owners, they said yes to me coming. I left Gomer in the care of some friends and flew back down. Shortly after, those friends drove him all the way down there for me. It was really a cool place, very nice folks and very nice horses, but it just didn't go fast enough for me. At Gillian's we worked every minute we were there. At the farm we mostly leisured away the winter. There were all these horses to train; why weren't we doing it?

I had terrible allergies there. I could barely breathe and have to go to bed. Finally I went to the doctor who gave me an antihistamine shot, which cleared things up. I had to get shots once or twice more. The trainer was probably glad when I was bedridden, as it meant I was not bugging her to teach me how to train all those beautiful horses.

Spring rolled around and so did show season. I was really upset because we had some really nice horses, but they didn't do well because, *duh,* they weren't all that trained! Isn't that what we should have been doing over the winter? The trainer and the owners didn't seem nearly as concerned about it as *I* was. Something was said about the trainer being the victim of some trauma at a barn in *her* past, and the owners had taken her in to shelter her. Looking back, they probably did her a wonderful turn and I should have seen it for what it was. But I was young and ambitious and driven, too selfish to see the greater good going on. The barn owners were especially kind to me, and so were their daughter and her husband. They were really decent folks. No doubt Abba was looking out for this headstrong girl of his who took off for parts unknown, and could have ended up in a bad situation like that trainer. Abba, please forgive the errors of my youth! I hope that trainer has forgiven me too.

After one dismal horse show I got into a huge fight with the trainer about her work ethic. I came down on her pretty hard. It was decided I needed to go. I was angry. The trainer was angry. The owners had taken her in as a daughter, and the daughter said I had to go. The owners were sad. They were kind enough to send me home with my horse in their truck and trailer, driven by one of their employees. God bless them; I wasn't always nice to them, either.

I ended up keeping Gomer at the same stable where I had first taken summer camp as a nine year old. They had bought a big, new property with nice indoor and outdoor arenas and a cross-country course! I ended up working there as a stall cleaner. I took some jump and dressage lessons. It was heavenly.

Chapter Seventeen

BACK HOME IN CARY, a *big* change took place. I gave my life to Jesus. I had always believed in God; took it as a given that He existed. I went to church here and there and thought it was great. I even went down front at a Billy Graham crusade in High School with a horse-loving friend from Gillian's. I never really took it seriously, like Christianity was something you actually *practiced*.

That summer I went to see the movie *Tommy* with a very cute boy from high school. I didn't know it, but I guess he was kind of a wild child who had come to Jesus a few times and had backslidden the same amount. The movie really did a number on him. He talked to me at length about Jesus and we both prayed for him to take over our lives. For the boy it was a heavy moment, but for me it was, "*Sure!* Why not?" the way I had approached this belief in God thing my whole life.

That boy took me to a prayer meeting that he knew of in a house on Pond Street in Cary, between where we lived now and where we used to live on Rose Street. After my parents' divorce my mom had rented an apartment quite close to Gillian's so that I could walk to the barn. Of course, *what did this headstrong daughter do?* Leave Gillian's for a barn on the other side of Raleigh. Poor Momma. Bless her heart.

The prayer meeting was made up of high school and college kids mixed in with a few misfits. It was led by some young and middle-aged adults, some married with young children. It was toward the end of the Charismatic movement, and these folks were the products of it. "Regular" church didn't do it for them. The earlier Pentecostal movement had devolved into the Pentecostal *Church*. This new shift and shake by Father had resulted in the House Church Movement. People sure like to put labels on things.

These folks were serious about God. About getting *right* with God. In response I said, "Sure! *Why not?*"

My friend didn't stay long with the group, as was his usual m.o., but I did. These people were friendly. These people were passionate about God. These people showed love and concern for one another. These people spoke truth and life. These people gave *hugs*. That was sure different for me. It took some getting used to. I even learned to hug back.

After I had been home for a couple of months, I took a job as a working student with a trainer about 50 miles from home. Dan McHale was a nice man, and so was his wife. They had a couple little kids. They also raised tobacco. They set me up in an Airstream trailer to live, and I brought Gomer along to live in the barn. In the morning I would clean the barn. After lunch I would ride several horses, sometimes with Dan watching. Often he would be in the tobacco fields, and his wife was busy with the kids. So much for being a working student. I was the work*ER*. I worked incredibly hard.

During breakfast, lunch and supper I also devoured a youth bible I had purchased, *The Way*. Having never really read the Bible, I couldn't get enough. I read myself to sleep each night. I was alone I in a little Airstream camper way out in the country. There wasn't much else to do. There was nobody to talk to except God and the horses. I found myself lonely and longing for my day off, Sunday, so I could drive home Saturday night and go to the house church Sunday morning. I would be sad to go back to my isolation. I loved riding the horses, but the work was exhausting. I was lonely. My Mom sent me to her doctor, and he thought I might have mononucleosis. He prescribed rest. I thought "*Sure*, uh-huh", but I could barely function. I ended up quitting that job, selling my dear Gomer, and moving back home. It broke my heart to sell my baby, but it seemed right to do it. A girl sort of appeared out of nowhere and really wanted to buy him. She did. As soon as we closed the deal over the phone, I wailed so loudly Mom thought something was terribly wrong. Well, it *was*!

I was horseless for the first time since I got my first horse when I was eleven. I was totally burned out, too. I took a job at a clothing store at Cameron Village, Raleigh's little shopping center before the big malls took over. I went to the house church and pondered life. My family thought … *who knows what they thought.* Poor mama. I bet she was really tired of parenting by then. Her last two, me and my older brother, Garret, just did not fit the family mold. We were both pretty different, but the fact we were *different* was the same.

In the very early spring, a position came open over in Chapel Hill, about an hour west of Cary. A couple needed someone to help with a horse farm they had just purchased. I was to teach, ride, and help out with chores. It sounded good to me! I left Mama and lived in the house with the owners. I was twenty-one. Before long I had a neat little group of Saddle-Seat students. Before long they learned to ride, and before long quite a few bought horses.

We started going to horse shows. First we went to little local shows and then bigger shows. We did well! How I loved those girls. One of my best and funniest memories is when the owners of Azalea Glen Farm hosted a Halloween party. In North Carolina it is usually pretty mild on Halloween. Most of the festivities were in the backyard, which was between the house and the barn. The rest of it would be held in the cute mother-in-law apartment which was attached to the house. Everyone expected me to come, but I told them I was going to another party and would drop in later.

I would drop in, *all right.* That night after dark, I drove my little Toyota Corolla to Azalea Glen, but parked it across the street out of sight. Then I carefully found my way along the north fence line back to the barn, where Lou Brinkley and her mom were waiting next to their horse's stall. Darq One was a big black Half-Arabian, Half-Saddlebred, bred long before National Show Horses became such a sensation.

We tacked him up in pitch black dark. He snorted a little as if to say, "What on *earth?!?,*" but was otherwise a good boy. I donned a cape and stuck a plastic pumpkin over my head. Then I mounted up, stuck a flashlight through the bottom of the pumpkin, and galloped to the backyard where all the kids were playing spooky Halloween games.

Through the eyeholes cut in the pumpkin head I saw looks of shock and disbelief come over everyone's faces. Then sheer terror. Screaming, they all made a beeline for the apartment. I tried to canter around like I was going to gather everyone up, but all my fiery Halloween steed would do was rear. In the dark we had accidentally criss-crossed the reins under his head, and the more I tried turning Darq One, the more confused he got. We didn't manage to round anyone up, but the rearing was rather spectacular. I couldn't have planned it any better. Finally I pulled the pumpkin head off so all my terrified students could see it was just lil' ol' me. As relief flooded their young faces (and some not so young) we all had a good, good laugh. And what a good boy Darq One was to play along!

Before long a set of parents fixed me up with a really great young man, Stuart Smith. He loved the Lord. We started going to the Chapel Hill Bible Church. I really liked it. I joined the choir; made some great friends. I still went home often to visit family and go to the house church. I was very happy and life was full.

I started evangelizing my students; that's just what you do when you are an on-fire, young believer. Many gave their lives to Jesus. I was young, zealous and innocent; I didn't realize I was turning up the heat and the pot would soon boil over onto the stove. Two sisters were Jewish and one girl came from a Catholic family. Their parents became alarmed when their kids came home talking about their conversion. They complained to the owners.

One day the barn owner sat me down in a lawn chair in their backyard and calmly explained to me why the parents had voiced their concerns. He said I needed to stop telling students about Jesus. I said, "No. I won't stop sharing." He became pretty agitated. I was dead calm. He ended up grabbing my collar, lifting me out of the chair as it toppled backward, and shoving me up against the side of their house. His face was in my face and it was furious. I never did back down. Finally he dropped me and stomped away. The grace of God was all over me. That is how Stephen must have felt at his stoning.

Later, when I was up in my room, the wife came and issued an ultimatum. "Teach riding or teach Jesus!," she snarled. I chose riding. Shortly afterward I got the opportunity to move into a really cool apartment in a lovely house just down the road. The house was on a hill in the woods, and the apartment faced the steep slope with a deck built over it. It was my first apartment, and it was fabulous. I held prayer meetings there for my students. Amazingly enough their parents let them come. One Christmas I had a birthday party for Jesus. I held communion. I didn't think a thing about it; we did that at the house church in Raleigh all the time. That did not go over well at *all* with the Catholics!

I had an awful lot to learn. I didn't know anything about different religions and the *faux pas* one could commit by breaking rules and traditions. I didn't know most Jewish people did not recognize Jesus as their Messiah. Ignorance was bliss, I guess.

As time went by, Stuart and I fell deeply in love and dreamed of marriage. He was still in college so we would have to wait. It tore my heart out when he would leave in the fall to go back to school. I thought he was perfect. He thought I was pretty okay, too. I took him with me to the house church one time, both to let him have the experience and to show him off a bit. Everything seemed hunky-dory, but when I went back to house church (we called it *The Church at Raleigh* back then) one of the women, Constance Easterton, pulled me aside and told me not to marry Stuart. There was nothing wrong with him, she said, but if I married him, we would be unequally yoked. She said my calling was higher than his, that he wouldn't, couldn't go where I was called. I thought she was nuts. I thought she was rude. Stuart was a wonderful young man; my family loved him. They were all *for* us marrying. I was stunned; I didn't want to hear her words! I went back to Chapel Hill and I ran straight to the Lord. I gave Him my heart. I gave him Constance's words. I gave Stuart back to him. I waited.

Incredibly, in less than two weeks I felt free. I ended my relationship with Stuart. That was hard and painful for both of us. Neither of us really understood what was happening and he felt very rejected. He was away at school; when he came back he said an official goodbye. That was really, *really* hard. What a grand soul he was, and probably still is. I have often wondered how he has faired in life. I recently found him on Facebook. He looks wonderful. He is married and has three beautiful children. I've always wanted to tell him how sorry I was that I hurt him. I hope I can do that. Hey Stuart, if you're reading this:

I'm sorry.

Another thing Constance told me was that I should move back to Raleigh and become more involved in the church. After I broke up with Stuart, I pondered that. I didn't want to though, as I was enjoying my life and my work in Chapel Hill. Before long the owners of Azalea Glen announced that they had sold the stables to a young couple. I met them and they invited me to stay. She was a hunter/ jumper rider, but she said I could stay and keep teaching saddle-seat. I did, but it soon became uncomfortable. It was obvious she didn't think much of saddle-seat. We got a new boarder who was a graduate of Pacific Horse Center in California. She was a fabulous dressage and jumping rider. She and the new owner became best buds.

After awhile it seemed best to move on. I had to tie up some loose ends. I had part ownership in that lovely Half-Arabian gelding, so I sold my half to the other owners, Lou and her mom, who owned the cool black gelding I rode for my Halloween prank. I had Frankie, an Arabian stallion Azalea Glen's owner's had given to me. I brought him home and kept him at a barn very close to my Mom's house that she had bought in Raleigh. It boarded on a state park. I spent many happy hours trail riding him there. The barn had a rental string of horses so sometimes some of my church friends came along. I felt sorry for the rental horses though. They seemed bored and sad tied up to the hitching post all day in the hot sun. I would often visit and bring them water.

Some guys from the church helped move all my stuff back to Mom's. One of them just happened to be Caleb. I have to laugh. How many times has Caleb helped me move all my stuff since then?

Poor Mom. Was she *ever* going to have a house to herself after all these years? It was her very own house that she had managed to buy all by herself after renting an apartment for several years. She sighed and very lovingly let me pick out colors and bedclothes for my room. She put up shelves for all my china horses. Mom tried not to get too angry when I dumped India ink all over her new carpet in her new home.

Chapter Eighteen

I IMMERSED MYSELF IN THE Church at Raleigh. It wasn't like anything I had ever experienced. These people had stopped in their tracks when they met Jesus. They had given their lives over to God and each other. Some had opened their homes to whoever needed a place to stay. On Triune Road in Raleigh, not far from Mom's, there was an older couple, Mr. and Mrs. Gretson, with a grown son who was in the church. They had a small farm with an old barn and a few cows.

Constance and Rowan Easterton rented a spacious apartment in their attic. They had two little boys and a little girl. Across the street from them were three brick duplexes. Eventually all of them were rented by young couples in the church. On Triune Road were five church families; the Gretson's home with the upstairs apartment and various young singles living with young married couples in the duplexes. Caleb was one of the single dudes, living with Mike and Shelly Fountain. Caleb's first wife said "don't come back" after he finished his basic training for the Army Reserves at Fort Leonard Wood, Missouri. Caleb had lived with her in Raleigh a few years earlier. They had hitch-hiked across the United States and southern Canada to attend a spirit-filled church gathering North Carolina, met some folks from The Church at Raleigh, and ended up staying. They had been a part of the church until the church "burped" and broke up, then they returned to Seattle. Their daughter Colleen Maera was born in nearby Durham, North Carolina during their time in the south. Caleb came to Raleigh after completing basic training to get advice on how to save his marriage. He ended up staying and moving in with Mike and Shelly. Each apartment held a different story. It was Christian community, *The Early Church* revisited.

I was floundering a little after having moved home. I wasn't quite sure what to do. I was having trouble with an eating disorder and I needed a job. I finally did get one at Hickory Farms at North Hills Mall selling cheese and stuff. It was kind of fun. One evening I accidentally locked my keys in my car, and who should come rescue me but *Knight in Shining Armor* Caleb. He lived in a house near the mall with Mike and Shelly at the time, before they moved to Triune Road. That was the start of our "courting" days. We still laugh about that, especially when I continued to lock my keys in our cars. Nowadays, they design them so you can't, unless you take the keys out of the ignition and put them in the cupholder like I do sometimes.

Poor Mom. I must have been pretty annoying to have around. When was she ever going to have an empty nest? Rowan and Constance Easterton had moved in with their 3 kids to help a lady who was struggling with her teenage daughter and her life. They thought I should come live there too, so I did. I became the Easterton kids' nanny. My mom thought it was weird, but she was probably glad to get rid of me!

The Eastertons, the woman, her daughter and I had the usual conflicts of communal living. I thought it would be nicer to fly the coop back to my Mom. I almost did, but I humbly went back and decided to slog it out.

The Eastertons eventually moved out of that lady's house and rented a big old farmhouse on Triune Road just down from the older Gretson's farm and the young couples' duplexes. Bonnie Gunderson, whose husband had left her and her young son, came to live there too and eventually a young couple with their three beautiful children, Murphy and Maryanne Rockwell. They had become Mennonites but weren't sure if that is what they should keep doing. They moved into a house trailer on the property.

I still had my Arabian stallion Frankie at the stable near my mom's house. I got permission to move him over to Gretson's farm, but the church elders didn't think I should own a horse. I loved horses so much they considered it a form of idol worship. I wanted to love God more than anything, so I put Frankie up for sale. I didn't have any takers except for one man who wanted to trade a diamond ring for my horse. I laughed about that. How little he knew of a true centaur! I ended up leasing him to a family I knew in Hillsboro, and he went to their farm for awhile. Rowan got a large flock of hens and a rooster. The rooster died of heart failure from trying to mate with all those hens. At least he died happy! Our head elder's wife wrote a hilarious song about the rooster's demise. It was all about restraining one's lusts and passions of the flesh, or you might go the way of Mr.Cocky!

In spite of the trials and tribulations of living in a full and very diverse household, we had some very wonderful times. Maryanne Rockwell used to be a Chicago nightclub blues singer before giving her life over to God and becoming a Mennonite. She now only sang Godly songs, but that wonderful, soulful voice was still there. We would sing together while washing dinner dishes. We discovered we harmonized beautifully. Many nights that old farmhouse would be filled to the rafters with God's praises. I know He really enjoyed the love songs we sang to Him.

Chapter Nineteen

The Church at Raleigh decided to start a school for all the kids in our fellowship. We rented a Full Gospel Assembly church during the week for our school building. I was Ramona Easterton and John Rockwell's kindergarten teacher. I had no training. We just used *A Beka Book* home school materials. Two of the older kids' teachers, Jim Monroe and Victoria Gretson, were certified public school teachers. We called it *Harmony School*.

Every morning we would start the day with worship in the church chapel. Jim was a great guitar player. One song we would always sing was *Give us a Song* on an album of Jonathan Edwards. Jim and I both liked his music a lot. It was a great song to start the day.

How that song has sustained me over the last forty years. I sang it with melancholy longing as we wandered in the "desert", wondering what *happened* to the glorious vision we beheld back in the Church at Raleigh era. One verse became very appropriate for me over the years:

You'll never know how hard I tried to find you,
I traveled here and ended up out there.
The devil has tried to sing the song of evil,
But he'll never know the kind of music people share.

The farmhouse and property we were renting was for sale, and before long it got sold. A couple in our church had a big house on a couple of acres in Raleigh. They were moving in to something smaller, as most of their kids were grown, so they rented it to our "family."

There were a couple of outbuildings that we turned into rabbit and chicken housing. The biggest shed caught my eye. It looked like a **HORSE BARN.** I guess Rowan and Constance thought I had given up horses long enough. We fixed it up a bit, I brought Frankie back from where he was living, and I leased an old pony from a lady I knew for all the kids to ride. That made it *easy* to be a nanny. I loved giving pony rides!

During that time an extension of U.S. Highway 64 was going in right beside the house. I rode Frankie up and down the steep embankment to the road under construction. On weekends when the workers were gone, I rode him on the level, graded packed red clay for miles. It felt like heaven.

Bonnie worked in Durham and Constance was bedridden with her third pregnancy, so I looked after all the kids a lot. My idea of great babysitting was to take the kids for long bareback rides on Dolly, the little white pony. The kids thought it was pretty cool too. I took care of the kids, took care of the house, took care of the horses, chickens, and rabbits. The rooster was an ornery Barred Rock that would come after me, Constance or the kids talons first. One day he got out of the chicken pen and went after the kids. Constance picked up a two-by-four and bashed him over the head like a pro. That stopped him. He seemed stunned, but he didn't die. Soon after we corrected that little issue and enjoyed Ornery Barred Rock Rooster Stew.

It was a *lot* of work butchering and plucking chickens. The rabbits had babies, well, like *rabbits,* and soon it was time to eat some. I tried doing one in. You hold them by their back legs and whack them hard and swift on the back of their head, so they die instantly. Nobody told me rabbits scream bloody murder as they are hanging upside down before you whack them. Nobody told me their eyes pop out. I only killed one and that was enough. I could handle butchering them. It was a whole lot easier than plucking chickens. Caleb started coming over to bop the bunnies. I guess those were our first "dates." *Romantic*, huh.

Caleb had a growing interest in me, and I in him, but the elders said absolutely ***not.*** After all, he was still a married man. His wife was fighting for a divorce, but Caleb and the church elders thought he should fight back to keep the marriage together, especially since they had a child. We did our best to just stay friends.

The harder Caleb fought to stay married to his wife, the worse she fought to get a divorce. Finally the church elders told Caleb to let her go. Caleb gave her up, but he also gave up on me! I was terribly hurt. I said, "Huh. What a *jerk!* Fine, then!" We both went our separate ways, as much as we *could* in a tight and small church community.

Chapter Twenty

SEVERAL MONTHS PASSED. CONSTANCE HAD "seen" Caleb and me as a couple in the Spirit, but she didn't say a word to anyone. Caleb cast his eye on a couple of cuties and so did I. Either nothing came of it, or those cuties up and married someone else!

Late that summer, when Caleb returned from South Carolina where he fulfilled his two week Army Reserve commitment, he stopped by the house where we all lived. He was in full uniform and he was proud of it. He had been to Drill Sergeant School. He *liked* being a Drill Sergeant. I guess he thought I might be impressed. I wasn't. He should have had a premonition or something right then! But he went ahead and asked me to marry him, and as funny as he looked in his *Bad Outfit*, I said yes.

We got engaged with the blessing of the elders. Constance told us what she had seen in the spirit. At first we were thinking about a beautiful spring wedding, *but what did this girl do?* I found some scriptures in Leviticus:

When you enter the land and plant any kind of fruit trees,
Don't eat the fruit for three years; consider it inedible.
By the fourth year it's fruit is holy; an offering of praise to God.
Beginning in the fifth year you shall eat its' fruit;
You'll have richer harvests this way.
I am Lord, your God.

Leviticus 19; 23-25 The Message Bible

I thought those scriptures were from God for us concerning our lives and our wedding date. I have disregarded them over the years, but *by George*, I think they really were from Abba.

We decided to marry on November 25th, 1979, less than six months away.

My mom threw a hissy fit about the date. "Why *November?* That's right before Christmas!" she complained. "It's your birthday two days before! It's right around Jeanne's, Kay's, and Garret's birthdays too!" (My oldest brother Winston's birthday is in June, just to be different.) *Poor Mom*. She thought I'd picked the worst possible time. She was wondering how to pay for everything. And *do* everything.

My mom told me I should ask Dad for help with the wedding expenses, so I did. He wrote me a check for $500.00 and we made do with that. Couples marrying within our group had the ceremony as part of the Sunday morning service and that's what Caleb and I wanted. We needed a space bigger than a living room or the club house at one of the elder's apartment complex where we met sometimes. No church was going to rent us their building on Sunday morning. A new YWCA had just been built in Raleigh on Oberlin Road, and it had some spacious rooms available to rent. It was not a problem to rent one on a Sunday morning.

Everybody in our church pitched in to decorate for the wedding and cook for the reception. My mom didn't have to buy anything or even do much. I wonder if she didn't end up feeling just a little bit left out. My church family transformed a bare room into a very decent place to get hitched. They brought in lots of their big house plants for greenery. My dad's money paid to rent the room and pretty much anything else we needed, like flowers, rented chairs and a candle stand. I borrowed a gorgeous Mexican wedding dress from my dear sister in the Lord, Victoria Gretson. I borrowed a veil from another sister in the Lord. I borrowed a blue garter from someone and I'm sorry I don't remember who it was. I borrowed shoes from somebody else. I did wear my own underwear. And teeth. I still have them, too. *Teeth,* that is.

Our wedding turned out to be quite the musical production. It was not your typical wedding! It was our version of Sunday church … all two-*plus* hours of it. I had invited several friends to sing. Maryanne

Rockwell, with her wonderful Chicago nightclub blues voice, started the "show" with a stately hymn as my Dad walked me down the makeshift aisle. When we got halfway to the makeshift altar, she starting clapping and grinning mischievously. The piano player ramped it up. Maryanne turned that hymn into a Chicago bluesy blast. Everyone laughed and started to clap and dance. Even though we didn't see him in His *Bad Outfit*, I am sure Abba was there in his fussy muslin gown and Captain Kangaroo bangs, doing a little shimmy in His tire tread sandals.

Two girls in our fellowship sang Psalm 103 with guitar music I had composed for it. Psalm 103 is precious to Len and me. We put it in our wedding day program. It has been prophetic to us over the years, and still is, just like those scriptures in Leviticus.

Psalm 103 *The Message Bible*

O my soul, bless God.
From head to toe I'll bless his holy name!
Oh my soul, bless God,
Don't forget a single blessing!

He redeems you from hell---saves your life!
He crowns you with love and mercy---a paradise crown.
He wraps you in goodness---beauty eternal.
He renews your youth---you're always young in His presence.

God makes everything come out right,
He puts victims back on their feet.
He showed Moses how He went about His work;
Opened up his plans for all Israel.

God is sheer mercy and grace;
Not easily angered, he's rich in love.
He doesn't endlessly nag and scold,
Or hold grudges for ever.

He doesn't treat us as our sins deserve,
Nor pay us back in full for our wrongs.
As high as heaven is over the earth,
So strong is His love to those who fear him.

As far as sunrise is from sunset,
He has separated us from our sin.
As parents feel for their children,
God feels for those who fear Him.

He knows us inside and out,
Keeps in mind that we're made of mud.

Men and women don't live very long,
Like wildflowers they spring up and blossom,
But a storm snuffs them out just as quickly,
Leaving nothing to show they were here.

God's love though is ever and always.
Eternally present to all who fear Him,
Making everything right for them and their children
As they follow His covenant ways
And remember to do whatever He says.

God has set His throne in heaven,
He rules over us all.
He's the King!

So bless God, you angels,
Ready and able to fly at His bidding,
Quick to hear and do what he says.

Bless God, all you armies of angels,
Alert to respond to whatever he wills.
Bless God, all creatures, wherever you are---
Everything and everyone made by God.

And you, O my soul, bless God,
Translate His wonders into music!
Honor His holy name with Hallelujahs,
You who seek God.

Live a happy life!
Keep your eyes open for God;
Watch for His works,
Be alert for signs of His presence.

Remember the world of wonders he has made,
His miracles, and the verdicts he's rendered---
Oh seed of Abraham, His servant,
Oh child of Jacob, His chosen.

Another dear friend in our church sang *Honeytree's* song about Ruth. I had written my own vows about me being Ruth and Caleb being Boaz from the Old Testament. I sang my vows to Len as though I were Ruth singing to Boaz. Caleb took my hands and said vows he had written on his heart. We took communion. We lit candles. Rowan Easterton pronounced us man and wife. Then Caleb lifted my veil and we kissed, our very *first* kiss. Everyone hooted, stomped, cheered and clapped!

We had a wonderful potluck lunch at the apartment clubhouse where we had church sometimes. It was downright homey. My dear friend Makeda Ennishad had made us a beautiful 3-tiered wedding cake---and it was orange, to honor the fall foliage. Sorry, Victoria, for that little orange stain it left on your beautiful dress!

We spent our first night together at the Plantation Inn, a gorgeous old destination place in north Raleigh. The next morning we left for our honeymoon in the mountains of West Virginia. My dad had a business acquaintance that let us stay in his sweet little cabin for a week, free of charge. It was cold. It snowed. But *we* didn't care! We had a glorious time hiking and exploring our surroundings ... and each other.

Chapter Twenty-One

WHEN OUR HONEYMOON WAS OVER we came home to our apartment, a converted second floor of a large brick house just down the road from my mom's place. It was an old, stately-looking house owned by an elderly widow. She rented it to us for fifty dollars a month. I tried my best to turn our space into something featured in *Better Homes and Gardens*. I didn't quite hit the mark, but I sure tried. I found an interesting pod-like thingy that was caught in the bushes on one side of the house. I stuck it in with some dried flowers on our coffee table that Caleb made from an old door. One spring day I awoke and stumbled groggily into the kitchen to make coffee. Then I stumbled groggily into the living room to sit on the couch, sip coffee and wake up. I got help in that department. Hundreds of tiny newly hatched Praying Mantises were everywhere! By the time I had helped them find a new life outside in the balmy North Carolina spring weather, I was fully awake.

Caleb was full of surprises. One evening a short while after we "jumped the broom" Caleb brought home a bottle of champagne and poured us both a glass. Being a good little born-again Christian girl, I didn't drink, and I didn't think Caleb drank either. But I didn't argue with the one I loved, so I drank it down. Caleb refilled my glass. I was such a lightweight it shot straight to my head.

Soon I was giggling merrily, then laughing hysterically. Somehow we got into an argument that turned into an ugly fight. I started sobbing, then crying rather hysterically. Caleb thought it very entertaining. I dashed the wineglass on the floor and decided to leave. Caleb escorted me down the steps with my left arm twisted painfully across my back.

Somehow I got loose and got into our old station wagon. I high-tailed it over to the Easterton's little apartment over the Gretson's house, tears and snot running down my face. I wanted comfort and consolation, and maybe a couch for the night, but I walked right into an elder's meeting.

"Go home to your husband," I was firmly instructed. I was aghast. No comfort, no consolation. Only one man's firm orders while the others kept quiet like little pansies. I didn't know where Constance was, but she wouldn't have been allowed to intervene anyway. I turned and stumbled back down the stairs of *their* apartment. I didn't want to upset my Mom or impose on either of my brothers who lived nearby, so I went back home. I think Caleb had gone to bed. And so it began.

One morning the sheriff came to our door. He had a subpoena for Caleb for small claims court. He had joined a fitness club but hadn't used it, so he hadn't paid his monthly membership dues for a few months. The fitness club wanted their money.

I wasn't aware of that, or all the money that Caleb owed on student loans from going to college in Seattle. We hadn't discussed money matters before we married. It was all about love and serving Jesus, not the daily grind! I was shocked and dismayed. In my family, our religion was *Money and How to Manage it.* That meant you *always* paid your bills on time, *never* ran up credit cards, and had a hefty savings account, which you only added to, never subtracted from. I thought everyone lived that way. Poor Caleb was just trying to juggle dollars and survive; something I have gotten pretty good at by now. I think a lot of folks have in the current economy. Back then however, my Prince Charming suddenly turned into Prince *Alarming!*

So what did this girl do?

I sprung into action. I got my old job back at Hickory Farms. I also taught some riding lessons out at my friend's place, where I had taken Frankie to board after Caleb and I got married. We paid off the fitness center and started chipping away at the student loans. So much for Caleb's fantasy of having a sweet little thing who stayed barefoot and pregnant.

One Sunday morning our head elder stood up in our church meeting and announced that the Lord had told him to step away from church leadership for a season. He had heard correctly, but most of the young people under his discipleship reeled from that announcement as though they had been hit by a train. Our church came unglued and fell apart. At the same time the economy did the same thing and the United States fell into a recession. Caleb and the former Mennonite brother in our church had just started a new remodeling business and soon there was not a drop of work. *Poor Mom.* Caleb had borrowed a thousand dollars from her, and it took a very long time to pay her back. Caleb, still in the Army Reserves, gave serious consideration to enlisting full time.

Some glitches in Caleb's Reserve paperwork made full time enlistment challenging, but with Mom's help writing our Senator he finally got the green light to go down to Fort Benning, Georgia. Caleb left for Columbus first and found us an apartment near the post. They were the infamous, cockroach-infested Camilla Apartments, the very same infamous, cockroach-infested Camilla Apartments my sister Kay stayed in when her first husband went through basic training during the Vietnam War.

I packed up and drove a U-Haul truck down there with Len's little girl, six year old Colleen Maera. Colleen had come to live with us exactly nine months after Len and I married. Her mom was at a tricky place in her life and thought Colleen would be better off with us. Colleen's grandmother flew with her to Chicago. Caleb and I drove up there to fetch her home to Raleigh. I didn' know *nuthin'* 'bout babies, but I said "Sure! Why not?" In the airport bathroom Colleen asked if she could call me Mom, and I said, "Sure! Why not?"

After we left O'Hare we stopped for lunch. Colleen got a hot dog and a root beer, which she promptly threw up. *Motherhood 101,* baby. The rest of the trip was uneventful. Colleen and I sang our guts out the whole trip.

The day after we got back from Chicago I took her out to the barn where I boarded Frankie because I had to teach a lesson on him. The daughter of the barn owner asked if Colleen could take a little bareback ride on her very sweet, dependable Arabian gelding. I said, "Sure! Why not?" Colleen was having a wonderful time until the guys working on the roof next door dropped a big section of shingles off the roof to the ground. The horse shied hard at the end of the lead and Colleen slipped off. Her right forearm hurt badly. For someone just five years old she was extremely stoic about it.

"I'm in a great deal of pain", she moaned in her husky little voice. I ended up taking her to the local hospital emergency room, and sure enough it was broken. She cried as they reset it. So did I. I had to call Caleb. "Great!" I thought as I dialed the number. "I've had his kid in my care less than 24 hours and she's already broken." Of course we had to call her mom as well. What a stellar start to my motherhood! **Motherhood 101,** baby. Now Colleen Maera Estes is married with 4 babes of her own. Not one of them have broken their arms yet.

When we got to Columbus, we quickly made the tiny apartment a home and made friends with the cockroaches. Spring came early down there, making Fort Benning truly beautiful. Colleen and I decided this was a pretty cool adventure. If we were driving onto the post to pick up Caleb or go to the commissary, often we would have to pull over for platoons of recruits jogging by, the drill sergeant leading, singing lusty running tunes. Colleen would love to yell "get **DOWN,** meat!" She especially loved it if I had the windows open! Sometimes we would be on post at five o'clock when the post loudspeakers broadcast Taps being played on bugles to close the day. You were supposed to pull over, get out of your vehicle and solemnly salute the nearest American flag. Colleen thought it was awesome.

To my amazement and excitement, I discovered the post had really nice riding facilities. They had a large stable area with a barn, and lots of run-in sheds with paddocks where military families could keep horses. There were two outdoor riding arenas, one filled with stadium jumps. There was a round pen. On one of their parade fields, they had several field jumps. Best of all, alongside one of their endless tank trails, was a several-level cross country jump course!

I made arrangements for Frankie to be shipped down after we moved and checked out the stabling. Fort Benning did not allow stallions on the post stables. I had to have him gelded at nine years of age, poor guy. Once he arrived at Fort Benning he had to spend a couple weeks in quarantine so he would not transport any deadly, nasty diseases down from North Carolina; you know, that *Yankee* southern state. The quarantine area was isolated, but beautiful. It was an old unused amphitheatre in the woods. Frankie hated it because he was all alone, but he was a trooper and made it through. After quarantine he got a nice loafing shed with a run right next to a bunch of other horses. His neighbor's owners were concerned that he was recently gelded, but I assured them that Frankie had been a very nice gentleman when he was a stallion. He didn't cause any problems.

I had left behind my saddle-seat riding days when I left Azalea Glen Stables in Chapel Hill. After moving Frankie and me back to Raleigh, I had dabbled a little with jumping and dressage whenever I could afford lessons and had the opportunity, Years earlier at one big all-breed show at the Dorton Arena in Raleigh, a woman did a half-time Musical Kur dressage demonstration on her Grand Prix dressage horse. Even though my church friend who rode dressage pointed out many errors in the performance, I was totally spellbound. Right then and there I told myself, "*that* is what I will do someday!" It set the stage for a big change in my life. That demo was one of the most beautiful things I had ever seen.

Showing Arabians and Saddlebreds was not the Oneness with horses my heart longed for. It was more like animosity between man and beast. It was scaring the pants off them so that their performance looked flashy and animated. Often that degenerated into abuse. I had a few experiences that told my heart and soul it was *so* very wrong. It was certainly not what my heart desired when I was a little girl practicing neighing so the neighbor's horse would answer. I wanted *communion* with horses. Almost forty years down the road, I am a little bit closer to that goal.

Chapter Twenty-Two

THERE WERE SOME WONDERFUL PEOPLE at Fort Benning that I worked with to learn more about dressage and jumping. There were two older ladies down there who helped me with dressage. They were absolutely fabulous. I took a couple of jumping lessons from the post commander's daughter, but I mostly muddled about on my own. I am sure it would make any experienced event trainer's hair stand up, but I often took Frankie down the tank trails and clandestinely asked him to jump some of the cross-country jumps. God was really looking after me, back then, apparently, as I really had no idea what I was doing, other than watching and reading, and Frankie had no jump training.

I taught Colleen how to ride a little bit (no more broken bones!) and we were able to lease a small pony for her from a retired Colonel who helped run the barn. Her name was Penny Pony. She was fun for Colleen when she wasn't doing pushy pony mare stuff, like running Colleen over! The guy who was in charge of the stable, an old curmudgeon retired Sergeant Major, had a great quarter horse that he wasn't riding and he would loan him out to us. Caleb would plop Colleen on the back of that boy and off we would go for hours on the tank trails. It was wonderful.

The barn area had that nice round pen, and often I would put Frankie in there and ride him without a saddle or bridle, simply working on balance and being one with him. I had read enough books to know *that* is what you do if you want to be one with your horse as you ride. I didn't have anyone to longe me, but the round pen worked great. I went round and round at walk, trot, canter, doing the suppling exercises I had seen in my books.

That summer I heard about a little horse trials not far from Fort Benning. A young captain's wife asked me if I wanted to go along with her. I said "Sure! Why not?" and so we went. I rode in the 2-foot Hopeful Division. Frankie was awesome and we won first place. We have an old 8mm movie of that event, and it shows Frankie absolutely *throwing* himself into the water complex. Usually Hopefuls don't do water, so I wonder if I just added that in for fun. In stadium a little dog came galloping into the arena and jumped with us. It was *so* much fun. I was hooked.

In the fall the Old Guard Ceremonial Unit from Fort Meyer, Va. was down recruiting. Caleb put in his request and was accepted. Soon we had our traveling papers. Caleb went up ahead of us while I packed up our apartment, making sure we didn't have any stowaway cockroaches. I left Frankie in the good care of one of those terrific dressage ladies. Then Colleen, myself and the three coon hound puppies we had acquired sang and bayed our way up to my Mom's house. We stayed just long enough for one of the puppies, a beautiful Walker hound named Dancer, to eat a piece of carpet in his kennel and become violently ill. A big vet bill later, he was on the mend. A short time after that we were on our way to Arlington, Virginia.

It was a big jump going from sleepy little Raleigh and even sleepier little Columbus, Georgia, up to buzzing and crackling Washington, D.C.. It was terribly exciting and terribly expensive. We had rented a town house in Reston, Virginia, a planned community. There was a long waiting list to get into post housing. It was a nice townhouse and Reston was a nice suburb and they even let us bring the three coonhound pups. We began the process of settling in and exploring our new home. There was so much to do, so much to see!

Most of my day was spent with Colleen Maera and the coonhound puppies. The three of them were a lot of hound dog for our little postage stamp backyard. We would take them for walks in a large nearby park that was mostly in its' natural state. The puppies would follow their noses, hit a scent, and then give voice in the beautiful way that Caleb and I loved. It took quite a bit to round them all up to come home, but we all got plenty of exercise.

Caleb had come to Fort Meyer not sure what he would do. There were lots of options. He could be a guard at the Tomb of the Unknown Soldier. He could be in the Presidential Color Guard. He could be in the Reconnaissance Platoon. He could be in the Caisson Platoon. There were even more choices. The Old Guard was basically a ceremonial unit, a real "dog and pony show" if you ask *real* soldiers. It made the Armed Forces look good to visitors. The *real* stuff is invisible.

Caleb chose to work in the Caisson Platoon, the only live, *real* horse unit left in the U.S. military. The horses pulled the funeral caissons bearing caskets to Arlington National Cemetery. They did parades and ceremonial stuff. The soldiers that worked in the Caisson Platoon had to clean the barn every morning, feed and water the horses, check them over, exercise them and keep their harnesses sparkling. They had to have the horses spotlessly clean and show groomed for the funeral processions and other ceremonial functions. They had to ride them in those functions. They had to hold them for the vet and farrier. They had to be, well, *horse people*. Mostly horse *dudes*. I never saw any girls there. I did end up helping them a little bit with their riding. For a *very* short time. I don't think they wanted some dumb *girl* teaching them stuff.

It was a very good thing I had taught Caleb to ride down at Fort Benning. New recruits had to pass an audition of sorts with which the soldiers working in the Caisson platoon had a field day. They would do things to try and trip up the applicants, like putting a pine cone under the saddle, or bringing a horse for a new recruit to ride with a very loose girth, or *no* girth. Then you could tell who truly knew a few things about riding, or at least how to stay in the saddle most of the time!

Caleb spotted all their devious little tricks and passed his audition with flying colors. He ended up being one of the best riders in the bunch. He worked in the Caisson platoon for over a year and managed to escape some very scary caisson wrecks. Imagine six terrified horses galloping with a caisson through the crowded streets of Roslyn, a good-sized metropolis right next to Fort Meyer!

After a while Colleen began to get disturbing phone calls and letters from her mom. She was really missing her daughter and her letters really upset Colleen and made her cry. This upset me too. I finally got angry enough to write a letter to her mom asking her to "cease and desist." Her mom's reaction was to insist that Colleen return home at once. Poor Colleen, she was caught in the middle. She was happy with us, but missed her mom terribly. Caleb was very upset, but we put her on a plane back to Seattle.

Suddenly I had all this free time on my hands. I kept house and walked the pups in the large nearby park. I looked into boarding Frankie, who was still in Georgia, but the prices were astronomical compared to Fort Benning.

When some officers found out Caleb was actually intelligent, they transferred him from the Caisson platoon to Hotel company to be the training NCO. In that position he managed training for the Caisson platoon, the Guns Platoon, the Recon platoon, and the Fife and Drum Corps. After a while they sent him over to the Public Affairs office, where he stayed for the next four years. Caleb worked there as NCO-In-Charge, carrying out the orders of the officer in charge and overseeing the lesser ranked enlisted soldiers who worked in the office. They managed *all* the public relations of the Old Guard which were many, quite varied, and interesting. Caleb loved it. He was really good at it, too.

I kept telling Caleb I wanted to visit the *Potomac Horse Center* in Gaithersburg, Maryland. Back when I was I was living in Chapel Hill, a girl my age came to board her horse when the new owners took over. That girl ended up partnering with the new owner instead of "little ol' saddle seat" me. That girl could *ride like stink*. That means "you ride REAL good." I had also seen a girl riding a horse at the rental string barn where I kept Frankie after I moved back to my Mom's. She was riding a boarder's horse that was for sale. I wasn't interested in the horse, but what struck me was the fact that girl could *ride like stink!* I asked her where she learned to ride like that, and she said, *"Potomac Horse Center."* Years later, when I worked at the horse-rental office at Fort Benning, I was cleaning out a desk. I ran across a job request from a girl who said she'd trained at *Potomac Horse Center.* I bet you anything she could ride like stink.

So we went up to Gaithersburg, about 45 minutes from our townhouse. What a beautiful horse-heaven that was! Green, rolling hills, the Potomac River flowing lazily by, majestic oak trees. Hunt country. Lots of coops and stone walls built right into the fence lines. Horse farm after horse farm. Old, majestic, and *expensive.*

Potomac Horse Center was huge. The main barn had about 75 stalls surrounding a huge indoor arena with offices and a lounge/viewing room upstairs. There were several more barns, two more indoor arenas and two outdoor arenas as well. Built into the pastures were lots and lots of cross country jumps. There were trails and a level grassy spot for setting up dressage arenas for outdoor shows. And that was even after selling off 200 of the almost 300 acres of it a few years prior! Did I mention housing for the students? And a swimming pool? And a cafeteria?

I decided right then and there that I was going. I set about finding out how to make that happen. Tuition was expensive, but they had a working student program. I signed up for that. I was worried I was too old to learn a new way of riding (I was only 26) but the head instructor, Tomasia Jettson, laughed and said I would be fine.

I started that fall, with Frankie still in Georgia. I had to be in the barn by six a.m., which meant I had to get up early enough for the 45 minute commute from Reston to Gaithersburg. When I got there I had to feed 8 horses, clean 8 stalls, scrub 16 water buckets, and help sweep the aisles. We had to keep the horses in our care spotlessly groomed, our tack cleaned and conditioned, and all the stalls, feed tubs and water buckets in pristine shape. We had to have the lesson horses ready for any and all students that came. We fed the horses lunch and dinner too. Sometimes the stable managers and instructors would hold impromptu inspections on everything. We had an hour-long mounted lesson every day, six days a week, and we had a daily lecture on riding theory or horse management. We helped the staff with horse show preparations. We picked endless buckets of stones out of the outdoor arena.

The down side of being at the Horse Center all day was we had to find our beautiful coon hound puppies new homes. They had turned the tiny back yard into a wasteland. They had learned to jump on the air conditioning unit and over the fence. Neighbors started to complain. We kept them in the house from then on, but they annihilated our couch and were bent on destroying the rest of the furniture. It wasn't fair to expect three hunting hounds of a tender exuberant age to lie quietly about and play nicely with their toys while we were gone. They were beautiful, quality hounds so it didn't take us long to re-home them. It was hard to see them go.

Back at the Horse Center our group sang and "talked trash" as we swept the aisles, tidied the muck heap and picked rocks. We would make up our own songs about certain staff members and put them to popular tunes. *You're so Vain* by Carly Simon was one of my favorites at the time. We reworked the song to fit one of our instructors who was on the Olympic team and seemed to think rather highly of himself. It seemed plainly obvious to us that teaching scumbag working students was beneath him. We sang loud and long as we swept aisles and picked rocks. We drew smiles and comfort from that song and the Negro spirituals we sang as we slaved away. I don't know if the object of the Carly Simon remix ever knew about it. If he reads this he will recognize himself, no doubt. But that was almost 40 years ago, and thank God time has matured both of us.

Riding in the A.I. (assistant instructor's) course meant getting rid of all prior muscle memory for whatever way you used to ride, and learn new muscle memory for the way you were *going* to learn to ride. That meant most of our lessons were spent riding without stirrups or reins, doing lots of suppling exercises. There were too many of us for longe line lessons, but fortunately the school horses knew their job. They would trot and canter quietly around the huge indoor arena on their own, rarely missing a beat, while Tomasia drilled us for 45 minutes. My crotch got so raw from all that work without stirrups that I started wearing Caleb's thick olive drab Army Issue underwear just to get through those lessons. But man, *we learned to ride like stink*. My crowning achievement was sitting little Y-Knot's incredibly jarring trot. Y-knot was a retired, funny-looking little buckskin, but I guess he had been an incredible jumper in his day. It was a Horse Center golden achievement to say you could sit Y-knot's trot in a saddle with stirrups. I *did* it. I haven't been able to sit the trot like that since, but I'm still working on it.

I was able to graduate three months early from the Assistant Instructor's course. My dear friend brought Frankie up to the Horse Center from Georgia in her truck and trailer. She was visiting family in North Carolina and decided to bring my horse, and while she was visiting I drove Frankie the rest of the way. God bless her! The Horse Center took him in trade for the Horsemaster's course tuition. This time I didn't have to be a working student! Instead of taking care of eight horses, I only had two. I got *two* riding lessons and *two* lectures a day instead of one each. My friend Cheryl, who was in my A.I. course, snuck in on my coat tails with the same deal, 3 months ahead of schedule. We added a third girl, Betsie, who was returning for her Horsemasters after being away for a time.

We became *The Three Musketeers*. Depending on who you were talking to, we were also The Three Stooges!

In the mornings during stall cleaning time, we would get really silly, playing air guitars and jamming in the barn aisles. *Very* different for me, the usually quiet and serious young woman that I was! One morning Betsie, Cheryl and I snuck an old 2 person horse costume out of a closet upstairs and we crashed the A.I. formal inspection. Cheryl dressed up in her *Bad* formal riding *Outfit* and Betsy and I donned the horse costume. Cheryl put a nice clean halter on the paper mache head, trotted us in, and stood us up with the other students and their real horses. She was totally serious, but her horse was a little naughty. We caused quite a stir; the real horses thought we were downright terrifying! Betsy and I were laughing our guts out underneath that costume while Cheryl deadpanned it. Through the eyeholes I could see Tomasia Jettson trying very hard not to laugh. It was truly a great moment in Potomac Horse Center History.

I wonder how those girls are now. Cheryl went to California to work for a well-known dressage trainer. I don't know what happened to

Betsy. After we graduated, I stayed on as an assistant instructor. I had to get back to being serious. But girls, wherever you are, my time with you was *SO* much fun.

As an assistant instructor, I mostly taught kids' group lessons. I rode a few of the boarders' horses. It was interesting being on staff instead of being a student. I enjoyed both teaching and riding, but I began to see some things. Disturbing things. A young woman had taken over as Barn Manager a few months earlier, and her boyfriend was the Horse Center farrier. He was very talented and *very* expensive. Seems like the school horses needed shoeing an awful lot. Seems like the young woman didn't show up half the time, and yours truly would have to pitch in and do her job. I finally complained to the owner of Potomac Horse Center. who promptly fired the girl and gave me her job. Both my riding instructors through the programs pitched hissy fits; they thought I should pursue a training and teaching career. That is what I wanted too, but I couldn't stand watching the Horse Center and its' horses get ripped off. Besides, I did get a nice raise.

Shortly after that the owner of Potomac Horse Center hired Bunnie Ascott to be the head honcho. She used to help run the Horse Center and had gone on to manage Gladstone, headquarters of the USET. Bunnie was an extremely knowledgeable horsewoman. She came back to Potomac Horse Center to get their financial situation under control. The Horse Center was hemorrhaging money, and Bunny had been hired to put clamps on the leaks. The teaching staff at PHC were elated, as they knew how experienced Bunny was and how inexperienced *I* was. I think the horses breathed a sigh of relief, too. I remember meeting Sally O'Connor, David's mom, up in the office one day. What a remarkable woman she was. I was in awe and I wanted her autograph! She looked me over and when she found out I was the barn manager, she said gently, "You are *very* young."

One of the first things Bunnie had me do was find out why our shoeing bill for the school horses was so astronomically high. I did some sleuthing. The farrier for PHC *was* quite expensive. He took his work very seriously, made an art form out of it, and hand made all of his shoes. He was enormously talented and enormously arrogant. Several of the school horses were getting shod every four weeks and several were getting very expensive orthopedic shoes. It was way over our budget. I ended up hiring a different farrier for the school horses. He did a good job and was a hundred times less expensive than the "artist". That other guy stayed on to shoe private client's horses; the ones who could afford his fees.

Bunny broke the news to "the artist" that they could no longer afford his services, He cornered me in a dark barn aisle that evening as I was finishing for the day. I was scared to death and he was furious. He did his best to scare the pants off me. I was worried that I might get bludgeoned with a pair of nippers. But God was with me. I stood my ground.

Remember the confrontation I told you about when I was a young, on-fire Christian, evangelizing all the kids at Azalea Glen Stables in Chapel Hill? There it was again. Different era, different location, same issue. A person's income was threatened by what I was saying and doing. I don't think Azalea Glen's owners were busy ripping the boarders off. And most likely "the artist" did not intentionally rip the Horse Center off. The Center desperately needed to save some money, and they charged me with plugging the leaks. "The artist's" prices had caused a hemorrhage. When I put clamps on the torn artery, he howled with pain and rage.

That was the hardest thing I had ever done in my life, but I did it. I've gotten much better at it over the years. Whenever I have to do or say something that is difficult and possibly confrontational, I always remember that night. I have gotten *way* better at it, but I still hate doing it.

Chapter Twenty Three

THEN CALEB AND I HAD a big surprise! I became pregnant. We had found a nice church in northern Virginia, and they held an annual spring church retreat. The guest pastor was someone who had visited the Church at Raleigh frequently. He was the guy who told us about the church. At the end of one of his talks at the retreat he had an alter call for anyone who felt like they were holding anything back from God. We were to come forward and release it to the Lord. Caleb nudged me. He really wanted us to have kids, and he knew I was reluctant.

I kept my bottom glued to the plastic chair. I thought, "Sure *you* want kids! You'll have all the fun, but *I'll* do all the work". I was never keen on having kids, and now I *especially* didn't want them after experiencing four years of a painfully difficult marriage. I saw the writing on the wall and said "NO THANKS".

I had just devoted my life to going through horsey boot camp and earning my Horsemaster's certificate! I was finally jumping, which is what I had *always* wanted to do since I was a little girl. I just graduated with top honors! I was Horse Center *staff!* I was on my way! I wasn't interested in being a broodmare.

Sigh. Finally I peeled my fanny off the chair and went down front. I confessed in front of everybody what I was holding back. On my wedding day back in 1979, my dear friend Makeda Ennishad was helping me get dressed. As she helped me fuss with the dress and veil, she started to prophesy. *"The reason for this union is to reproduce"*, the word of the Lord came forth. *"Thou shalt have many children, and they shall rise up and bless you."*

I was pregnant less than a month after the church retreat. Caleb and I weren't even trying to make a baby. Talk about *Fertile Myrtle*. God showed me lots of little signs that I was with child a long time before I went to the clinic at Fort Meyer. One day I had a foreshadowing of having a special needs child. I prayed that I would love the baby with God's love *no matter what.* Then I forgot all about it.

I had a great pregnancy and kept right on managing the barns at Potomac Horse Center. Lots of folks didn't even know I was pregnant till I shed my big down jacket in the spring when I was about 8 months along. Early in my pregnancy I would be in the barn at 6 a.m. and clean stalls along with the grooms and students. I had morning sickness for the first 3 months. I would barf right in the stall I was cleaning, scoop it up along with the poop and toss it in the aisle for the tractor to push to the muck heap. No one knew. Then I would eat a huge 3-egg breakfast and keep *gittin'* it the rest of the day. Late in my pregnancy, I would have to take a nap, which my assistant thought pretty wimpy. Huh. I wonder if *she* ever had kids after the Horse Center.

Everybody threw me a big baby shower and send off party at the Horse Center about a month before my due date. It was bittersweet, for I knew that my horsing around days would soon be over. The barn manager when I first arrived at the horse Center had a baby. That baby came to work with her mom. That baby stayed strapped in a back-pack while her mom mixed feeds, checked horses and supervised students. I never saw the baby out of the back-pack. I am sure she came out to eat and get changed. That baby was a trooper, and so was the mom.

I had no intentions of doing that. I knew that I was *so* into the horses my baby would suffer from my divided attention. I thought I should quit horses cold turkey and just be a mom. It was a tough decision, but a no-brainer for me. Having babies meant *not* having horses. At that church retreat where I gave up my resistance to God, I gave my horse dreams up to Him, too.

But---*arrrgh*--the staff at the Horse Center had just brought me to "take off". I was ready to fly, and fulfill my lifelong riding goals and dreams.

Chapter Twenty Four

SINCE WE WERE LIVING AT the Horse Center, we had to move. With another young couple in our church we rented a house in Manassas, Virginia. It was a split foyer, so for the most part we comfortably lived downstairs, and Tom and Wendy and their kids lived upstairs. We did it to save money and also to practice Christian community. Hey, we had done that back in Raleigh. Our current church family thought we were a little crazy, as they were much more conservative than the Church at Raleigh had been, but they were also a lot less controlling! Tom and Wendy were in worse financial shape than we were, if that were possible. They had a handsome son and two beautiful daughters.

We got settled in our new digs. After we were done making the downstairs into a home for us and transforming one of the bedrooms into a nursery, I starting walking. I walked and I walked and I walked. I walked and waited for my baby to come. She came on April 14th, 1984. Our beautiful Enya was born.

In the recovery room two sweet young doctors asked me if I had any Chinese relatives. "Not that know I of," was my wondering reply. Then they told me they suspected my baby had Down Syndrome. I really didn't know what that was. They told me in the sweetest, most gentle way. Good job, young Army docs on the G.I. bill.

Then followed several weeks of confused joy and sadness. Enya seemed perfect except that she slept a lot more than other newborns I knew. Caleb and I were thrilled with Enya. We were in love with our new little girl! Our birth announcements read:

This is the Lord's doing;
It is marvelous in our eyes.
Psalm 128 NAS

We were flooded with sympathetic cards and phone calls. Why was everyone feeling so sorry for us? A social worker came to counsel us on what programs were available in our area for a handicapped baby. The look on her face as I rocked Enya in our living room was one of compassion and concern, as though I might dump Enya in her lap any second and go slit my wrists. I just kept patiently rocking Enya until she left, surrounded by a warm cloud of grace. I think she thought I was disturbed.

One of the grooms from the Horse Center asked if we might look after her Australian Shepherd. We happily agreed to look after Marbles, as the house we rented had a big fenced-in back yard. Caleb and I were both dog lovers and still sad that we had to give up our three coon hound puppies when we moved to D.C..

So then we were three. Enya, Marbles and me. The three of us started walking. First Enya was in a Snuggly, then a backpack, then a stroller. When I was at the Horse Center I was used to putting in 12 hour days, 6 or 7 days a week. I walked the barn aisles, taught lessons or rode horses all day long. Here I was in the suburbs with not a whole lot to do except keep house and baby and dog. I walked to keep from going stir crazy. Caleb did all the shopping and errands on post, and he commuted with our only car. I walked through town, but I never went in the stores because we had the dog with us, and we never had any spending money anyway. Once I went alone to town on the weekend when Caleb was home with Enya. As I walked through the grocery store I had a little panic attack. Talk about sensory overload! So much *stuff*. I preferred to walk in the neighborhoods or nearby parks. I could handle grass and trees, not shelves and shelves of man-made stuff screaming, "BUY ME! BUY ME!"

On one rare trip through town, however, I found a treasure that I still treasure 30 years later. I walked into a thrift store to look around.

Thrift stores were more my style back then and they still are; I love poppin' tags! Occasionally I go shopping and find great bargains. That day back in 1984 there was a painting hanging on the wall of that thrift store. It was a print by an old Dutch master. It was a picture of a shepherd girl walking along holding a lamb while its mother walked closely beside; making sure her babe was all right. I knew that painting was for me. It *was* me. The price was seventy dollars; too much. When the shop keeper saw me admiring the painting, he let me know it would go on sale for half-price in a few days. I thanked him profusely for the information and left the store, asking God to please hold the painting for me.

I knew He would. I knew I was meant to see it that day. I knew it was mine. I knew it had significance. I bought it as soon as it went on sale. It has hung in every living room we've lived in since then. The shepherd girl in the painting is *me.* How many kids have I "held" in riding lessons as their moms looked on anxiously? How many have I carried through the years? They were not my flesh and blood kids. Their moms were right at my elbow, making sure I would take good care of their precious child, especially in jumping lessons. I think I have done pretty well. Their parents do, too. After I woke up I read what they put on my Caring Bridge webpage as I lay unconscious in Intensive Care. All the love poured out in those pages went straight to my heart. I had no idea people felt that way about me. It was life changing.

As Enya grew, my walking turned to jogging which turned to running. I ran and ran. I felt like Forrest Gump! I certainly lost all my "baby weight" and I have not been in as fit since then. The crowning achievement of all that sidewalk pounding was a 6K Caleb and I ran in Washington, D.C. A lot of Army guys ran in it. Caleb's boss's wife held Enya while the three of us ran. It was awesome.

My precious son Ryan was born two years later on March 14th, 1986. He seemed "normal" whatever *that* is. After he was born, I kept right on walking. I kept right on *gettin it.* We bought a double stroller for the kids, as Enya took a little longer to learn how to walk, but not *too* much longer. There was no way she could have kept pace with her mamma's Power Walk, though. I took her to Early Intervention classes for parents of children with special needs. I was very diligent to do all the recommended exercises and activities with Enya. It was a great help in just being a *Mom*, period. Guess the Lord knew I needed help!

One of the highlights of Caleb's time at Fort Meyer was getting to be a Technical Advisor on the set of a movie filmed right on post. *Gardens of Stone* was based on a novel written by Nicolas Sparks. It was set in the Vietnam War era, and took place at Fort Meyer. It was a story of a gung-ho young soldier training for Vietnam and the grizzled old sergeant who mentors him and tries to get the young recruit to see the reality behind the dog and pony show. It's a good movie.

Francis Ford Coppola directed it. Just as the filming commenced Francis' son was killed in a boating accident on the Chesapeake Bay. It was a stunning blow to Francis. Somehow he recovered enough to make the film. It was ironic that most of the film focused on losing a loved one. The cast was full of current movie stars and budding stars that would become famous.

Colleen Maera was visiting with us at the time and got to be a flower girl in a big wedding scene. One of the actresses practically adopted her while the movie was being shot. For quite awhile after the filming wrapped up they wrote letters back and forth. Caleb got to be an extra in a bar room brawl scene. Ryan was a baby and Enya was a wild handful, so I didn't get to see much of the filming or be in it as an extra, but I did manage to hire a babysitter once to go watch a scene be filmed and eat the lunch supplied by the caterers. I got to meet all the actors and actresses. It was *waaaay* cool. Frances gave Caleb a painting used on the set, an original watercolor of a shepherd leading some sheep down a quiet path by a pond. Hmmm, let's see. That would be our own kids, and countless other children he has shepherded while working at Arby's. It was a prophetic painting for Caleb.

Riding and caring for horses all my life and particularly going through the Horse Center had given me an outrageous work ethic. The Horse Center's owner always made a point to say that going through the courses at the Horse Center prepared all the young girls for motherhood. Us young horse-girlies loathed that speech, as at the time we had no intentions of having children (who had time for babies when there were Olympic Games to strive for?), but P.H.C.'s owner was right. Good food, good grooming, good exercise. Those were the first ABC's/1-2-3's I lavished on our kids. The Early Intervention classes filled in the details. But best of all, Abba supplied the love. Pure, glorious, unconditional love. How I loved my babies! Horses became a fond, poignant memory.

We had asked to live in military enlisted housing at Fort Meyer when we first moved to Virginia but there was a very long waiting period. Finally a three bedroom apartment in the Fort Meyer Enlisted Personnel high-rise apartment tower became available. Caleb was tired of the long, knarly Beltway commute, and I was tired of sharing a home with another family. When you live in Community, one of the best things it does is show you the worst of yourselves. That is, *if* you have eyes to see. Caleb and I didn't at the time. Neither did Tom or Wendy. We began to fight and argue about everything like getting the bills paid on time, keeping the house clean and raising the children. Caleb and I thought *we* were right, of course. Tom and Wendy thought *they* were right. The kids thought *they* were right! I think Marbles was the only one who saw the light.

The owner of the house decided to put it up for sale and none too soon. We were polluting it with anger and misunderstanding. We couldn't wait to move. I don't know exactly what became of Tom and Wendy and their kids. I think we saw them once or twice more at our fellowship. I sure wish them well. And I *apologize.*

We sadly returned Marbles to her girl, who was now in a place where she could keep her. Then we moved to Fort Meyer.

Fort Meyer was a really gorgeous Army post. Aside from the high-rise and some modern looking office buildings on the south end, it had an ancient, majestic look and feel. Most of the main office buildings, the stabling for the caisson horses, and officers' housing were quite old and made of brick. Some new additions kept to the traditional look. To the Southeast was Arlington National Cemetery, home of thousands of soldiers who gave their lives for their country. The Kennedy brothers' graves were there. So were the tomb of the Unknown Soldier and the remains of the 1986 Space Shuttle disaster, along with thousands of others. If you stood on a hill on the north side, you could see the promenade all lined up with the reflecting pool, the Capitol Building, and the Washington monument. Sitting on that hill on the fourth of July watching fireworks go off made unforgettable memories. Before we moved there, I would go walking in the cemetery with Enya every chance I got. I named Ryan after a fallen Confederate soldier whose name I saw on an old, old tombstone.

Our family felt complete. I had my hands full. Caleb and I were talking about getting two good ten speed bikes with baby carriers on the back so we could explore the D.C. area with the kids. We could avoid the congested traffic, lack of parking, and get great exercise to boot. Enya would be contained and entertained for long periods! There was so much to explore in D.C. and the surrounding areas, but getting there could be a nightmare, with *or* without young children.

We were almost ready to make the purchase of the bikes when I woke up one morning in a pool of blood. It was very odd. I felt fine, and had never had a problem with my periods or pregnancies, not even menstrual cramps. I made an appointment with a doctor at the post medical clinic. After I got checked out, the doc told me with a little grin, "You're pregnant."

It was Maeve, a.k.a. *The Girl with the Shotgun,* making her presence known. She probably just swung her tiny, developing shotgun around and poked a tiny hole in my uterus.

I nearly fell over. That didn't even seem possible. Probable, I guess! The doctor said to take it easy and make a follow-up appointment for my first pre-natal visit. I did, still shaking my head in disbelief. What was really funny and ironic, however, was that just a couple of weeks earlier I had called my Mom on April Fool's day to tell her I was pregnant! She nearly dropped the phone and fell over. It was too, *too* funny when I had to call her back and tell her it was true!

I'll always wonder what that heavy bleeding was about. Sometimes Maeve and I wonder if I didn't lose her twin. She is such a tiny thing compared to the rest of us. Or maybe her shotgun went off in there.

Enya and Ryan were born in the spring, like their Dad, but Maeve was due in early November. Well, *that* was in keeping with my side of the family … mine is November 23rd; my sister Jeanne's is the 24th and her oldest son Dan's is the 22nd. My sister Kay's is December 2nd and my brother Garret's is December 9th. On Caleb's side, Colleen Maera's is on November 29th, as is her fourth child's, and her husband Mitchell's is on the 30th. I forget what Maeve's exact due date was, but she didn't miss it by much. She was born November 9th. She's a Scorpio, and she knows how to whip that stinger. Maybe *that's* what caused the bleeding.

While I was pregnant with Maeve, Caleb's enlistment was up and so was his time at Fort Meyer. If Caleb had chosen to stay in the Army, his next destination would have been Korea without us. I would have given birth to Maeve with him half a world away. Most career military families seem to do that easily, but it made Caleb decide *not* to become an Army career NCO. He made up his mind to discharge from the Army so he would be home for Maeve's birth. Home for me and the kids. *Good man.*

Maeve came along pretty much on time. She emerged aiming her shotgun with her tiny hands but it evaporated the moment the cord was cut. There is a picture of me sitting in bed at Walter Reed Hospital holding a very wild-looking Enya with a darling, dreamy-eyed Ryan sitting close by. Colleen Maera is sitting by on the bed holding tiny newborn Maeve. I look very happy but pretty tired. Colleen recently sent us a picture of her and her three kids ages 5, 3 and 6 months. (Now she has a fourth.) I don't think she meant it to be, but the picture is amazingly similar to the one taken of us back in 1987. Colleen looks very happy but pretty tired, too. I knew just how she felt.

Chapter Twenty-Five

SHORTLY AFTER MAEVE WAS BORN, Caleb discharged from the Army and off we went to Portland, Maine. Caleb wanted to go up there and be a part of a house church movement. The leader of the group was an ex-Baptist preacher who had written some fabulous spirit-filled books. On the advice of his doctor, John Goddard and his wife moved from California to Maine, and several of his church members followed him. People from as far away as New Zealand and Holland came to be a part of the church.

Caleb was really pumped to go to Maine and pursue this new spiritual adventure. Me, I was scared. *"Maine?"* I thought. "Why not pull out all the stops and just move to Siberia!" I really loved the guy's books and agreed with the messages, but *move to the frozen North?* What I really wanted was to move back to N.C. to be close to family. Good Lord, I had all these babies, and babies need a grandma! And aunties! And uncles! And cousins!

But there was no changing of Caleb's mind.

Finally I thought, "Hmmmm, this *could* be God's will for us, and I am not going with the flow. I'm damming the river. Not only am I supposed to give up riding to be a Mom, I am supposed to give up my family and my homeland, too!" When Caleb and I were first engaged, he carved two wooden plaques as a gift to me. One was a hand holding a tiny black box. That represented my hand giving my life, my hopes, my dreams to God. The other carving was God's hand holding a *huge* box. He wanted me to trade my life for His. I needed to trust Him for what was inside that big box in his hand.

Once again I yielded all to God. Caleb wrote to John that we were going to come. Some of the church elders gave us a call. They said we probably *shouldn't* come, as the economy was horrible in Portland and the entire state of Maine. The church was also doing very poorly, with lots of misunderstandings amongst the group, in spite of their hopes and dreams. By that time Caleb was so intent on going that there was no stopping him and I had climbed on board as well. We rented a duplex sight unseen in Portland (some folks in the church were moving out, and some folks in the church were still downstairs), arranged for the Army to ship all our stuff from D.C., and made one last visit to my family in Raleigh. It was Christmas time.

They thought we were completely nuts to go up there. Who could blame them? I thought we were a little crazy too. We had three young children; the oldest was special needs, the youngest only a couple months old. Caleb had no job, and our vehicle to Maine was a big old rickety Plymouth station wagon. Neither of us had family up there, except *God's* family.

Maeve was tiny, so tiny. She was barely 6 weeks old when I went home for Christmas for the very last time. By that time in my life I had pulled a bunch of totally loony stunts. I was loony about horses, dogs, and cats. I enrolled in college but bailed at the last minute. Then I struck out for Alabama to a farm and people I knew only from a magazine. Then I opened my mouth too wide and got deported back to Raleigh. Then I got religion and became a Jesus freak. Then I went to Hillsboro and lived in an Airstream trailer. Then I came home for a few months, worked in a clothing store and tried to act normal, but no dice. Soon I flew off to Chapel Hill like a crazy bird and ran a riding school at age 20. It seemed that I might settle down there and feather my nest, but nothing doing. I came home and joined a crazy, holy-roller commune!! I got out of horses! I married "Cosmic Guy" Caleb. Then I got back *into* horses. Then I started having all these kids and got back *out* of horses.

No wonder my family looked on numbly as we made plans to go to Upper East Siberia in an old clunker with 3 little kids. I just remember my dear, sweet sister-in-law Sunni crying as we got ready to leave for

Maine. "We'll never see you again!" she wailed. She made it sound so ... so *final*. I am happy to report that is not true. We've been back to N.C. lots of times; at least six. But never for Christmas.

Off to Portland we sailed. It was like launching a boat---that Plymouth was a big old whale that swayed and rolled as we drove along. I was pretty scared to be heading north, in January, in a whale. I felt like Jonah. I felt really little. I felt really vulnerable. I clung to an old prayer I had run across many times; "Help us, O Lord!!! *For Thy sea is so great and our ship is so small.*"

We pitched and rolled north through Virginia, Maryland, Pennsylvania ... all places I had lived ... and loved. Then the familiar faded as we pressed on. We didn't run into any snow, and the kids were fabulous little travelers. We skirted the skyscrapers of New York City, marveled at the beauty of the Hudson River Valley, and stared wide-eyed at Harvard University in Connecticut. On we sailed through Vermont and New Hampshire on a wing and a prayer. We finally docked in Portland, a little rumpled, but otherwise okay. We arrived ahead of our stuff ... by about two weeks.

Some of the church folks lent us a mattress and blankets. We camped on the floor. Our duplex was really nice, but it was huge and old and drafty. Thank God there was a woodstove. While we waited for our stuff to arrive, we met everyone and explored Portland briefly until the kids and I came down with nasty pink-eye. Then we holed up with stuck-shut eyes and waited to get better. I wondered if a yurt in Siberia felt any cozier.

Caleb searched for work. Our stuff came. We got better. It snowed a ton. The drifts were higher than Ryan and Enya's heads.

We fell into a routine of sorts. Caleb would go out looking for work. I would stay home and change diapers, and nurse Maeve, and change diapers, nurse Maeve ....

Mixed in there was a little unpacking and a little fellowshipping. With 3 kids in diapers and a nursing infant, that is what filled up my days.

The church group was quite a diverse lot. There were people from the east and west coast of the United States and several people from other countries. Everybody lived close together; lots of us lived on the same street. There were young singles, young childless couples, young couples with young kids, older couples with older kids. Pretty much everybody was in survival mode. Everyone had left something behind to come to Portland, hoping to find a deeper revelation of God's body, His church. But now most folks were just hoping to find a job! The church had fallen into disagreement; people were disgruntled and starting to lose hope. Bitter disappointment was sneaking its way through the cracks in the old houses and the cracks in folk's hearts. Some handled it better than others. Everyone made good effort to stay connected and brave. I took it all in between nursing and changing diapers. People did their sorry best to welcome us and make us feel supported, but everyone was also dealing with the little demons named Disillusionment, Discouragement, and Despair.

Before too much time passed, we ran out of money. One of the guys in the church who had a house painting business gave Caleb some work out of pity. We also applied for food stamps and WIC. Maine was a good state to go broke in, as that was the norm for most folks. The state was pretty well set up to take care of you. On the front of our wedding invitation we had printed a verse from Jeremiah 29;1. *"For I know the plans that I have for you," declares the Lord, "plans for welfare and not for calamity to give you a future and a hope."* At the time of our wedding, Caleb thought it was a word from the Lord regarding the break-up of his first marriage and being given the chance to start over. It probably was. Many years later as I was looking at the yellowed and curled invitation, I sarcastically pointed out that the Lord really did have WELFARE plans for us.

Heh, heh, heh.

Very funny, Abba.

Chapter Twenty-six

I MADE GOOD FRIENDS WITH the gal that lived on the first floor of our duplex downstairs. A lovely young woman named Naomi, she hailed from a small town in Texas. She already had two rowdy little boys and was pregnant with her third child. Her sons would act like, well, *boys*. Ryan had instant buddies, and Naomi fell in love with baby girl Maeve. We did a lot of stuff together. We tried to keep Enya, who had wanderlust, from escaping the house. We babysat each other's kids. We talked about missing the South. We talked about our crazy husbands and our crazy church, crazy relatives and our crazy lives. We are still friends to this day, though we both have traveled far and wide. Especially Naomi!

When the calendar said it was spring, I was on the verge of a panic attack. In North Carolina, spring rolls in when the calendar says so. The weather warms up, the grass starts growing and the trees and flowers start blooming. Spring in Portland was slightly less cold than winter. Instead of snow, rain. Lots and lots of rain. Lots of black flies, too. When the end of May rolled by and the trees were still naked, it was hard not to freak out. I thought, "Whatever will we do?" They don't have spring or summer up here. Just cold, snow, and rain forever! *AHHHHH!!!!!"*

Every day the kids and I looked out the window to see if there were any buds on the tree branches. Nope, nope, nope, nope ....yes!!! *Finally!* What joy to see those tender shoots. Very soon after that, it got *hot*. Summertime arrived with a vengeance. My mom came to see us, and without her customary N.C. air conditioning, I can't say it was a great visit for her. Me? I was just happy to be sweating instead of freezing!

Summer came and went really fast. And summer lasted 'till about six o'clock every evening, then it got really chilly. I was used to stinkin' hot humid days turning into pleasantly warm humid nights. In Portland, whatever summery stuff you were wearing needed to be exchanged for pants and a sweater! Fall was short and beautiful but on it's heels came the long winter. I would get all the kids dressed in their snow suits, tape their gloves to their sleeves and their boots to their leggings so the snow would stay out. About the time I was ready to open the door to the outside world, one of them would have to pee. Then the other one. Then the other one. Some days I would say, "Just go in your snow suit! That's what the washing machine is for!!!" And after all that potty training.

When we finally got outside, we had lots of fun making snow men and snow angels. I made the kids a little ice rink in the back yard one winter, and they learned to ice skate with buckle-on, double runner skates. Some of the parks had ponds that were frozen over so sometimes we went there to skate. We had a blast sledding at the local golf course. It was a busy place for kids, their mommies and daddies. We had acquired an Australian shepherd puppy and aptly named her *Rugby*. She would chase our sled to the bottom of the hill and grab at our ankles. Fortunately the kids' snowsuits were bulky enough to keep them from getting nipped! Maeve's first word was *Wugby*. I was holding Maeve out on the sidewalk one evening and calling "Rugby! Rugby!" for she had wandered up the street. Pretty soon Maeve was calling her, too! Now *that* is a very precious memory.

Another spring slowly rolled around, followed by summer. We were pretty close to the ocean, so we church ladies would pack up our cars and head for the beaches once or twice a week. We Southern and California gals thought the water *pretty* cold, but the kids didn't care. There was one beach, Higgin's Beach, that was a little farther to get to, but worth it. It was wide and sandy, and the Gulf Stream ran close by, making the water tolerably warm. That one was my favorite. Ryan and Maeve stayed put, but somehow I would always lose Enya. Panic would set in, then embarrassment when other people brought her back to me, especially if the same people did it more than once! *Man,* she was quick to disappear. I would look on enviously as the other Moms chatted and relaxed while their kids stayed put and played together for hours. Me, I chased Enya for hours. She is still with us though, thank God.

Colleen Maera came the first summer we were in Maine. She came the following fall for the school year. Colleen is a true survivor and an *Unsinkable Molly Brown,* like both her mommas. Her birth mom would put her on a plane and she would fly 3,000 miles to us, then we would put her on a plane and she would fly 3,000 miles back. What a plucky kid! She handled the traveling, the separations from her Dad, two very different Moms, and 3 new sibs with grace and aplomb, even as a hormonal junior-higher. She *lived* in the grace of God. Poor thing, I cut my parenting teeth on her before I had babes of my own. I think you can still see the marks.

One flight out east to stay with us, her plane was delayed. She got into Boston so late they put her up in a motel for the night as there were no more flights till the next day. The taxi driver gave her a tour of Boston before depositing her at the motel. Colleen loved every minute of it, but we were pretty freaked out. She was only fourteen!

All those plane rides might be why Colleen worked at Sea-tac Airport in Seattle for awhile before finishing college, and why she got into airline stewardess school. She didn't end up going because she busted her ankle leaping out of a grocery cart one night in a parking lot with some wild and crazy friends from high school. Now she's a pastor's wife with a Master's degree in Marriage and Family counseling, with four babes of her own. Joseph, her first, came after a very short labor. Gillian was born in the bathtub at home because she was even quicker than Joseph. Ester Halah also came into this world in the bathtub … but on purpose. Her fourth child, Asher, was planned to arrive at home with a mid-wife, since his sisters didn't wait for Mom to get to a hospital. Four kids and a pastor-author husband are a platter-full for her, but nothing much fazes Colleen.

Chapter Twenty-seven

THE OLD PLYMOUTH STATION WHALE finally died. I have to say I was thrilled. We scraped enough money together to buy a little green used Volvo station wagon. We christened it **The Green Volvo**, and it suited us perfectly. I felt almost like a yuppie! In the summer I would pack the kids in it and we would head for Portland's amazing parks and playgrounds. They had many wooden play structures; each new one more elaborate than the last.

Some mornings I would pile the kids in The Green Volvo and head out for the day. I would turn the car radio on to only static. We would pretend we were in a spaceship, and as we backed out of the driveway and headed up the street, I would turn the volume up louder and louder to sound like the spaceship was lifting off. We would spend the whole day flying from planet to planet to check out all the alien playgrounds. Sometimes I lost Enya and it would be scary, but she always turned up in some nook or hideaway cranny in the play structure. I got a lot of exercise tracking her down.

One of our very favorite places to go was Mackworth Island, just north of Portland. It was a beautiful island connected to the mainland by a car bridge. Once a privately owned estate, it had become a state park. A perimeter trail went around the island and past a very peaceful cemetery where the original family members, including their Golden Retrievers were buried. It hosted a very nice school for the deaf. We would walk the trail around the island and in the summer when school was out, go to the school's playground. They had a very cool slide made of pipes that rolled when you sat on them, and therefore rolled you gently to the bottom. We especially loved it when Caleb had a day off and went with us---what a treat that was.

Life got really busy with the kids and the dog and the church and the house. I took odd jobs here and there to try to make ends meet. I didn't have much time to miss horses, but they were always in the back of my mind and heart. Sometimes I would see a horse in a pasture or on the movie screen, and I would just start bawling. Though I loved being a Mom and threw all my energy joyfully into it, horses still pulled at my heartstrings.

One rainy spring I met a lady with a riding stable who said I could work off lessons. I was so thrilled, I agreed without really thinking. I made arrangements to go up there as soon as I could. Caleb kept the kids and I high-tailed it for the barn. I worked hard shoveling poop and hauling it through deep, sticky mud to the muck pile. I often tipped the full wheelbarrow over and had to start over. At the end of four grueling hours she thought I had earned a lesson. I drove an hour to get there and an hour back home, so I never took it and I never went back. I was sad.

I was sad about living in Maine, period. I was very homesick. I felt like a stranger in a strange land. The church was having lots of problems and slowly dying. People were starting to move away. The economy was miserable, and so was the climate. Summer was short and hot. Fall was nice but way too short. Winter was freezing and spring was cold and rainy. We tried a different church after ours fell apart but that one fell apart too! So much drama. It was exhausting. I started wondering if *we* made the churches go under.

Keagan White, Naomi's husband, started a business tearing asbestos out of homes. The old houses in Portland were full of it, and it had become illegal to sell a home with asbestos in it. It was hazardous but financially lucrative. Caleb helped Keagen, and we enjoyed the income until Caleb ruptured a lumbar vertebral disc hauling heavy equipment around. He spent his fortieth birthday in the hospital having back surgery. Soon some bigger, competing abatement companies lobbied the state legislature about the need to put into law regulations requiring very expensive special safety equipment, which of course they already had or could afford but small companies like Keagen and Caleb's could not. It passed and very neatly put Keagen and Caleb out of business.

Another thing we tried to do was start a Community Supported Agriculture co-op. Caleb had met an older farm woman at a week long organic farming training camp in Vermont given by Eliot Coleman. We ended up calling her "Aunt Hettie." She was a tough old bird. It was hard to say if she liked having us around, or if we highly annoyed her. I think she liked Caleb pretty well, because he went out to her farm and helped her. Occasionally I brought the kids out. It was just about impossible to find a babysitter for my three, especially Enya. What a wild thing she was!!

Aunt Hettie taught me how to milk her goats. That was a sure fire way to experience pain in your arms and become exhausted in a hurry. Aunt Hettie could milk five goats in the time it took me to do one. We tried drinking goat's milk, but the smell and the taste was a real turn off. I thought it smelled and tasted just like their little round pooties.

At one point we discussed buying a piece of Aunt Hettie's farm. That would give her some money and get us on a farm. I was cleaning house for a lady whose husband was a real estate agent. We all agreed to meet and discuss the possibility. The guy seemed really harmless to me, but for some reason Aunt Hettie got really agitated and called the whole thing to a screeching halt. I still can't tell you to this day why she got so angry. I think it was just Abba saying *"NOT YET."*

By that time I was feeling really *done* with Portland. I was feeling really done with being married to Caleb as well. I called my mom to see if the kids and I could come home. "**NO**", was her reply, but she did send me $500.00 to start college. She said to learn a skill so I could get a job and *then* I could come home.

I am *sure* what my Momma had in mind was for me to spend that hard-earned $500.00 of hers going to a community college to learn a quick and marketable skill, but I was thinking of becoming a nurse. There was a big shortage of nurses in America, and the pay was good. I was used to caring for livestock, and I *was* getting used to caring for people, a.k.a. my kids, so that seemed like a good and logical plan. *Heh, heh, heh.* Yes Abba. I hear you chuckling as I write this.

So what did this girl do? I defied all logic, of course. I split the money with Caleb and we both enrolled at the University of Southern Maine, which was walking distance from our house. It was a four-year liberal arts college, not a community college! Caleb wanted to finish the bachelor's degree he had started several years ago at Seattle Pacific College. I signed on for the bachelor's degree program in nursing. Nothing quick or cheap about that. And why on earth did I split the money with Caleb, when I was planning on leaving him? It was probably a really good thing I was way up in Maine. My momma must have wanted to bean me with her big cast iron frying pan!

Because we were both "adults" and broke, we qualified for every student loan in the book. We applied, and we got 'em. We both enrolled full time---Caleb as a junior in the School of Psychology, and me as a freshman in the School of Nursing. We worked our class schedules so that we could take turns staying home with the kids. On rare occasions we took a class together and used the school's good daycare system.

Caleb had very good study smarts, so I knew he would do well. Me, I am totally hands-on. I was never a great student in high-school, except in Art class, where I *could* use my hands. In my other classes, I fretted in my chair and looked out the window, dreamed about riding and waited for the bell to ring. I graduated by the skin of my teeth, something I was embarrassed about, because I thought I must be stupid. I didn't think I was smart enough for college, so I chickened out at the last minute. Now I was 33 years old and a new freshman at university. I rolled up my sleeves and took a deep breath.

I had to take remedial Algebra, because I flunked it in high school. I took a high-school chemistry class I needed, through community education. I took freshman college English, and guitar lessons as an elective. In spite of my fears, I did pretty well. I made sure I went for math tutoring as much as the poor work-study students could stand. I had always avoided chemistry like the plague, but now I found it interesting. The first song I learned on my guitar was *Amazing Grace.* Amen to that.

English was one of my better subjects. I liked to write. I could spell, and my grammar was pretty good, too. My English 101 teacher was a very outspoken liberal. She had us write on current events after reading her handouts and doing research. Our first essay was on abortion. Being a good little Christian girl, I was anti-abortion and a conservative. We were supposed to write a pro-life or pro-choice piece. The teacher was very pro-choice; so was most of the class. We would read articles and discuss what we had read. I felt very alone. I didn't believe in baby-killing. I had seen horrible pictures and read horrible things, but all the pro-choice people made me think. Their arguments were valid. I started out to write a very pro-life paper but it ended up being a paper about how gut wrenching the whole issue is; how it's not black and white at all. It shook my foundations. My teacher loved it and gave me an "A".

That class rocked my world the whole semester. I had been programmed by very well-meaning people to believe certain things as the gospel truth. My English teacher was the polar opposite. She rang my chimes. She shook me up. She made me think and question what I thought was as solid as rock. I told her, and she said that made her very happy! I loved her spiciness; she reminded me of a spirited chestnut mare. While she was quite talented at dismantling my little universe, she was also supportive and kind. I tell you what, there was a whole lot more going on in that class besides learning to write a paper! I was learning to think outside the "churchianity" box. For that I will be forever grateful, both to my feisty, red-headed, wonderful human teacher, and to God, who set the whole thing up.

I ended up learning lots of great stuff both inside and outside the classroom. I learned I wasn't as stupid as I thought. I learned I could still be a pretty good Mom *and* go to college *and* get some different perspectives. I learned that people outside my church were actually really cool! *And* that it was okay to make friends with them. *And* that it was okay to read non-Christian books, and that some of them were really helpful. *And* a little daycare/preschool wasn't going to ruin my kids. They actually liked it! The teachers were wonderful. It was good for them.

Caleb and I made the dean's list every semester. I made a lot of wonderful friends. Not all of them were Christians, but it was **OKAY**. I blossomed in every way. I worked out with weights in a PE class I took as an elective, so my muscles blossomed, too!

My guitar playing improved to the point where I could finger pick pretty well. Even though my summer intensive French class was really hard and I almost flunked it, one night that summer I had a dream … in French.

Chapter Twenty-eight

As our second year of college came to a close in late spring, we got a call from Caleb's mom Evie out in Washington State. Caleb's grandpa Ogden had recently had gone to the hospital for prostate surgery. At first it appeared successful, but over a three week period he gradually lost sensation and use of his legs. He was now facing the rest of his 94 year old life in a wheelchair. He was angry and distraught, as before the surgery he was still driving, going fishing and keeping up with his bills and yard. His wife of 65 years had passed away a year earlier. He missed her terribly.

Evie didn't know what to do. Ogden could no longer live alone. He was totally opposed to living in a nursing home, or going to live with *any* of his remaining children. They weren't thrilled with the idea, either. According to Evie, some of her siblings suggested that he give them an early inheritance so that he would qualify for Medicaid and go to a nursing home. As brothers and sisters tend to do at times like this, they began to argue and fight about it. As she talked that night she shed tears as she shared her version of the story.

After Caleb told me about it I brought it before Abba. We were 3,000 miles away and doing well in college. But school would be out soon for the summer, and Caleb and I both needed jobs. So far, we had looked but found *nothing*. Maine's economy was always in recession. What if we came out to Washington just for the summer break? Since I was in nursing school and approaching the time to do my hands-on clinical education, taking care of an elderly paraplegic would be good practice. We were currently broke with no job prospects. Could Grandpa maybe fly us out for the summer? Could we bring the dog? Could we trade room and board for his care? I was excited at the opportunity to leave Siberia for awhile.

We asked all these questions and Grandpa Anderson said yes to all of them. We gave notice on our apartment, asked church friends to store our stuff. We put out on the curbside what we didn't want anymore. We left a couple of weeks after school got out for the summer. That was May of 1991. Twenty-four years later, we're still here.

When we landed at SeaTac airport, who did I run into but a girl I'd known from Potomac Horse Center. She was originally from the Seattle area and had moved back a few years ago. What are the chances of that happening?

We stayed at Caleb's mom and step-dad's house in Marysville for a few days. Evie taught me how to do Grandpa Anderson's basic daily care, as he had been staying with them since leaving the hospital. A visiting nurse, whose husband was a longtime buddy of Ogden's, came and showed me how to do the more involved medical care. In a few more days we all moved with Grandpa Anderson to his little house in Snohomish.

We were packed in that tiny place like sardines, but we didn't care. What we cared about was the weather. It was fabulous! It was sunny and warm but not humid. Grandpa's house had oodles of flowers and a big cherry tree that was perfect for the kids to climb. The house was old and settled. The floor was so unleveled we had to keep the brakes locked on Grandpa's wheelchair or it would roll toward the kitchen. It was a very typical Grandma and Grandpa's house with lots of knick-knacks that had been gifts from their kids and grandkids over the years.

Our kids loved it. It had a teeny-tiny, very steep curved staircase to the second floor bedrooms. The kids would put on dress-up clothes and model up and down those stairs. It's a miracle no one ever took a fall and bonked *their* head!

The summer flew by. We hung out a lot with Evie and Rafe, Len's stepdad. We saw a little notice in the paper for the Pat Flynn Memorial Horse Show for riders with disabilities. We went to watch and were totally impressed. A short time later a local therapeutic riding program placed a notice in the local paper seeking volunteers. Away I went to the volunteer orientation. I got Enya enrolled as a student. I fell madly in love with Snohomish and the Pacific Northwest.

As long as I could remember I had wanted to live close to mountains in a little town. Huge snow-capped mountains were all around us and only an hour's drive away. I was involved with horses again, to the benefit of my child! Being in the Pacific Northwest was a gift from God.

As summer began to end and fall approached, I calmly announced to Caleb that the kids and I would not be returning to Maine. We were staying right here. Evie and Rafe agreed. Grandpa Anderson agreed. The kids and the dog agreed. Only Caleb wanted to go back. But he was outnumbered and I was determined. It felt like God's doing. We stayed.

Chapter Twenty-nine

THAT FALL I ENROLLED AT Everett Community College to keep my education rolling, or at least trickling along. Caleb transferred to Seattle Pacific University, the very same college in which he started his bachelor's degree back in 1976. Enya started a new experimental integrated kindergarten at the local public school where special needs kids were in the same class as "normal" ones. Ryan started kindergarten in a different classroom. Maeve was to go the following year.

I kept volunteering for Equifriends and Enya kept riding in their program. Before long I was asked to teach a little bit. Before long I was teaching a lot. Equifriends started letting me trade teaching for letting Ryan and Maeve learn to ride on their fabulous ponies, one of which became *our* pony, the fabulous Firecracker. In the spring I became a North American Riding for the Handicapped Association certified instructor.

Then, on Mother's Day 1992, the director of Equifriends gave me one of their horses, a bay thoroughbred mare named Velvet. I had admired her greatly when she was donated to the program. When Velvet came to Equifriends her feet were a real mess. The director's husband was a farrier, and through careful trimming and shoeing, brought her back to soundness. Once Velvet was better, I rode her for them. We fit like a hand in a perfect size glove. I fell in love. A lovely lady with a debilitating back injury rode Velvet in the Equifriends program. She improved so much she was able to return to riding her own horse, for her horse and riding was what gave her happiness. I knew exactly how she felt.

Velvet was a bit tall to be a therapy horse. The director had considered selling her, but she felt Abba, *her* Abba as well as mine, wanted her to give Velvet to me. I'm so thankful for that fateful day, and for holy sisters who listen to their heavenly father. After all these years it still overwhelms me with thanksgiving and joyful tears. Thank you Abba! Thank you, my sisters in the Lord!

Just to complicate matters, Caleb and I were not in a position to own a horse because we were really broke. I had to go home and break the news to Caleb about my wonderful Mother's Day gift. I was *so* nervous. I was worried he might have a big hissy fit. But hey, I had just been given a horse! A perfect horse at that! Oh Holy Day! When I told Caleb about it with a trembling heart, wonder of wonders, he was actually very calm about it. When something is *God's* doing, it always has a way of working out.

The Equifriends staff members were loving, caring people. Not only did they agree to give Velvet to me, they also agreed to let me keep her there in exchange for teaching their program students. I did that for almost two dreamy years. And during that time God sent us Jim, the Wonder Dog.

Chapter Thirty

I WAS OUT TEACHING AT Equifriends one summer day. A volunteer out in the paddock across the street from a little restaurant saw a pickup truck leave the parking lot with a black dog in hot pursuit. The dog ran like crazy after the truck, which had accelerated down Highway 2 West. The volunteer went out and rescued the dog, who had finally given up the chase and was now wandering on the side of the very busy highway. The sweet dog stayed tied to a rope all day in the barn hallway, waiting for the return of its' master. He never came. When it came time for everyone to go home for the day, the dog's fate was undecided. No one was willing or able to take the dog. But I think the sweet Lab cross knew she was to be the *Green* family's special friend. I took her home.

We had just given away Rugby, our Australian Shepherd we brought from Maine, three months ago. Our neighbors accused her of killing their epileptic cat when it was having a seizure in their yard and asked that she go away. I didn't tell Caleb I was bringing home another dog; I just showed up with her. Grouchy old Grandpa Anderson was none too pleased with yet another Green dog in his currently pet-free home. Caleb was furious. The neighbors weren't happy either.

Caleb wouldn't speak to me for three days. The neighbors and Grandpa Anderson wouldn't speak to me anyway, so there was nothing unusual about that. I wasn't allowed to bring Jim in the house. We tried keeping her on the back porch, but it was too cold. We tried her in the root cellar, but it was too lonely. Soon she was happily in the kitchen, and within a short amount of time had the run of the house. When something is *God's* doing, it always has a way of working out.

So why did we name a girl dog *Jim?* A Jonathan Edward's song, of course! Jonathan had a big black setter type dog that traveled with him to his gigs. He stayed underneath Jonathan's big black piano during the show. Jonathan wrote a song about him:

I got a dog and his name is Jim,
I've got a dog and his name is Jim.
I've got a dog and his name is Jiiiiiiiiiiiiiiim,
Now I betcha five dollars, he's a good dog, him!

Heeeere, old Jim! You're a good dog, him.

You can listen to it and see John sing it on YouTube. You can even see the original Jim. I was lucky enough to see the original Jim live in concert way back in 1975 when I was an apprentice at that farm in Alabama. Some nice neighbor girls whisked me away from the farm to the concert, and there was Jim, up on stage with Jonathan.

The song was on Jonathan's children's CD along with *Little Hands,* which became Enya's theme song. There's a song for Ryan and a song for Maeve on John's CDs, too. And don't forget *People Get Ready* and *Give Us a Song.* John's music has been an absolutely *huge* part of our lives. Thank you so much, Jonathan.

When I saw the sweet black lab tied to the wall at Equifriends, I thought, "Oh, there's Jim!" The name stuck even when we found out *he* was a *she.*

What a grand dog Jim was. She never looked back. We never found her owner, not that we looked very hard. We did put an ad in the paper. But I really didn't want anyone to come claim her. Nobody ever did.

We had a vet check her out. She was healthy and about nine years old. She was probably a lab mix. She was spayed. That softened Len's heart a little. She was loyal, kind, and quiet. She stayed put. She never bothered any cats. The only thing she would do was sometimes steal the neighbor's cat food tins they had left lying about. Caleb's parents had sent us a very nice computer when we lived in Maine. One of the programs on it was *Spell-a-Saurus*. You could write stories and poems on there, and this really funky, robotic sounding, computerized voice would read it back to you. Remember, this was way back in the early 90's, the dark ages, ha-ha. Here is a poem the kids and I wrote about Jim. It's so much better when the *Spell-a-Saurus* voice reads it, though.

Jim, oh Jim,
I know why you are
Fat.
You eat up all the
Cat food
When you go out at night.

When you go out at night,
Your little eyes
Glow green,
In the beam of our
Flashlight.

Chapter Thirty-One

EQUIFRIENDS, BLESS ALL THE STAFF, students and volunteers, had given me back my life with horses. Velvet was absolutely fabulous. She fit me perfectly. She was just the right size--16 h.h., medium bone, (built neither spindly nor chunky), with a flat rib cage. That meant my leg would stay put, right where it belonged. I wouldn't have to struggle to keep my position balanced on her. She was a beautiful bright bay with a tiny white star on her kind, alert Thoroughbred face. She was a very nice mover, too. The first time I saw her eating hay in her stall, I thought "*Wow*. That's a nice mare!" Now she was *my* mare. It had been ten years since I had been on a horse. I wondered if I could still ride at all. Going through Potomac Horse Center had given me a beautiful seat and lovely hands, and I could sit the trot on every horse there, even the notoriously bouncy "Why Not?." I had not ridden for 10 years. I didn't know how rusty I would be. I didn't want to embarrass myself.

But Glory to God! It was almost like I'd never quit. Those ten years of "mommying" had taken off a little finesse, but I wasn't half bad. Velvet made good riding easy. I was in *heaven*. I cried for pure joy every time I rode her. I rode her in my NARHA certification videos---the ones we had to submit to become certified instructors---and I passed easily.

Being the perfectionist that I am, I thought I needed further education in therapeutic riding. Equifriends had several severely palsied adult students, and I really wanted to know how to help them and make riding less painful for them. I started volunteering at Little Bits, one of the top handicapped riding centers in the United States, so I could learn

113

more. It was not too far from our home, about thirty minutes south. I thought it was a good idea, because I intended to stay at Equifriends and use everything I learned at Little Bit, but the program director of Equifriends felt slighted. She had started out at Little Bit, but had broken off to start her own program. I guess my going over there rubbed a raw spot. Soon she asked me to start paying board on Velvet. She didn't think I was working enough hours to justify keeping her at Equifriends in a trade situation. I was going to Little Bit once a week.

I had to figure out what to do, as we could not afford to pay board, and I didn't want to work in what had become a hostile environment. I wanted to teach special needs riders, but I didn't feel experienced enough to help the more physically challenged participants. I also wanted to teach able-bodied students, but NARHA guidelines prohibited that.

We had filmed our NARHA certification videos at Pebble Creek Stables in Snohomish. It was a beautiful place with an amazing outdoor arena and cross country jumps in a big field. The owner's daughter helped support Equifriends. I asked her about boarding and she gave me a reasonable rate on self-care. It was closer to our house than Equifriends, so I could actually do the care. She also said I could teach there if I got liability insurance.

I shyly asked my oldest brother if I could borrow money to pay for liability insurance. In our family we don't ask each other for financial help, or if we do, no one talks about it to anyone else. I was desperately motivated, so I asked, and he said yes. That really wonderful woman who had ridden Velvet at Equifriends had a horse trailer and moved her for me. A very mildly disabled student left the Equifriends program to ride with me on Velvet at Pebble Creek. That helped pay her board. *Whew.* The transition was made, and I was on my way.

I started out tentatively. I was still taking care of Grandpa Anderson, Caleb went to college most days, and the kids were still little. I went out to take care of Velvet every day and ride as much as I could. Most days I took the kids with me. I gave them longe line rides on Velvet. Even teeny-tiny four year old Maeve rode her. Velvet took everything in long, lovely strides. She was amazing.

Chapter Thirty-two

ENYA AND RYAN BEGAN ANOTHER year of public school; Maeve started kindergarten. Enya was in an "integrated" first grade classroom like she was in kindergarten. Ryan was in a very large class taught by two teachers.

Maeve loved her teacher and thrived in kindergarten. Enya's going was rough, and Ryan was lost in the crowd. While Ryan and Enya both had wonderful years in Kindergarten, first grade was disappointing for them *and* me.

Enya's teacher could not handle the stress of mainstreaming a special needs child. Enya was indeed a handful and a spent a good part of her school day in the timeout chair. At recess kids on the playground were often cruel. Once or twice a week we were called to come pick her up early, as she was just too much for her teacher to handle. There was an aide in the classroom when funds were available, but both the aides and the funds were inconsistent.

I volunteered in Ryan's class just so I could be with him, but the teachers obviously did not want a mom hanging out in their classroom. I mostly ended up in a desk in the hallway outside the classroom cutting out paper shapes for the teachers.

I missed my kids. I had been a devoted mom, playing with them and educating them during their preschool years. As my lesson program grew I was concerned that I would be teaching after school and weekends and I would never get to be with them. I was worried about the stress on Enya, not to mention the stress on that poor teacher. It seems I had choices between being an obnoxious mom bucking the school system,

115

rolling over belly up and doing nothing, or take the kids out of school and do it myself.

So what did this girl do?

I let Maeve finish her kindergarten year, but I pulled the others out before the school year ended. Enya was ready to read when she started kindergarten, but all progress had come to a halt. In just a few months Enya was reading like a champ. I was very happy to be immersed in my kids' lives again. I missed them terribly when they went to school.

Grandpa Anderson's house became Grandpa Anderson's *Little School House.* I dropped out of college. Taking care of Grandpa Anderson, teaching at Equifriends, owning a horse, starting a business and now home schooling the kids left no time for taking classes. I was slightly resentful that I had to quit while Caleb kept going to college, but I was so thrilled to be riding, teaching at Equifriends and back with my kids I didn't mind too much. I wasn't sure how I was going to take harder classes and start the clinical part of nursing school, anyway.

Caleb and I shared Grandpa's care and home schooling the kids. He went off to university when I was home, and I went off to the barn when he got home.

Grandpa Ogden Anderson started to fade the winter of 1993 just before his 97th birthday. We took him to see his family doctor of many years, who had become our family doctor too. Dr. Henley carefully examined Ogden, pulled me quietly aside and said, "He's dying". It was Ogden's time to go on home. We took Grandpa back to his *earthly* home, tucked him in bed and made him as comfortable as could be. Within a day the angels came for him. I was at the barn looking after Velvet with the kids, but Caleb was there. He said Grandpa seemed to be meeting folks he knew as he left his body. No doubt his beloved wife of 65 years and two of his kids who had gone on before him. His body is buried beside her and near his two sons at a lovely cemetery in Snohomish.

Caleb graduated cum laude earlier that spring from Seattle Pacific University with a bachelor's degree in psychology. Originally he had planned to be a shrink, but one of the upper level classes he took had him working with pre-school aged special needs children at the University of Washington. He was charmed by the kids and good at working with them. He decided to go for a master's degree in Early Childhood Special Education in the fall.

Chapter Thirty-three

I KEPT THINKING ABOUT THE stout red pony the kids had ridden at Equifriends. Firecracker the Quarter Pony was born on the Fourth of July. He was as bright as a newly minted copper penny, about fourteen hands high and about fourteen years old. He would be lovely for my kids to ride and I could teach lessons on him too. I knew he hadn't worked out at Equifriends and had gone home to his owners. The clanking metal of the wheelchairs frightened him and he felt claustrophobic in the close quarters of the wheelchair ramp. One day I called his young owner, one of the Equifriends volunteers, who had long outgrown him. Would she be interested in leasing her pony? She talked to her folks and they said, "Yes, I *could* lease him!" Fire was absolutely terrific and small enough for my kids to ride independently. I jumped at the chance, but I needed to find more students to help pay his expenses! I put an ad in the *Little Nickel*, a local classified weekly publication.

I felt like I was jumping off a cliff. I felt like Much Afraid in *Hind's Feet on High Places*. Would anyone answer the ad? Would anyone come? Who was I to think I could do such a thing? I was a nobody and I hadn't taught in a very long time, save Equifriends. Now I had *two* terrific horses to feed and care for, and I needed students. I jumped off the edge and hoped the Lord would catch me on the way down.

He did. One of my very first new students whose mom answered my ad was a teeny-tiny Korean girl who had been adopted by a wonderful couple. She was five years old, horse crazy, and full of unpredictable energy. Her mom brought her out one day to meet us and see the horses and farm. I brought Fire out and one of the first things little Rosalind did was dart right under his soft round belly. Fire stood patiently while Rosalind flitted around him like a little hummingbird. Her mom and I raised our eyebrows and laughed. That was the first day of many wonderful pony-filled days for Rosalind and her family. She was a wonderful, wiggly handful of joy. She learned safety around horses and she learned to ride quite well. She became my kids' bestest pal. They are still friends to this day.

My kids really enjoyed riding Firecracker. People answered my ad. My lesson program grew. Fire was a perfect starter pony for the little kids that came, and Velvet took care of the leggier, older students.

Pretty soon I leased another pony from one of my student's parents. We made a deal that she would take lessons and we would incorporate their pony into my lesson program so he could get some training, then eventually their child and their pony could be partners. Their daughter was young and inexperienced. Crisco was a middle-aged pony with a mind of his own.

What a funny looking fellow he was! Pure white, like an Albino, but he had dark eyes. He was about 13.2 h.h., a good size, and a good mover too. But what a nose he had! It was a big convex nose. Kind of like a draft horse---or a Lipizzaner. In fact, Crisco seemed like a *mini-*Lipizzaner. He had been used as a pack pony in the mountains and was broke to ride, but not really trained for the arena. He often used his roman nose to go wherever he wanted! But in spite of his funny looks and antics, Crisco grew on us. We worked with him, his girl learned to ride on Fire, and they both made great progress.

The barn manager at Pebble Creek had a lovely Arabian gelding that he offered to lease me for lessons, as he was seldom ridden. What a great horse T.C. turned out to be. With these excellent kids' mounts we tried some little local shows. Whoever was riding Crisco usually won the walk-trot class, with the others close behind.

Chapter Thirty-four

AFTER GRANDPA WENT TO HIS heavenly home, we had to find a new home. Ogden's children wanted to sell his house, and they wanted us out. I had no idea how on earth we were gonna pay rent somewhere, because we were broke. I asked the Lord for help. One day I picked up a Little Nickel just for fun, not really believing I would find anything we could afford to rent. An ad for a duplex on acreage caught my eye. I showed it to Caleb, and we called the agent and made an appointment to see it. It was halfway between Grandpa's old house and Pebble Creek Stables. It was a family dairy farm, but they had gotten out of the business. The duplex had originally been a big single-dwelling family home, but as the kids grew up and married they converted it to two side-by-side apartments. Downstairs was an apartment for the dairy farm workers. The farm was 150 pastured acres on both sides on Highway 2 with a tunnel underneath the highway for the cows to access the pastures. There was also an additional dwelling for farm workers slightly east of the main house.

I was so in awe of the land I barely took notice of the duplex for rent, but it was quite nice. It had a fireplace, three bedrooms and a huge room on the west end. A deck off sliding doors invited one out to an amazing view of the Snohomish River Valley and the Olympic Mountain Range to the west. The farm owner's oldest son and family had lived there and helped run the dairy, but he had started a construction company and moved away. His parents, a family doctor and an orthodontic surgeon, were getting old. Since their three sons weren't interested in being dairy farmers, they were selling all their cows and equipment, and renting the empty side of their house.

After we looked at the duplex, we fearfully asked what the rent was, expecting something astronomical. It was $700.00 a month. After we put our teeth back in we said we'd love it, and the owners said yes. There was no credit check, just a deposit required. We had no idea where we would come up with that and our first month's rent, but we had just seen our miraculous new home. We asked the Lord to supply the money and planned our move.

My lessons increased to the point where we could pay the deposit and first month's rent. We packed our things, scrubbed the house and hugged it and the beautiful flowers and cherry tree goodbye.

Every month thereafter we had to trust the Lord for the rent. Sometimes we were late, but the owners were patient. They were fine about Jim the dog, and she sure loved the farm.

Chapter Thirty-five

I HAD COLLECTED ENOUGH PONIES and horses to host summer camps. I thought *my* kids should go to summer camp, so why not have one that they could go to for free, right at Pebble Creek? I asked the older students to be camp counselors in trade for a daily lesson, and they were eager to do it. I kept an ad in the Little Nickel and got plenty of campers as well as weekly students. It was a lot of work, but a *lot* of fun. During camp weeks I taught the campers a lesson in the morning and we had a fun ride in the afternoon. One group did crafts while the other group rode. We cleaned stalls. We cleaned tack. On hot afternoons we went to the nearby lake. We had a dress-up day for the horses and ponies, and after they were done up in ribbons and be-sparkled, we had a parade up and down the road of the Pebble Creek neighborhood. Once the local paper came and took pictures.

The game "Pony Town" was born. The middle of the outdoor arena turned into a village complete with fast food, a gas station, a police station and whatever else the campers and counselors could dream up. The outside track of the arena was the freeway; one had to trot or canter on it, but once you came into town one must walk or face getting a speeding ticket---on your horse. We had a blast with Pony Town. Every time we played we added new shops and new drama. A jail was built out of jump standards and poles, mostly to house speed demons and careless and reckless riders. There were quite a few jail breaks and police chases too.

That fall we started looking for a pony for Maeve, as Ryan had claimed Fire and Enya decided that Velvet was *her* horse. We tried a few, but ponies can be tricky. I'm pretty sure it's because they have Short Horse Syndrome. We finally settled on one of them, a petite, pretty black mare named Rita Mae. We told Maeve she was for the lesson program, but she was really for Maeve on her birthday if she worked out. After a short trial period she became Maeve's pony on Maeve's seventh birthday, and what a birthday it was. We had a big barn party with fun mounted games and a kitten race, as Maeve's adopted *Equifriends* kitten had grown up and had given birth to several adorable kittens of her own. They were about 8 weeks old at the time. Each kid chose a kitten and a bag of catnip on a string. They lined up on a starting line I had made across the barn hallway. When I said "Go! whoever got their kitten to chase their catnip bag across the finish line was the winner. Well, one kitty sank its' claws in the bag and got *drug* across the finish line. We hadn't given much thought to the rules of the race, so we declared that kitty the winner.

Things started out pretty well for Maeve and her newly renamed *Spunky Like Me,* interspersed with some spectacular crashes when Rita decided to be a little *too* spunky. We learned that bike helmets aren't the best thing to be wearing when you get bucked off, as Maeve's split in half as she landed on her head in the (thank God!) cushy footing of Pebble Creek's outdoor arena. In the end, Maeve felt safer riding Fire, and I don't blame her one bit. I felt safer with Maeve on him too! Rita was unpredictable. Ryan could handle her, but he was a little too tall. We tried her as a lesson pony, but every now and then she would buck some poor kid off. We put her up for sale.

Chapter Thirty-six

After Maeve's November birthday the dad of Firecracker's girl gave me a call. They had decided to sell him. Would I be interested in buying him? My heart skipped a beat. Of course I was, but I didn't know how we would pull it off. Money was tight, and we had just bought Maeve a pony. But, it was *Fire!* I asked how much, expecting a price tag way over our heads. Fire's price was seven hundred and fifty dollars, and we could make payments. I checked with Caleb, and we closed the deal with joyful hearts. To us, Fire was worth seven hundred and fifty *million.*

Ryan had mentioned several times to me that he wished Fire could be *his* pony; maybe get him for Christmas? Christmas was just around the corner. Caleb and I didn't say a word to the kids about purchasing Fire, but we made plans.

On Christmas morning, Ryan unwrapped a small box that contained a red bandana; nothing else. He looked at us inquisitively, and I said, "It's for later," so he set it aside. After all the presents had been distributed and unwrapped by everyone, we had the kids get dressed and ready to go outside. I tied the red bandana over Ryan's eyes. I told the kids, "We are off on a big *adventure."* That was fine by Ryan. He liked adventures. The girls were excited too! Caleb drove to the barn, with a few odd turns here and there just to throw Ryan off in case he could tell where we were going. The girls had been sworn to secrecy and they did a great job not spilling the beans. When we pulled into Pebble Creek, Caleb parked down by the arena while I headed up to the barn. I groomed Fire, tacked him up, and put a big red velvet ribbon on his bridle. Then I led him down to the car where Ryan was sitting, still blindfolded.

The girls' faces broke into huge smiles when they saw, and I put my finger to my lips. Caleb helped Ryan out of the car and led him over to Fire and me. I guided Ryan's hand to Fire's face, and Caleb untied the red bandana. Ryan's face was full of wonder, full of questions, so we shouted, "Merry Christmas! He's all yours now!" Ryan threw his arms around Fire's neck. The girls spilled out of the car to celebrate.

I had brought down Ryan's helmet, so he put it on and I threw him up on Fire's back. Ryan had been learning to ride on Firecracker for a few months, so I thought I'd let him take Fire for a short spin on the track that ran around the pond and outdoor arena. I told him to walk Fire on the track a little ways, then turn around and walk back. On the way back, Fire's ears pricked and he picked up a little trot. All seemed fine until I realized Fire had plans to trot on up to the barn to have some hot apple cider around the fireplace with his friends. Ryan realized this too, and executed a lovely Aikido roll right off his back before Fire crossed the paved road that separated the track and outdoor arena from the driveway to the barn. Fire was surprised by this, as we all were, and stopped in his tracks. Ryan could have pulled Fire up, but he thought bailing was a better idea! I was impressed by his great Aikido roll off Fire's back. He and the girls had been taking Aikido lessons for a few months, and they had been taught to roll away from their opponents. It took a while after that to convince Ryan to stay on and manage his new pony! I plopped him back on and we finished that awesome Christmas day ride and adventure. It was the first of many to come for that pair.

Another adventurous pair came together that very same Christmas. Tiny Rosalind got her own pony too. She had conquered *all* the school ponies and horses, so her wonderful parents decided it was time for her to have her own pal and partner in crime. It was a tall order to find the right pony for Rosalind; it had to be a very special soul. It had to be small enough for Rosalind to manage, but not devious and cranky as small ponies can be.

One of my student's parents owned a few horses and ponies. They had an older gentleman they wanted to sell. They brought him over for Jaime to try. His name was Dexter. He was twenty-something, almost black, with lots and lots of gray hair on his face. He was right around thirteen hands high. He looked and acted like Eeyore from *Winnie the Pooh*; kind of sad but very, very wise.

He was perfect for Rosalind.

I have an old picture of Rosalind on Dexter and Ryan on Fire that Christmas. Both ponies have big red bows tied on their bridles. Both kids have great big smiles on their faces. Fire and Dexter do too, if you look hard enough.

Chapter Thirty-seven

MAEVE SHARED FIRE WITH RYAN and rode various and sundry other ponies and small horses; the ones in my lesson program and others who came through Pebble Creek as well. Maeve was a very talented yet *tiny* young rider, so people welcomed her to ride their horses and ponies, especially the ones that needed a capable rider on their back.

Now that the kids had plenty of ponies and horses to ride I had Velvet more to myself, although I still put the kids up on her and taught on her occasionally. I was finally making enough money to take dressage lessons on Velvet from a wonderful instructor that came out to Pebble Creek. At that time John Lyons with his *Natural Horsemanship* was breaking onto the horse scene. Caleb and I rented some of his videos and finally bought the whole series. We went to see him when he came to a nearby city to give a weekend clinic. Deep in my soul I knew this stuff was a really big deal. I knew I had to study and learn. I knew it was the wave of the future. Caleb bought the books written by the masters that had inspired John Lyons, Ray Hunt and Tom Dorrance. A boarder at Pebble Creek wanted two of her Arabians started. Caleb and I agreed to do it for a nominal fee if she would let us practice the John Lyons techniques on her mares. She agreed, and it was fabulous. Caleb took one horse, I took the other. In spite of our inexperience, they came along quite easily. The owner was pleased.

I started using the "baby give" technique to supple Velvet's very stiff neck. Being fourteen years old and having been ridden only as a hunter, she was pretty set in her muscle memory. After about three weeks, my dressage instructor could not believe the difference in her. I told him what I had been doing. Unfortunately he completely dismissed it. But I kept right on *gettin' it,* and I have been *gettin'it* ever since, in spite of what unenlightened horse people have to say. Actually, the "baby give" is a classically correct method of suppling a horse. They just had another name for it. I hadn't yet learned the technique, and stumbled upon it through the John Lyon's stuff. I betcha John Lyons didn't learn it through dressage masters. Good training is good training. It doesn't matter who you learn it from or whether you ride English or Western.

All the while I was working on Velvet's stiff neck, the Lord let me know He was working on mine! It was a hoot. God is a real *Funny Man.*

The following fall, we heard about a little one-day event on Whidbey Island, and we thought we'd check it out. The ferry ride over to the island was exciting and beautiful enough, but the event totally rang my chimes.

There were all kinds of horses there, from scrubby ponies to elegant warm bloods and all ages of boys, girls, men and women riding them. I knew about eventing from reading and watching, from trying it in Georgia on Frankie and from my days at Potomac Horse Center, but I wasn't aware of the local eventing community. I was now! And I knew this was where we were meant to be. We had gone to little local shows as an introduction for my kids and my students, but they were bland compared to this! My kids were just a bit young for eventing and the ponies weren't exactly trained for it. Neither was Velvet, who had been a show hunter, but I was sure game to try.

The following spring I heard about a cross-country clinic about two hours south of Snohomish at a place called Camas Meadows. I don't remember how we pulled it off financially, but I took Velvet to it. We borrowed a trailer and loaded up Velvet, the kids, and my mom, who had flown out for a visit. I had played around a little on the cross-country jumps at Pebble Creek, and Velvet was very good, so I wanted to see what she could do on a real course. The clinician was excellent, and so was my mare. I had a blast. I asked if she thought Velvet and I could go to an event, and her response was, "I don't see why not!" I started to look for our first event. I was *pumped.*

There was a little one day event at Camas Meadows later that summer. Just to be on the safe side, I entered Hopeful, the two-foot division. Velvet had a lovely dressage test. Cross-country was easy, fun, and *way* too short. Stadium was a snap. I wished I could do it over ... and over and over!

I wish I could say I was sensible and decided to go up one level, Beginner Novice, at the next event I found. *But what did this girl do?* Bumped on up to Novice. I was game. Velvet was game. Why not?

So we did. We went to as many one-day events as I could find and we could afford; Vashon Island, Whidbey Island, Lincoln Creek in Centralia. All the rest of that summer we borrowed a trailer, packed camping gear, and away we went. Often little Rosalind was in tow, as she had become best pals with my kids. They had fine adventures and we slept out under the stars most nights.

Velvet was excellent and we were always in the ribbons. I set my sights on Training Level. She was now sixteen; could she do it? I took her to a clinic on Vashon Island. We jumped some Training Level fences. It seemed like a stretch for Velvet. The clinician said I looked scared. I didn't want to hear that, but I was, a little. Maybe it was too much for *both* of us.

So what did this girl do? I decided to breed Velvet. I drooled over fancy Warmblood stallions in magazines. Their stud fees were out of reach. The owner of Pebble Creek Stables had a paint stallion, and she offered to trade the stud fee for lessons for her daughter, who was the same age as Maeve. It was probably a pretty dumb thing to do, but I rationalized it by telling myself (and anyone who cared to listen) that maiden mares' first foals were not their best and they tended to be small. So why waste money on a fancy stud when I could breed her for free and see what she would produce and if she could even get pregnant?

So that is what this girl did. We bred Velvet in August, live cover, right outside the barn. The stallion's owner handled him and I held Velvet. The kids watched. That was how they learned about the birds and the bees. I said to them, "You know how Velvet and Spooks mated?

Well, people do it in almost the same way. That's how babies get made." Ryan looked thoughtful, and Maeve exclaimed *"YUCK!"* Not sure about Enya.

Spooks covered Velvet two or three times. It was easy. And sure enough, she easily got in foal. She was *Fertile Myrtle*, just like me. The long wait for next July began.

Chapter Thirty-eight

AFTER WE MOVED TO THE farm on Roosevelt Road, we would drive up Uber Road to get to Pebble Creek Stables. One summer day we saw a magnificent sight. The loudest colored Appaloosa I had ever seen in my life was grazing in a field. The kids and I started to watch for him every time we drove by. He was there with two other Appys, but they did not hold a candle to him. He was a near leopard, with huge round spots over most of his body. His legs, face and neck were dark roan. He had a blaze and white socks, too. He seemed tall as well, with a beautiful, arched neck. What a handsome beast he was!

When I was a student at Potomac Horse Center in Maryland, I had the privilege of riding and getting to know several Appaloosas. There was *PT Barnum*, a very loud-colored leopard sweetheart of an old school horse. There was *Calypso,* a small Appy mare who was great fun and could jump the moon. And there was *Raisin Bran*, a very pretty young mare, a beautiful leopard, that I had the privilege of schooling for her owner after I graduated from the program. Even though I brought my Arabian gelding *Frankie* to Potomac Horse Center, and had ridden Arabians for most of my life, it was Appaloosas that won my heart. I fell for the spots.

When I or one of the kids noticed the Appy on Uber Road, we would exclaim **"Appy Alert!"** and everyone would look for him until they "spotted" him. I just couldn't stop talking about him to Caleb. One day Caleb stopped and talked to the owners and found out they called him *Meathead*. He was 14 years old and barely broke. They owned his mom and about the only times he had been ridden were when friends came over and everyone had too much to drink. Then they would hop on him bareback and drunkenly ride him around the pasture until they fell off. Caleb, undaunted, asked if we could lease him. They said we surely could but take him for a month on trial first.

In August I went to pick him up. He was a lot shorter than I thought; only about 14.3, where I thought he was 16 hands high. He jumped right in the trailer. We took him to Pebble Creek and turned him out, where he pranced around the field. He was kind of funny looking---hugely overweight, totally out of shape, and with that *great big neck!* He trotted around with a huge amount of knee action, like he was a Saddlebred or something. I had a tiny sliver of misgiving, but I sure didn't tell anyone. The barn owner came down and made fun of him. There sure is a lot of prejudice against Appaloosas. You either adore or despise them. Well, it figures. They are *horses of color,* and they were bred by Native Americans, the *Nez Perce* people; the indigenes.

He was woefully fat. Although his name was Barbarossa Sundance and Ryan nicked named him "Sump", we also called him *Marshmallow Man.* There wasn't a mean bone in his rotund body. Neither was there any training. The kids liked riding him bareback because he was so nice and squishy and had a very comfortable trot. He would jog politely once or twice around the outdoor arena, then make a polite but determined beeline (a *faster* jog) for the gate and the nearby grass. If the flimsy gate was closed, he would press on it with his chest, hoping to pop it open. It was just a 1"x6" board in sliders. It never broke completely, but he did succeed in cracking it pretty well. He never did anything we couldn't handle. He never bucked or had dangerous moves, but he was strong as an ox and it took Ryan some time to build up the strength to keep him in the ring. Ryan and I got him legged up, better mannered, and before long some of my students were riding him.

Walk, trot and canter. Sump had no right lead, and no intention of ever having one! So we schooled him and schooled him over a slanted ground pole, asking for the canter just as he went over. If he chose the right lead, it would feel less awkward, and all would be well. It worked eventually. Pretty soon he was a very busy boy giving lots of lessons.

Because he was quite stout and strong he could carry adults. In fact he was a bit *too* stout and *too* strong for little kids. He became quite popular especially with two high-school aged sisters, Estelle and Hannah Borge. They helped me with his training. Before long we were teaching him to jump. He was very game until he thought he'd done enough, then he would just carry his stout, strong self and whomever was on his back *around* the jump---just as pretty as you please.

But that boy had a lot of jump in him. As his training continued he continued to impress us with his jumping skills. He folded his knees tight as ticks and was careful behind. He was a flat-backed jumper, meaning he didn't round his back over fences. That wouldn't earn him any points in the show hunter ring, but it earned him major points with all his riders. He was extremely easy to sit on over a fence. We got him up to three-foot-nine before a rail dropped.

One of the Borge sisters who truly loved Sump was diagnosed with Hodgkin's disease. Her mom asked if she could please ride Sump for therapy through the long dark days of chemo. We said of course and no charge. Sump wouldn't have had it any other way. The girl recovered, and it warms my soul to know that Sump played a part in her healing.

Before long another horse came into the family; an older thoroughbred named *Pete.* I got him free from a gal who more or less rescued him. She was coping with two kids and no money after her husband left her. She brought him to Pebble Creek with another horse. She would ride Pete in the outdoor arena with draw reins. He really caught my eye. What a beautiful, elegant boy he was. He was tall and a whole lot of horse to sit on even at eighteen years old. I found out he used to be a Grand Prix jumper in his youth, and he knew some dressage. He had been passed from barn to barn, going more and more downhill until she took him.

After a couple months his owner told me she was going to have to part with Pete because she was out of money. When she told me she was going to have to take him to auction if she couldn't find a home for him soon, my heart lurched. I talked to Caleb. We took Pete.

I took dressage lessons on him for a couple years with my wonderful dressage instructor who absolutely loved him. He was not 100% sound; injections would have helped him a lot, but that was very costly. I couldn't justify the expense because he was way too hot to be a school horse. So I only rode him occasionally and wished I had the money to fix him.

Chapter Thirty-nine

AT SUMMER'S END CALEB AND I were playing with the kids on the living room rug. We started an impromptu wrestling match. Len was on his back and the kids and I were pretending to conquer him. I went in for an "attack" and Caleb deflected me by grabbing at my hands. I lost my balance and I fell on his chest with a thud. There was a cracking sound, then the sound of Caleb howling in pain. I had cracked the poor guy's ribs! Caleb went off to our medical clinic for a diagnosis. Sure enough, cracked ribs. The doctor who examined him admonished him to get in better shape. I thought I should lose some weight!

Caleb slowly and painfully recovered. Later in the fall he was out raking leaves in the front yard when **CRACK!** Ribs in a different place buckled. Back to the doctor's office, but this time our regular doctor; one we knew and trusted. He ordered some lab work. When it came back, it showed that Caleb had Stage Three Multiple Myeloma. Cancer of the bone marrow. The cancer was rapidly multiplying inside his bones and causing them to become thin and fragile. And break.

We were stunned. Our good family doctor sent us off to see an oncologist. More blood tests. Then, a meeting. The oncologist was a lovely man; in a very nice, professional manner he delivered to Caleb a death sentence with a small ray of hope: treatment.

Then came the exhausting and frightening processes of radiation and chemotherapy. After a year, the results were disappointing. His oncologist encouraged Caleb to go to The Fred Hutchison Cancer Treatment Center in Seattle, where he agreed to have an experimental bone marrow transplant. The doctors didn't give us much hope, but the bone marrow transplant was the one possibility of surviving *if* the treatment didn't kill him. I doubted Caleb would make it. In a morbid way I thought that could be God's mercy on me, since our marriage was so difficult and I couldn't find a way out of it. I felt horrible for the kids, though, because Caleb was an incredible father to them.

Fred Hutchison located an anonymous donor, and the treatment began.

Caleb was in the hospital for five weeks. Our incredible friend and sister in the Lord, Makeda Ennishad, flew out from North Carolina for an entire month to take care of the kids and horses so I could stay at Caleb's bedside. She had raised enough money to keep us and the horses fed and the bills paid during that time. I have never in my life met anyone like her. She is so strong in the Lord, and so unselfishly devoted to helping those in need that God puts in her path. She is *amazing*. She'll probably blush and deny her sainthood when she reads this, but don't let that fool you. That is sincere humility in all its' glory. She is **The Real Deal.**

The days by Caleb's side at Fred Hutchinson crawled slowly by. The way a bone marrow transplant works is it nearly kills you. They give cancer patients enough chemo to kill a moose. It hopefully kills all the cancer cells in your body. It also kills tons of healthy cells; too many die, and so do you. You get healthy bone marrow from an anonymous donor with the same blood type. Then you get lots and lots of drugs to deal with Graft vs. Host disease, a by-product of the transplant which can also kill you. Your immune system is decimated by all the chemo, so you are wide open to all kinds of infections and diseases which can also kill you.

Patients dropped like flies on Caleb's floor. They died of complications, secondary infections and liver failure. We wondered if Caleb was next. I spent a lot of time praying in the hospital chapel. I prayed in any quiet spot I could find. I prayed for Caleb, for his fellow patients. I prayed for the patients' families. I prayed for my family. I prayed for the horses. I prayed for myself.

Caleb looked like Uncle Fester from the *Adam's Family*. He blew up like a balloon from all the prednisone in his system. He was bald. He had thrown up so much and so violently his eyes were very bloodshot. The lining of his throat died and sloughed off, leaving his throat incredibly raw and sore. It was all he could do to eat or drink anything, then somehow make it to the bathroom to throw up or have projectile diarrhea. He didn't always make it. My job was to try and help him get there, or clean up when he didn't. I took blankets to the dryer to heat them; one for Caleb, one for me. When Caleb was sleeping I snuck in a little TV. Ironically I got hooked on *E.R.* and *Chicago Hope.* Caleb was not amused to wake up to those shows. Sometimes I left The Hutch and went for walks. I became very familiar with that part of Seattle. My favorite place was The Freeway Park over I-5, which Caleb had shown me years ago on our trip out to get Colleen Maera.

Caleb slowly, slowly improved. He rejected all attempts by therapists to get him to do stuff, but we walked and walked the floor of the hospital. Other patients walked as well. I had taped our favorite picture of Jesus giving a thumb's-up sign by the door to Caleb's room. One day a lovely patient we had befriended was slowly walking by. He saw the picture and stopped. He placed his thumb on Jesus's thumb. Caleb and I looked wide-eyed at each other and smiled. He didn't notice we were watching. He stood there with his thumb on the picture for some time, and then he shuffled down the hall. After the guys' discharge from the hospital a couple weeks before Caleb went home, he got a nasty secondary infection. Before long he was in heaven with the Lord, touching His real thumb.

Then it was Caleb's turn to be discharged from the Fred Hutchison. Makeda went home to her family. My dear friend from Maine, Naomi White, came to stay for a week. My mom came for a week after that. Colleen Maera dropped out of college in Oklahoma and came to live with us and help out. We made weekly trips to Fred Hutchison's outpatient clinic so Caleb could be checked on and receive medicine to prevent Graft vs. Host disease. Visiting nurses came and went. We made sure the house was very clean and Caleb had minimum exposure to anything that would make him sick. It was hard, but we made it. By the grace of God, we made it. And Caleb lived.

Chapter Forty

ALL THE TIME I WAS with Caleb at the hospital Makeda and the kids looked after the horses. Sometimes I would drive home, hug the kids, drive to the barn, hug the horses, and drive back to the Hutch. Makeda was an incredible blessing. She loved on my anxious kids and took such good care of them, Jim, the horses and the kitties that I never worried about them. She said that was her plan when she came out to stay with us.

My mare Velvet was about nine months pregnant when Caleb came home; due in early July. Fortunately she had a very easy, very horsy-like pregnancy, not requiring much more than the normal good care we gave her and routine vet checks. She carried her foal quietly through Caleb's outpatient chemotherapy, then his bone-marrow transplant and recovery. By the time Velvet was due I felt comfortable leaving Caleb with Colleen and sleeping at the barn. I strung up a hammock in the grooming stall across from the large foaling stall. We had it thickly bedded with straw for the new arrival. I didn't sleep a whole lot, but I was thoroughly enjoying staying in the barn with my ponies. I just had to open my eyes a crack to check on Velvet and heard the beautiful, haunting call of the Swainson's Thrush all through the night. Those tremulous notes are forever imbedded in my soul.

One evening I finished up at the barn and went home for a quick supper before returning to stay the night near Velvet. The kids had camped out in sleeping bags the previous two evenings hoping to see the birth, but that night all three opted for a good night's sleep in their own beds. When I got back to the barn Velvet was in early labor. I very excitedly called my vet. He was cute. *"I can tell you are pretty excited!* he chuckled. I agreed! He said call him back if necessary, but carry on.

Velvet went into harder labor, and the foal's forefeet appeared. They were white. Were they socks, stockings, or did they keep on going, meaning she had color? As the forelegs slowly slid forward, they remained white past the midpoint of her cannons. Then Velvet laid down, rolled, and got cast (stuck) against the wall of her stall.

Yikes! What to do? I had seen in a book how to dislodge a cast horse, so I got a hose and wrapped it around her front and hind pasterns that were on the stall floor. Try as I might, I was not quite strong enough to roll her over so she could get up. No one was there except for Mark, a wiry, elderly gentleman from Scotland. He lived in a tiny apartment next to the barn and did farm maintenance. Mark is an outstanding fellow. He has never owned a car, but has a good bicycle and rides it everywhere, including a trip once across the United States. He has to be in his early eighties now, but I still see him peddling around town.

I roused Mark, and with his help we rolled Velvet over, and she got to her feet. During that time I even more excitedly rang my vet! As soon as Velvet was on her feet she lay back down and finished bringing her new filly into the world.

Talk about color! She was a gorgeous bay and white tobiano, with just the right amount of brown and white. Her legs were white, her tail was white, her mane was two-toned, and in the middle of her lovely bay forehead was a perfect star in shape and size. She was *exquisite*.

I named her Gracie because of the circumstances into which she was conceived and born. When I bred Velvet, we had no idea of the coming storm called Multiple Myeloma that was gathering on the horizon. We just thought having a baby from Velvet would be fun, and having Spooks right there, and trading lessons for his stud fee was incredibly convenient. We didn't know what the coming months would bring. It was possible that Caleb would die and leave me a single mom with three kids and several horses. Teaching riding was a shaky kind of way to make a buck.

Gracie was named that because Velvet was an older maiden mare, yet she got pregnant so easily. Gracie was Gracie because Velvet carried her through all those dark months when Caleb was sick and we didn't think he would make it. Gracie was Gracie because I was not at the barn a whole lot when Caleb was at the Hutch. My dear friend Makeda was not a horse person. My young children were well, *young.* But they all took good care of her mom and the others for four weeks. Gracie was Gracie because she was basically a free horse. All she cost was a few hours of my labor teaching a young girl and a few vet visits. Gracie was Gracie because she had an easy birth even though her mom was stuck upside down for part of the birth process!

Gracie was Gracie because it was the grace of God Caleb lived. There he was taking pictures of Velvet and Gracie their first day out in the pasture at Pebble Creek. The pictures show me in exhausted happiness sitting cross-legged in the grass. I was wearing a pink tank top because it was nice and warm, watching that beautiful, loud-colored, wobbly-legged filly explore her beautiful new world with her plain bay but beautiful mom.

Chapter Forty-One

AFTER CALEB GOT HOME FROM the hospital and we settled into a routine, I slowly started to teach lessons again. We were always a bit nervous about Caleb getting an infection or Graft vs. Host disease taking over, but neither was a problem. Colleen did a great job holding down the fort while I was at the barn, and the kids usually came with me to help clean stalls and ride. Slowly but surely Caleb got stronger and healthier to the point he could come out to the barn as well, and being at the barn made him stronger and healthier.

We got two new boarder families; a very nice young woman and young man, their beautiful mare and gelding, and their lovely respective parents. The girl had been a Pony Clubber until she aged out of the club requirement, twenty-one. The boy was still in Stillaguamish Pony Club, although it was reduced to two members, him and a different girl who kept her horse at home. As we got to know these folks, the possibility of taking over their club came up. I had often thought about Pony Club and thought it would be great to have my kids join and be involved myself. Before long I was the new District Commissioner (D.C.) of the newly formed Pebble Creek Pony Club. We decided to rename the club because Pebble Creek ran right through Pebble Creek Stables, and Pebble Creek Pony Club sounded cool. I raised a few eyebrows at the Regional Pony Club level, because I wasn't supposed to name a club after a stable. But since we named it after a creek that flowed through the farm, it was somewhat justified. It was just a bit tricky, and I was to learn Pony Club was more than just a bit tricky.

I was strongly discouraged from teaching Pony Club lessons because I wasn't a Pony Club alumnus. That was a bit of a setback, but I didn't argue. We had guest Pony Club graduate instructors. I rented the ponies and horses out to my students who didn't own their own horse but had joined Pony Club. Once a month we had a mounted meeting that took up a Saturday. We had unmounted meetings once or twice a month. We had a rating that took up a weekend. Ratings tested the member's riding ability and knowledge so that they could move up the Pony Club levels.

We also took teams to a couple of different Pony Club Rallies. Those were competitions between clubs. Each club sent a team of three or four riders and a stable manager. Teams were scored on their riding performance, their horses' care throughout the day, and their ability to answer questions on horse management. At our first rally Ryan rode Fire, Rosalind rode Dexter, the farm owner's daughter rode her pony, and one of my students rode Maeve's feisty little pony mare. Maeve had opted out of competing Spunky Like Me because of too many involuntary dismounts. I had an older student who bravely volunteered to be the Stable Manager.

By far we had the youngest team members. We also had the most nervous parents! We stood behind the rope barring parents from helping and wrung our hands. One of our moms was even tearful. We watched Fire sit back on his lead rope and break his halter while tied to the trailer, as he was prone to do. A nice Pony Club volunteer let Fire stay in a portable pen the rest of the day. Spunky Like Me dumped her spunky little rider in their stadium jumping round, confirming Maeve's decision not to ride her in the Rally. Rosalind's and Ryan's rides went well, and the stable manager did a stellar job. At the end of the Rally our team came in next to last. But not last!

We took another team to a Dressage Rally. It was Ryan on Fire, Rosalind on Dexter, and two talented students of mine on their own cute horses. Another older Pony Clubber was our stable manager. This time we were more prepared. Ryan stayed with Fire so he wouldn't pull back and break his halter. No parents had nervous breakdowns or shed tears. Having been to one Rally, we had our trailer more organized. We were much more prepared than last time.

Everyone did pretty well in their dressage tests. When it was Rosalind's turn, all was going fine until Dexter neatly picked up his canter exactly where he was supposed to, between K and A. He then promptly left the arena at A and proceeded to hightail it back to the trailer! Rosalind stayed on, little monkey that she was. She probably thought it was pretty cool, since she wanted to be a jockey when she got older. At least Dexter galloped as fast as he could but did not buck! So Rosalind stayed on and brought Dexter back to the arena. She and Dexter got a do-over, and he stayed put this time. And the end of the day our team came in third from the bottom. Hey, we moved up a notch!

Chapter Forty-two

We cranked up our summer camps again. Caleb was coming to the barn to help every day, and he was a wonderful addition to our camp staff. He was superb with the kids and added so much to their day. That summer we had the best camps ever. I'll never forget Caleb running a seafood restaurant in Pony Town. He would pace back and forth like he was holding a sandwich board yelling "**Fried Fricasseed Frog Legs! Get 'em while they're hot!**" That was in fond memory of a great seafood house in Virginia where we *did* eat delicious fried frog legs.

We went to Flowing Lake nearly every afternoon. The lake started having problems with goose poop causing skin irritations on swimmers, so when we brought the campers back to the barn we would have them soap up in the wash rack with their swimsuits on, then hose them down like horses. They thought it was awesome. Caleb made Breyer Horse-sized barns with the kids as part of their crafts. We held an advanced camp for my year-round students with a trip to a local training track. The kids had a blast galloping around on their ponies. Fire proved to be quite competitive! No way was he going to let any horse get ahead of *him*.

Towards summer's end we taught a Back-to-School camp. We found this particularly fun to do since we were home schooling our own kids. We incorporated different subjects like poetry and math into the camp activities. On poetry day the campers chose to write cinquains, haikus, acrostic poems or sonnets about their favorite horse or pony. On history day they learned about the evolution of the horse from fox-sized Eohippus to the majestic Equus about whom they were writing poetry.

On math day they weighed and measured out a horse's daily hay and grain ration, then calculated what it would cost to feed that horse for a month. On science day they built horses' 100 foot long digestive system using panty hose and barn rags. On Friday we had a little show and the kids proudly showed off their newly acquired or improved riding skills and their academic achievements as well. It was my favorite camp of all.

We spent most of our time at Pebble Creek Stables. A trainer left and we had the opportunity to move down to the nice main barn that had about 16 stalls and an apartment attached to it. We moved the computer there so the kids could "barn school" instead of home school. They did spend a *little* time doing the 3 R's in that apartment, but really the whole farm was their classroom. Their imaginations were keen. They romped and played outside all day. Sometimes their adventures were with friends on horseback, sometimes it was just on foot with brother, sisters, Jim and friends. They played out epic adventures, as they had just been introduced to the fledgling *World of Warcraft* game on the computer. They took that game from the computer to fields and woods of Pebble Creek. They played it mounted on their trusty steeds and on their trusty feet. While riding their trusty steeds the kids would challenge each other to tackle the up and down bank on Pebble Creek's little cross-country course. Always our dog Jim would be in the background quietly standing guard over her young charges. The kids gave her a Warcraft name: *Lone Wolfe*.

We also added a second dog to the family. Caleb came back from a trip to the grocery store with groceries and a black and tan coonhound. A boy was holding the hound's leash in front of the grocery store, hoping someone would take him. The boy's family bred the hounds to hunt bear and cougar in the mountains. The young dog was terrified of gunshots so flunked out of hunting hound school. Since we loved coonhounds and missed the three we gave up in Virginia, Caleb was happy to bring him back to the barn. The kids were delighted. They promptly named him *Hank* after all the *Hank the Cow Dog* stories they were reading. Jim stoically bore with his puppy antics. Caleb tried to train him to come to a dog whistle, but Hank's nose took him far a-field. He always came back, though we worried about him getting hit by a car on Westwick Road. He was also a notorious horse brush stealer. Anyone leaving their grooming kit out while Hank was loose was sure to be missing a brush or two. Hank ended up having to be tethered on a longe line most of the time, unless the kids took him out to play in one of Pebble Creek's wire-mesh paddocks. As long as one of them blocked the pipe-panel gate so Hank would not escape, he would play catch until the kids were exhausted.

We hosted "Barn Days," a kind of horse lover's daycare. If parents of my students had a busy day or had to work and find alternatives to school or regular day care, we let them come to the barn for a fee. They rode, played with my kids and did barn chores all day. They loved it.

My oldest daughter Enya rode for three years in Little Bit's annual therapeutic horse show. She had a blast and won some blue ribbons. The first year she rode a darling buckskin pony from Equifriends; the second year she rode Velvet. The third summer she rode Fire. Little Bit always had a costume class. *The Lion King* movie was out the spring before the third show, and Enya was totally into it. We dressed Fire as Pumba and Enya as Timon. Fire sported tusks made from paper towel tubes wrapped in masking tape. I wrapped his tail with black self-sticking wrap to look just like a tail belonging to a warthog. I painted his soft muzzle pink with theater cake make-up. He was already a stout red boy, so it wasn't too much of a stretch to transform him into the movie star. With a little makeup Enya transformed into Timon, complete with a grass skirt and coconut bra. She sang that song from the movie as loud as she could and shimmied her hips as she rode Fire around the arena. It was hilarious and perfect. They won first place.

Ryan and Rosalind had some grand adventures on horseback. Maeve was more conservative with Spunky Like Me with good reason. Ryan and Rosalind were constantly in the saddle. One day they were riding together out on the exercise track. They picked up a trot, then a little canter. I was watching the scene from a distance and enjoying every minute of it. Fire put on a little speed and Dexter kept up. On the far side of the track it turned into a hand-gallop. Then Dexter proceeded to buck while galloping as fast as his old short legs would carry him. Rosalind went flying and Ryan bailed off Fire in support. Soon I was flying across the pasture to the rescue. By the time I got to the scene the ponies were quietly munching grass and Ryan and Rosalind were laughing as they brushed off dirt and grass from their shirts and pants.

Maeve shared Fire with Ryan and rode the other school horses. I had a cute pinto in training for awhile and we ended up leasing him for Maeve to ride in Pony Club. Enya enjoyed riding Fire and T.C.. One winter we had a big snowstorm. We knew our two wheel drive truck wouldn't make it around the turns and up the hills to Pebble Creek so all of us walked the three miles to the barn. The arena looked pristine with over a foot of snow covering it. I thought it might be fun for the kids to play Fox and Geese on horseback. I greased up the soles of their hooves so the snow wouldn't stick. We got down to the arena and started the game. T.C. gently lay down to have a snow-roll. I helped Enya roll clear and we watched T.C. in amusement (except for Enya) as he enjoyed the fluffy white stuff. The snow was too deep for the saddle to get damaged and Enya was fine. The only thing hurt was her "diggity"!

When the kids had ridden enough we headed back up to the barn. Maeve was riding Dexter; Rosalind couldn't get out to Snohomish from Bothell. Once out of the arena Dexter bolted and bucked. He wanted to go to the barn as fast as possible in case there was hot toddy! Maeve went airborne and was deposited in the deep snow. It made for a very soft landing.

Chapter Forty-three

DEXTER WAS NO SPRING CHICKEN when Rosalind got him, and he wasn't getting any younger. Rosalind needed a new pony to match her growing abilities as a rider. Rosalind loved Dexter, but she was ready to do more than Dexter could do. We put out feelers for a new pony. We found one on Whidbey Island. He belonged to a Pony Clubber who was willing to let Jaime have him on trial for a month. His owners were honest; the pony was a good one but had a few quirks as he had been rescued from a bad situation. They wanted to give Jaime time to see if he was the right pony for her.

He was a darling chestnut pinto, about thirteen hands high. He could be shy, but Rosalind was careful and gentle with him. After about three weeks it seemed they would be best buddies. Rosalind's parents closed the deal. They gave Dexter to us to use gently as a lesson pony. That way Rosalind could still be close to her beloved old guy.

Kids enjoyed riding Dexter in lessons, and Rosalind loved riding her new guy. Dexter was great as a school pony with one exception. I would often walk about 30 feet away from him down the track of the arena and then let Dexter's rider canter to me. Dexter had a nice little canter and the nice little kids who rode him loved to canter a nice little distance to me. It was a perfect way to let kids experience their first few canters, until one day Dexter exploded like a rocket launcher, depositing his rider at my feet! After that you never knew when he was going to do that. Most of the time he would be perfect, but occasionally it would happen. We started calling it being *Dexterized*. I'll never forget one day when we had to do a lesson in the indoor arena because it was raining so hard outside. The footing was old; mostly dirt, and it was either very dry and dusty, or wet and slippery if we watered it. That day it was dry and dusty. Dexter was being ridden by a young girl named Meribeth who was a pretty capable little rider. When it came time to canter Dexter, she tried and tried to get him to canter unsuccessfully. Finally I went and got a longe whip to help motivate Dexter. Just the sight of it in my hands was all it took. He turned into a little black torpedo. Just before he turned the corner he "Dexterized" her with some major dolphin-like moves! Meribeth turned into a human torpedo, skimming through the dirt and dust until she disappeared in it. She quickly surfaced, coughing and spitting out dirt. I helped her clean up as best I could. I got her a drink of water and a washcloth for her face. I dusted off her clothes; I felt like I was beating a rug on a clothesline. Meribeth was quite the trooper. Any other kid would have had a meltdown. Needless to say she has kept riding all these years and is quite talented. Meribeth has trained a horse or two herself and is coaching now, so I guess I can thank you, Dexter. **No one can teach riding better than a horse.** (CS. Lewis)

Chapter Forty-four

Rosalind got along well with her new pony Cody until we tried jumping him. That proved to be quite the challenge. Cody did not want to get anywhere near jump poles. It took a long time for him to finally go over, and when he did, he would launch himself in the air like a cat. Rosalind came off a few times, but slowly and patiently we brought him along. Finally we thought Rosalind was ready to take him to a little event. We chose Whidbey Island; Rosalind had already had a successful go on Dexter there. She and Cody had a respectable dressage test, and while we held our breath for most of cross-country, Rosalind and Cody made it through. Stadium, however, proved disastrous. Rosalind struggled so much in the warm-up I decided to take Cody to a little stadium practice ring off to the side to see if I could get him settled. I got him over almost everything except one that I jumped instead of Cody. He galloped back to where Fire and Ryan were warming up. The practice arena was mostly obscured by shrubbery, so I showed up back at the warm-up momentarily, a little embarrassed. I got back on Cody, took him back to the ring by the bushes and got him over the jump. Then I brought him back to the show jumping warm-up area and gave Rosalind a leg up. She got him over a couple of warm-up fences and then it was her turn to show in the stadium ring.

Each jump was more awkward then the one before, until finally Rosalind and Cody finally parted company. Caleb was video-taping, and the video shows Rosalind sitting in a frustrated heap on her tiny bottom in the grass while Cody galloped away. Sadly we called it a day.

Rosalind's parents wanted a safer pony for her, and I agreed. Cody was sold and the hunt for a new pony began. Her parents found one that seemed nice, so we went for a look. This pony was a white Connemara mare named *Miss Marbles*. She was pretty, middle-aged, and experienced. She was opinionated, but what pony and what mare isn't? Marbles became Rosalind's third pony, and this time it was a very good match.

We kept going with lessons, camps, barn days, shows and spectacular mounted birthday party packages that parents bought for their children. Pony Club was in full swing, but I was becoming disillusioned with it. Being the D.C., I had quite a bit of administrative work to do, when what I wanted to do was teach. Because I couldn't, I rented ponies inexpensively to my students who were Pony Clubbers to be taught by guest instructors. I ended up losing money on Pony Club. Renting ponies for the day was a lot less income than teaching lessons, and when we had ratings and Rallies that took up an entire weekend, I not only lost money but time as well. I decided to quit being D.C.. Another mom took over, and very soon I felt pushed out to the margins. I felt I had so much to offer, but she didn't seem to want my help. That hurt. A *lot*.

Other things were going on too. Caleb and I were having major difficulties. He did not like working at the barn with me. He felt I was way too bossy. His disability checks ended. It was time for him to find a job. A psychology degree and three dollars will get you a latte. He looked for a job for awhile, but nothing materialized that seemed fulfilling or offered a decent wage. Finally he approached his old bosses from the late 60's where he had worked a year after high school. They were two brothers that owned a string of Arby's® Roast Beef restaurants. They hired him as an assistant manager.

I was *angry*. I had given up college so Caleb could finish college. We had borrowed a ton of money in student loans. Caleb had a bachelor's degree; fast food was the best he could do? Not only that, but all the money I was making at French Creek got spent on books; Caleb's book fetish. He had rung up big credit card bills. I owed a lot of money in B&O taxes. Suddenly we were very broke. I did not understand at all, at all. That added fuel to the fire of my anger. We declared bankruptcy. That nearly made me die from embarrassment. I never told my family.

I decided to divorce Caleb once and for all, and he was pretty tired of me too. I made arrangement with the owners of Pebble Creek to live with the kids in the attached barn apartment. Caleb's parents gave him their old motor home to live in.

To complicate matters, the guy we bought local hay from and who came to haul away Pebble Creek's huge manure pile became very attracted to me, and I to him. He was sweet, he was attentive, he was totally infatuated with me; basically everything I wanted Len to be but wasn't. I really struggled with it. I knew it wasn't right, but I was desperate for that kind of affection and attention.

The kids were aware of this and thought me ridiculous. They were very upset and angry with me for doing this to Caleb, who became deeply hurt and depressed. The kids were mad at me for breaking up the family. I prayed desperately to God for help in doing the right thing. He answered and gave me the strength I needed to turn away from this other guy's attentions and I did. I thank God it never went anywhere. Caleb and I decided to start over.

But the owner of Pebble Creek's daughter, who lived there and managed the place, did split up with her husband because she had a boyfriend. He was a horse trainer who trained horses to pull carts and buggies. He worked out of a stable just up the road. Once the husband was out of the picture he started showing up more and more. One day I was in the outdoor arena teaching three girls on three ponies. Suddenly, shod hooves rang out on the pavement. The driving guy was coming down the street in a buggy attached to a smartly trotting pinto pony.

My lesson ponies immediately spooked and bolted. Two of the girls promptly fell off but I caught the third frightened pony. No one was injured, but I was really annoyed with the trainer, whom I thought a careless and thoughtless jerk. As time went on things got worse. I wanted to find a new barn.

Chapter Forty-five

I STARTING ASKING MY FRIENDS about barns and looked around. One of my best buddies that I worked with at Equifriends lived across the street from a pretty cool place in Sultan, about a half-hour due east from us. The owners had bred Arabians for a number of years, but weren't doing much any more. It had been quite the show place. It needed some elbow grease and TLC, both of which I was happy to supply.

The owner was also open to the idea of us living there in the motor home Caleb's parents had given us. His eyebrows rose a little at the thought of two adults, three kids, two dogs and three cats living in that tiny space, but he agreed to it. Caleb and the kids were game to try, and so I gave notice at Pebble Creek which upset the owners. It also upset my students and boarders.

A couple of days before we were supposed to move the barn owner in Sultan called me. He had just talked to someone else and liked that person's situation and plans much better. He called off our deal. Needless to say I was devastated. I had to go up to the owner's house and beg permission to stay a little longer. They were not happy about it, but agreed to it. The rest of our time at Pebble Creek was extremely awkward. I loved my boarders and students and they loved me, but they felt betrayed and hurt that I would leave them. A few were going to come with us, but only one was committed. That was Rosalind's family.

There was a woman in nearby Murphy that had a booming lesson program. I found out about her through friends and approached her about a teaching position. She came out to watch me teach a lesson. After watching she hired me.

We had asked our landlords if we could stay on after the deal fell through in Sultan and they said yes. Since I was going to teach at a barn that was already packed with horses I needed to figure out what to do with mine. T.C. had been sold to one of my student's families and they decided they would try hauling over to the new place for lessons but keep T.C. at Pebble Creek. Since I leased Sump I had to take him back to his owners and that was brutal. His fan club piled in the truck when I borrowed a trailer to take him back. They cried all the way there, cried when they kissed his velvet muzzle and said goodbye, and cried all the way back to the barn. Dexter was leased by one of my students' families and went to live in Sultan. There he would have a nice life and little work. The rest of my horses, Velvet, Gracie, Fire, Pete and Rita went home to the dairy farm. We also brought home a thoroughbred mare I had bought with my fabulous working student Rachel. We also brought home Marbles. Rosalind's parents trusted us to care for her and find the right board and lesson situation for Jaime.

Our very last trip up the driveway from Pebble Creek was incredibly painful. I had expected most of my students to follow me but they did not. I felt rejected by the Pony Club. I was angry at the owner's daughter and her trainer boyfriend. When we got to the top of the driveway we stopped, got out, removed our boots, and shook them out. That is how we felt about it.

Chapter Forty-six

THE HORSES SETTLED IN FAIRLY well to their new home and became a herd. I was very worried about the fence, for it was barbed wire. That was the worst fence possible to keep horses in. We put hundreds of pieces of white tape along the fence line so the horses would see it. The only mishap was when Gracie ran into, then jumped a section of it between pastures when she was first let out. She didn't seem to see the flags, and when she hit it she leaped neatly over it. The old fence posts fell down along with the fence, and the only injury she received was a scrape across her chest from the barbs. She could have been seriously injured; even killed. I washed it, treated it and gave her a tetanus booster. That was the first experience of much, much grace as long as we had horses at the place. The horses loved all the grass to munch and communal living. I almost felt dismissed; no longer needed. There was plenty to eat, plenty to drink, room to roam and play, and shelter if they desired. They had each other and that was enough.

A couple of weeks passed peacefully. I closed down one pasture to recover and opened another after we checked it over and flagged the fence. I got busy teaching at Bonnie Colson's barn. Then one morning I went down to feed the horses and found the other horses fussing over Velvet. She had badly broken her leg. I knew it was the end for Velvet. I called my vet; watched and waited for him while the mare Sadie, that I owned with Rachel, licked Velvet's leg which was bleeding from the fracture. Sadie was absolutely wonderful, cleaning Velvet's wound and washing her all over with her tongue. Pete, my old thoroughbred, stood stoically on Velvet's other side in support. My vet came in a hurry and took x-rays. He rushed them down the street to a nearby veterinary hospital to have them developed. Her wound was devastating. Her left pastern was broken in five places. We talked about her chances of recovery, which were slim to none. It would be incredibly hard on her---and me. My vet went to his van to get the Phenobarbital. Through my tears I saw the other horses, whom I had put back in their old field for safety and shut the gate to the other one, get in file and one by one come to say goodbye. When they were all done they galloped to the far end of their pasture. It was the most amazing thing I have ever seen.

It happened early in the morning and I was scheduled to go teach at the new barn that afternoon. I called the owner to explain what happened and that I wouldn't be coming that day. Bonnie encouraged me very strongly to come anyway, as she thought it would be good therapy. I really did not think it would be at all, at all. But I was a chicken; a new employee, and she was my new boss. I went and somehow got through my classes.

The next day the kids and I went down the road a bit to help our farmer friend pick his gourds. We were all still reeling from Velvet's untimely death. My friend and his helper patiently taught us how to harvest the gourds so that the stems remained in tact. We worked a few hours till they were all picked. Now *that* was therapeutic. There was something about being in an amazingly lovely space, being quiet, working in a rhythm with the plants and soil that was healing. The Lord spoke to me from His word, *unless a seed fall into the ground and die, it cannot multiply and bear fruit,* from the book of Matthew. Something about harvesting the fruit of the ground was healing balm for my hurting heart. Something enormously close to my heart had fallen to the ground. Soon we would bury her in the same dirt that was capable of bearing forth the lovely gourds I was picking. A profound lesson on the rhythm of life was planted deep in my soul.

About two weeks later, I received a call on Saturday evening from the people who were leasing Dexter. He had been colicky all day; the vet had been out to treat him and it didn't look good. The mom and my friend wanted to know if we would come out and maybe help her keep vigil. I had been teaching all day and was exhausted. I had to be back at Bonnie's the next day, too. Dexter currently was loaded with drugs and feeling fairly comfortable under the influence. Feeling a bit guilty, I told my friend I wouldn't come out to Sultan that night. I told her to call me first thing in the morning with a report.

I told Caleb and the kids and called Rosalind's parents. I was prepared for the worst. Dexter had been experiencing tummy troubles for a long time at Pebble Creek. The kids wanted to go with me in the morning no matter what, to either cheer him on to recovery or kiss him goodbye. The vet was standing by in case she needed to come help Dexter slip away.

The call came at 6:00 a.m.. Dexter was worse. He wasn't showing signs of being in acute pain, but had severely bloated. He was standing very quietly and stoically still. I had my friend call the vet. I loaded up my kids in the motor home, as Caleb needed the truck to go to work. At least the kids could lie on the beds and snooze on the way. We arrived and soon after so did the vet. We walked Dexter slowly outside to a lovely meadow near the house and a big fir tree. The kids, mine and my friend's, kissed Dexter, hugged his neck and said goodbye. We moms did the same. We thanked Dexter for his years of patient service to us. We sat close by while the good lady vet sent him on his journey home. He was buried on the spot after we left. A month after that, Rosalind's parents wrote to say they had found a new riding teacher for Rosalind. It was a very kind letter, but it said they didn't think we had winterized the stabling area enough and they were worried about Marbles staying over the winter. The letter broke my heart, but I can't say that I blamed them. They picked Marbles up and took her to her new home.

T.C.'s family hauled him over to take lessons at the new place but decided it was too much work. Rachel, my fabulous working student and half-owner of the mare Sadie, also departed. She had gotten a job at Bonnie Colson's barn, but it was not a good place for her. She needed to look for something else. That broke my heart too.

There was a small reprieve from all these sad farewells, but after a few months I decided it was time to put Jim, our beloved old black lab, to sleep. She was 16, and covered with huge lipomas. Now that I look back, she possibly could have taken on Caleb's illness, maybe our families' ills, so we could live! I've heard of dogs doing that. There was no money to get the lipomas surgically removed at a vet clinic, and our house call vet said if she drained them, they would just come back. Before long the largest one opened and started to drain blood and fluids. Jim was becoming incontinent, and our house was carpeted. Between the drainage and the accidents that I was constantly cleaning up, I was overwhelmed. I called Dr. Currie, our wondrous small animal vet who makes house calls.

She came on a bitterly cold, dark, wet, windy day. The weather matched how we felt about saying goodbye to Jim. I decided to have Jim euthanized in the back of our old Dodge pickup; I guess so taking her down to the barn for burial would be easier for me than picking her up in the house and carrying her outside. I put a blanket on the truck bed and put Jim in my lap. My kids gathered around us. We were all shivering. Maybe it was from the cold, maybe from grief; probably some of both. It took a huge amount of Phenobarbital to stop her heart. I felt so guilty. I felt like a murderer.

So within a few short months I had lost my riding program I had invested my heart in, the Pony Club I had invested my soul in, and the barn where I and the kids had been so happy. I lost their best friend and all of my young riders. I lost that fabulous loud-colored, overweight, hunk of a handsome Appaloosa. I lost my lovely mare that meant so much to me, a fabulous old pony I was very fond of, and a fabulous old dog I dearly loved.

I had nearly destroyed my family. All the losses had nearly destroyed me.

Chapter Forty-seven

A SHORT WHILE AFTER WE returned Sump to his owners they called me and offered him to me for a very reasonable price. I thanked them but said I was so sorry; we were flat broke. Then they offered to give him to me! They said he was bored and they didn't really need another horse to feed. I joyously accepted and then Caleb drove me and the kids to Sump's house. It wasn't that far from our place. I threw the kids up on his back two at a time while the third walked along. They took turns riding him on the way home. Caleb had the truck flashers on and followed behind to keep us safe. We were so happy! It reminded me of Jesus' triumphal entry into Jerusalem, only my kids were riding on the back of ... Sump. I couldn't find any palm branches along the side of the road to wave; only some dead canary grass, but it didn't matter. Sump was **ours!**

I made good money teaching at Bonnie's barn. I would drive the motor home over there with the kids and the dogs when Len was at work. They were supposed to work on home school stuff, but they mostly played or took naps. I taught six to eight lessons per day, three days a week. I really liked one of the other teachers. I thought the school horses were great. What I didn't think so great was the number of hours each horse worked, and the way they were kept.

It was a very busy barn with lots of students coming from the Seattle area north. Bonnie was a very good teacher. So was the other gal I had befriended. The horses went to four or more lessons a day. A lot of them stood tied two to a stall with a board separating them. The rest had box stalls. The ones in tie stalls got turned out in the indoor arena at night, and everyone got a little pasture turn-out on their day off. This arrangement seemed like it was pushing the envelope of conscientious horse care, but not abusive, at least at first.

I enjoyed teaching the students there. The kids and I rode our horses at home around the farm and in the pasture. We made some jumps in the pasture out of whatever we could scrounge up. I particularly wanted to get Gracie going again, because I had started her under saddle briefly at Pebble Creek using the John Lyons techniques I had learned. She had been a good girl.

Ryan and I rode her and Fire in the pasture I was renting and she was good as gold. One day we decided to venture out into another empty pasture that was flatter and easier to ride in. Everything went swimmingly. We were just finishing up and heading for the gate when some people pulled up. They got out of their car to admire the horses. As we were chatting amicably something caught Gracie's eye and caused her to have a major hissy fit. I don't think I had ever been bucked off so hard. I have been since then, many times. But *that* one was a doozy. I went flying and landed on my back on the hard ground. As I staggered to my feet, Ryan and the admirers looked shocked and concerned. Gracie didn't go far. After all, Grandpa Fire was right there and the grass was pretty yummy. The admirers beat a gracious but hasty exit. I caught Gracie and got back on 'cause that's just what you do. I rode her a few more times at the farm.

Even though the money was good, I was experiencing more and more things that made me anxious about working at Bonnie Colson's barn. Students were getting injured negotiating the cramped quarters of the tie stalls. Horses were getting injured from working in an exhausted state.

I found myself in a situation that made me more and more uncomfortable. All the kids I taught were great. I liked the long-suffering school horses. But Bonnie at times was somewhat critical of my teaching methods. Some of the older students, especially ones that rode regularly with Bonnie, seemed a little disrespectful. I had to teach on the clock, which meant that the lesson began and ended at a certain time regardless of how things were going. I wasn't very good at that. As a result I had some irritated parents, especially if my lesson ran over the hour into *their* kid's lesson.

As fall turned to winter I saw some things that chilled my heart to the core. My favorite school horse was an absolutely fabulous half-Fjord, half quarter- horse. One day he went out four or five times. He started protesting in the last lesson. He did not want to work. His student whipped and whipped him. He just took it. I was appalled. She didn't whip him non-stop, but every time he shut down, which was very often. He was such a lovely, kind horse. It broke my heart to see him so tired.

One of the old school horses died in a stall in the barn in full view of all the clients. It was her time to go, but it made all the young kids so upset when they came to ride, as well as the adults. At least they could have tucked her away from the main aisle, I thought.

Another horse was kept outside in a pipe panel pen. He had gotten cast and lacerated his legs badly. The vet came out and treated him, but I did not think highly of his living situation, exposed to the weather like that.

A nice older pony had been bought as a possible school mount, but was lame in the shoulder area. The folks that had been leasing Dexter knew about him and wondered if Bonnie might give the pony to them, as he wasn't sound enough to do lessons. My friends just wanted to have a pony to walk their kids around on, so he would have been perfect. They approached Bonnie, and she wouldn't budge. She said she'd get some money for him at the auction, quoting current horse meat prices. That made us pretty mad.

The last straw came one cold night in mid-December. I was closing her barn down after lessons about nine p.m.. It had started to snow. I went to throw hay to that pony, who was living outside in the pasture. I found him down, unable to rise. He was cold and wet and covered with snow. I tried and tried to get him up on his feet, but no luck. I ran back into the barn and got a horse blanket to cover him. Then I went to Bonnie's house and rang her doorbell. No one came to the door. All their cars were in the driveway. I pounded on the door and screamed for them. Nothing. After awhile I gave up, burst into tears and sat in my car. I dialed Bonnie's number on my cell phone. No one answered, but I left a scathing, screeching message at the top of my lungs. Then I went home. I never went back.

Chapter Forty-eight

I QUIT RIGHT BEFORE CHRISTMAS. Caleb was not thrilled, but there was no way I would go back to a place like that, ever. We were going to have a small Christmas, but we were used to that. I now had time to make a few gifts. Then a mom from my lesson program at Pebble Creek decided to buy *Spunky Like Me* for her daughter for Christmas. Her daughter, one of my very dear students, had always loved that pony. She was just a bit big for her now, but her mom bought her as a pet. She was meant to be a friend and a healing balm to her new young owner, and she was. That such a wonderful family bought her was a healing balm to me.

After Christmas I made a little money traveling to a family's farm to teach them on their own horses and to ride one of them. Caleb had been promoted to Manager at the Leesburg Arby's®, and I went to work part-time there to make ends meet.

Caleb had to be at Arby's® very early in the morning. The motor home had died and was parked in front of our house. We had been given an old Toyota pick-up truck by one of my Pebble Creek student's dad, who was a great mechanic. Most of the time it ran fairly well, but sometimes in the morning it wouldn't start. Caleb would wake me up and have me push him with my diesel pick-up I had managed to lease. I would push him down the long drive and sometimes down the road a-ways before the engine cranked and then Caleb would be on his way. That would be the only time I managed to get up early in the morning, but I wasn't that happy about it.

I wasn't that happy about working at Arby's® either, but the horses needed hay, grain, shoes and vet care. I had to do *something*. I worked evenings so my days would be free to teach and ride. It would bring in a little money until I found a new barn.

I really liked most of the folks I worked with. I was the oldest except for Caleb. There were young American kids and young to middle-aged adults from other countries. I worked with people from Vietnam, Pakistan, Iran and Mexico. I learned a lot about their cultures. What was the same about all of us was that we were all struggling to survive as best we could, and we wanted to be valued, appreciated and loved. We needed to know that we *mattered*.

I mostly worked the drive-through window. I enjoyed greeting and serving most everyone, and I met some great people through that window. I have a deep appreciation for fast food workers now. Sometimes I would get silly and pull some joke through the headphones so that the other worker wearing headphones would hear it. They would do the same. That made work fun, and we never got too outrageous. At least *we* didn't think so. You'd have to ask my boss.

One drive-through customer did get out of hand. He ordered a lot of food in a rude tone of voice and kept changing the order. By the time he drove up to the window I was pretty irritated. At the window he ordered a few more things, again being quite rude. Finally he said, "Gimme some salt!" So I picked up a handful of little salt packets and chucked them through his open car window. He and his passengers were momentarily shocked. Then he yelled, "WITCH! You *hit* me, witch!" He reached down to grab something. I thought maybe it was a gun. All the rest of the employees, who had been watching this drama unfold, ducked down and dived under the counters. One gal rushed over and helped me lock the drive-thru window, and another called 911. It turned out the guy had reached for his cell phone and *he* called 911. So we ended up with a parking lot full of cop cars after the customer left. The rest of the evening was pretty quiet. The next day when I walked through the doors of that Arby's® to go to work, I got a standing ovation from the other employees.

At the family barn I went to teach occasionally, there was an Arabian gelding the owner wanted ridden. The horse had been trained to pull a cart and was fine with that, but not with someone riding him. Since the owners were less experienced than I and I had ridden Arabians as a young girl, I didn't think he'd be a problem. He wasn't, the first ride. About 20 minutes into the second ride something got to that horse. He tucked his little bay bottom and bolted around the arena like a house on fire. Flying around the short end of the arena, he pitched me into the wall. I was more stunned than hurt. Seriously, that is. I was seriously stunned and a *little* hurt. Enough so that I really didn't want to ride that horse again. I told the folks about a remarkable trainer in the area that I had seen around, who worked with a lot of Arabians. He had enormous success with all kinds of horses, particularly difficult ones. He had his own style and did a lot of liberty work with them. In the end he could do whatever he wanted with them, and the horses were happy to do it.

Those folks had him come out. I came to watch and it was amazing. Within twenty minutes the trainer was up on the horse and cantering around bridleless and bareback without a problem. Those twenty minutes was an amazing demonstration of communication between man and horse. Plus, that guy could leap on and off a horse going full tilt around the arena. I couldn't do that. The second time he came back he had me ride the horse. I did, but I was scared. It went fine, but I was still scared. And I couldn't ride or communicate to the horse like that guy. *Wow.*

Even though I knew I could never leap on and off a flying horse like that guy did, I wanted to learn more. I found the barn where he currently operated and found out about some short courses he was giving. I scraped up the money and signed up for one.

I don't recall the theme of the clinic. Whatever he called it, it was about being one with your horse. I soaked it up with a sponge. On the third day we were allowed to bring our own horses. I decided to bring Gracie, because she had been getting really pushy lately. I wanted to learn how to manage her without a huge fight and without getting hurt.

The trainer worked with our horses first. He spent a long time with Gracie. Finally he brought her to me, wiped his brow and said, *she's a lotta mare.* Then we worked with her together, getting her to move her feet and politely move out of my space. At one point he told me I was invisible and that's why she would run over me sometimes---she couldn't see me!

His words sucker punched me in the guts. Suddenly I knew I had not just been invisible to horses. I had been invisible in most areas of my life, to most people, since my high school days. I had learned to retire in the midst of a bunch of girls clamoring to be seen and heard. I just didn't want to fight that hard.

The trainer taught me how to be "big" so Gracie would see me. He taught me to have loud body language. Sometimes horse whisperers have to shout! That was an incredibly valuable lesson. It was definitely worth the price of the short course. Since then I have learned to "put my big girl pants on" and speak up in many ways, in many situations. I am still learning to be seen and heard.

Chapter Forty-nine

WHEN I HAD WORKED AT Arby's® four months I got a call from a mom of a former Pebble Creek student. She had found a really fun lesson program at Woodland Farm for her daughter. An instructor had just left and the owners and their daughter, who ran the barn, needed to find a new one. She gave me their number and encouraged me to call. I did, and we arranged for an interview.

It was a cute barn about half-way between Murphy and Coleville. I liked what I saw, especially when I saw Marbles! So *that* is where Rosalind went. And *Crisco* was there! Crisco the mini-Lipizzaner I leased at Pebble Creek. His owners had taken him back home before I left Pebble Creek and a short time later put him up for sale. I would have loved to buy him, but his price tag was pretty high. And here he was! He was back being a lesson pony. I left there that day with a new job and a joyful heart.

I started teaching right away and gave notice about quitting Arby's® to Caleb, my boss.

For the most part, things started out pretty well at Woodland. The farm was attractive and well-kept. The school ponies were nice, the owners were nice and so was their daughter, who ran the barn and was the head instructor. Their were tons of kids of all ages and some adults who rode as well. It was a small scale hunter-jumper barn. I told the daughter, Fiona, that I was a balanced seat instructor who liked eventing. She said that was fine.

I was overjoyed to see Rosalind and her parents at the barn. I was looking forward to picking up where we left off. I was to learn that was not going to happen. Rosalind was Fiona's student now. I was naïve to think it would be any different. Rosalind seemed uncomfortable around me; even my kids noticed a change. We did not feel the same easy bond we had with her at Pebble Creek. Her parents were the same warm, loving couple. But Rosalind had moved on. The kids and I felt we were not cool enough for her anymore.

It was the same with the girl whose mom had told me about Woodland. It hurt my feelings and I did not understand, but I settled in with my new students. One young girl, Meredith, stole my heart right from the beginning. She was the same age as Maeve and she was home schooled. I hit it off with her mom and we decided our two girls should meet. We thought for sure they would immediately become best friends. We got them together at the farm to meet and just about the opposite happened. Her mom Cayanna and I shrugged. We figured they would be together a lot Woodland Farm and we hoped in time they would become friends.

Cayanna told me about Westshore Home-school Networks. Her daughter was going there and she highly recommended it. It was a village of portable classrooms attached to a junior high school in Coleville. Students and parents worked with a group of public school teachers who saw the value of home-schooling. The teachers acted as guides and counselors. They also offered a variety of classes. Kids who went through the program could get their high school diplomas with the Westshore School District.

I liked the sound of it. The kids were getting older and needed a change. It wasn't enough for me to be their only teacher, and they had said goodbye to all their friends when we closed up shop at Pebble Creek. I checked out Home-school Networks and was pleased. I would still be involved in the kid's education, but I would have support and resources. The kids would have a chance to work with other adults and socialize with their peers. I got the kids enrolled to start that fall.

One of my new students and her mom met a woman named Sarah Anne up the street on the way to Woodland Farm. Sarah Anne had a homebred thoroughbred mare for sale. The girl had just begun learning to ride so I thought it was really premature, but her family bought the horse for her anyway. The mare was going to stay at Sarah Anne's place while her new people made payments. Sarah Anne convinced them to have me ride the mare a little bit at her house while her new owner continued to take lessons on the school ponies.

That's how I got to know Sarah Anne. She was a retired school teacher, still filling in as a substitute, and a long time horsewoman. She had been married to a thoroughbred racing industry man and had bred several of her own. She was still riding with the trainer across the street from where I was teaching, and still breeding her mares. She had just lost her stall cleaner and wanted to know if I and my kids would be interested. We always needed money, so I said sure.

Soon after we stated working for Sarah Anne, she bought a new truck and horse trailer. She offered to sell me her old rig, a pickup with a matching tan 3-horse bumper pull trailer. I had my nice Ford truck I was leasing, but I sure needed a trailer. The price on the trailer was $3,500.00. It might as well have been $3,000,000.00. First Sarah Anne tried to sell it to us, but I think she knew we couldn't afford it. Then she offered to let me and the kids work for it. I said *sure!* So we did work for it, for about 3 years.

During those years we cleaned her barn, took lessons from her (Sarah Anne turned out to be an excellent instructor), and sometimes I rode her horses. I was burning up the roads dragging that old tan Circle J trailer with my green Ford 250 Turbo Diesel. I hauled Little Fire over to help teach lessons and for Enya and Maeve to ride. I hauled Sump over to help teach lessons and for Maeve and Ryan to ride. I hauled Gracie over to train, and eventually for Ryan to ride. I would get up in the morning, feed the horses, feed the kids, load the horses, load the kids, and drive to Home-school Networks in Coleville. I would drop the kids off and take the horses to Woodland Farm. After I unloaded them and got them settled I would drive to Sarah Anne's place. Then I would drive back to Home-school Networks to get the kids. We would drive to Top Foods in Coleville to grab lunch, then either drive to Sarah Anne's barn to finish cleaning or drive to Woodland Farm. At that barn the kids would work, then ride or play with friends. I would teach lessons and ride Gracie. Then we would hitch-up, load up, drive home and reverse the morning's routine at night. We went to Home-school networks four days a week; Woodland Farm and Sarah Anne's six. No *wonder* my kids won't do horses anymore.

But we did take advantage of having a horse trailer and go trail riding and cross-country schooling. We explored Lord's Hill Park and Bridle Trails. We spent some time at a very nice horse park on Vashon Island. It was free except for the ferry ride, which the kids and I enjoyed. Once on the trip over to Vashon, Gracie urinated big-time in the trailer. It ran through the floorboards and made a big puddle on the ferry. The ferry crew treated it like it was a hazardous substance. It was embarrassing but funny.

At the horse park on the island Gracie learned the ABC's of cross-country jumping. We would sandwich her between Fire with Maeve aboard and Ryan up on Sump. Some of the jumps were wide enough for us to jump three-abreast. Gracie was happy to jump in-between her two buddies, or follow them over. Fire and Sumps' sides were so nice and squishy it didn't matter if we got too packed together---our legs folded into the ponies' sides like they were fluffy bread dough. It was a lot of fun.

Chapter Fifty

My kids joined a 4-H club with some of their friends from Westshore Home-school Networks, whom I was also teaching at Woodland Farm. Ryan rode Sump at Fair the first year and Maeve rode Fire. Ryan, who had outgrown Fire and then Sump, moved on to Gracie and Maeve took over Sump. That made Fire available to Enya as her project horse. Ryan, Maeve and Enya had a very successful second Fair. Ryan and Maeve did well in dressage and over fences. Enya had a great Fair on Fire. He took amazingly good care of her. No one would even suspect she had Down Syndrome with her show clothes and velvet helmet on. In her dressage test, I had permission to help her if she went off course. She only made a few small errors, and about the 3rd time I got her attention to correct her, she yelled ***WHAT?!?!?!?***

She also rode Fire in the trail class, in which she had to negotiate several obstacles. It was to be done in a pattern, but Enya had her own in mind, and enthusiastically attacked the course. The ring steward grinned and waved my concerns away. Enya and Fire did great until they came to a blue plastic barrel. It had a skinny PVC pipe about three feet long attached by a swivel to the top of the barrel. The rider was supposed to take one end of it and hold it while her mount walked around the barrel. That was exactly the kind of thing that frightened Fire. I held my breath. Enya walked Fire up to the barrel, grabbed the pipe, and proceeded to walk around it. Fire got a little too far away, but Enya held on to the pipe with a death grip. The barrel tipped over. My heart was in my throat, but Fire was steady as a rock. The kind ring steward put the barrel upright and had her try again, this time with success. By the end of Fair Enya had all kinds of danishes and ribbons to hang in her room. Hats off to angel pony Fire.

After that, I decided I had enough of 4-H. I'm not sure if the kids agreed, but they went along with my decision to stop participating. I had gotten the impression that trainers weren't welcome in 4-H, at least during that time period. I wasn't thrilled with layout of the jumping courses and I wasn't sure the people managing it knew what they were doing. When I offered to help they were not interested. I decided to pull my kids out of 4-H. I wanted to go eventing, anyway, and so did Ryan and Maeve.

Ryan quickly outgrew Gracie. She was the tallest horse we had. Ryan needed a new horse, but there certainly wasn't any money to buy one for him. God soon intervened on Ryan's behalf. Sarah Anne told us about a warmblood gelding that her friend had bred. He had good bloodlines and was a originally a high-priced young hunter prospect. She found a buyer, but the gelding flunked his pre-purchase exam. He had a small bone spur on his P2-P3 joint which is inside the hoof capsule, so nobody would pay much for him. The chances of him staying sound were questionable.

His breeder finally sold him inexpensively to a local gal. She wanted a horse for her boyfriend to ride. They were supposed to make monthly payments. After several months went by without seeing any money, his owner went to retrieve him, only to find him near death from starvation and neglect. She brought him home and slowly nursed him back to health. She wasn't sure what to do with him next. She asked Sarah Anne if she knew anyone who would give her horse a good home.

Sarah Anne thought he might be a good horse for Ryan, so we went to see him, taking the horse trailer with us. He was a big handsome chestnut with "chrome," that is, a blaze and stockings. We asked to ride him but his owner told us no, he hadn't been ridden in a long time; he once had a "little rear" and if it showed up again she didn't want the liability. But we could take him home, try him, and return him if he didn't seem suitable. After we loaded the horse in our trailer, I asked Ryan if he wanted to give his new horse a new name. His official name was the Spanish equivalent of John Deer Tractor. Ryan thought for a moment and then said in a very matter of fact way, "Bob." The movie *What About Bob* was a new release, and we liked it so much, we added the "What About" to Bob.

Sarah Anne told us we could keep Bob at her place and work off the board, so that's where we kept him when we first got him. Bob settled right in. The next day when we came out to work and visit Bob, he was napping on a horse blanket Sarah Anne had hung on the fence to air out. Bob had pulled it off the fence and then laid down on it to sleep. A few days later we saw him pick up an orange traffic cone and use the tip to scratch his belly. Those were the first signs of Bob's intelligence and eccentric personality.

The second day after Bob's arrival I longed him and then threw Ryan up on him bareback just to have a look-see. They looked very well suited for each other; two sandy-haired, long and lanky boys. Bob walked quietly around on a circle for a while. Then Ryan asked him to trot.

Bob trotted several steps and then reared sky-high. He went up so high he lost his balance and ended up half-falling, half sitting on his haunches. He kind of sat there like a big dog while I yelled at Ryan to jump off. Ryan's eyes were big as saucers and my heart was pounding in my chest. We both said "*DANG!* There's that *little* rear his owner told us about." After Ryan dusted himself off he got back on Bob and I led him around. I told Ryan there was no way he was getting back on that horse again until I had ridden Bob to see what the rear was about. I certainly wasn't looking forward to that. I *hate* rearing.

I equipped myself with my cross-country vest in case I hit the dirt, and it didn't take long. He would rear so high I would slide down his back like a fire pole. But he only reared once a ride when things got a little exciting, like *go forward*, and he didn't fall over backward as I feared. He seemed perfectly in control; in fact, he seemed to enjoy it. He thought it was great fun to rear sky high and walk around like that with me, and later Ryan, on his back, or without us, if we fell off. Ryan and I hit the dirt---a lot---until we figured out how to stay on. Then we progressed to riding him forward in the middle of it. Finally we learned the warning signs that he was going to rear … and ride preventively. He never quite stopped rearing; sometimes he would surprise us, but he did it less and less.

I was loading up Bob and trailering down to Woodland Farm where I was teaching a lot. The neighbors across from the barn offered us a stall for Bob in exchange for Ryan working for them. It was more convienient than the current situation, so we said yes. That worked for awhile and then we moved him across the street when a stall and a working position became available. Maeve and Enya helped Ryan with the work. I helped when I wasn't teaching.

I'll never forget the weekend Ryan took a clinic with a guest instructor at the barn. The first day Bob reared with such force he sent Ryan flying off his back like a projectile missile. The second day Ryan and Bob were cantering around the unfenced outdoor arena when Bob slipped on the grassy edge and fell down. Ryan rolled clear, but Bob just laid there. All of us watching were dismayed. Was Bob seriously hurt? While Ryan held the reins and waited to see if Bob would get up, Bob started placidly munching grass without a care in the world. Ryan started laughing and made Bob get to his feet. He seemed fine. They finished the clinic. I was *so* thankful Ryan seemed fine too!

Gracie was getting to be a big stout mare. She outgrew the saddle I was using. We didn't have the money to get a new one, but I knew the Lord knew I needed a saddle, and He would supply somehow, some way, at the right time. Gracie was comfy to sit on, so I rode her bareback. She was much easier without a saddle because the old one had been pinching her. She was still *a lotta mare,* especially when she was in estrus. Some days I hand-galloped her bareback her at least twenty times around the outdoor arena. I took a dressage lesson on her bareback. I jumped her bareback up to 3'9." My legs were like iron. I was fit as a fiddle. Within a few months Sarah Anne found me a nice forward-seat saddle that fit Gracie. I could make easy payments to its' owner. Problem solved, but riding bareback had proved to be a huge blessing.

Now that I had a saddle I could start competing Gracie. I took her, Maeve took Sump and Ryan took Bob to little one day competitions. We had so much fun. Gracie was green and she was *a lotta mare,* but showed promise. Ryan and Bob were a handsome team and managed to bring home some good ribbons.

Maeve and Sump were the cutest team ever! Sump's show name became *Spotteus Maximus.* They consistently came in third at almost every horse trial they went to. Eventing suited Sump. It was his *thing.* The first time we went to the old Camas Meadows Horse Trials at Beginner Novice, we thought the jumps looked huge. I wasn't sure Sump could do it, or if Maeve would be brave enough. Maeve loaded up her shotgun and put on her game face, and I sent up lots of prayers. I couldn't see the whole course, but I followed their progress by listening to the announcer. They were going clean over everything! Suddenly they came into view as Sump leaped off a bank and came boiling down the hill at Mach 10. What a glorious sight they were! Those giant spots, with tiny Maeve on board flew across the fields, over all the remaining jumps, and right through the finish flags. The sight is imprinted in my brain forever. The band *Afro-Celt* has a tune called "Big Cat' that goes with that scene perfectly. If only I had a video of the two of them set to that music! But I can play it in my mind whenever I want.

A couple of really funny moments stick in my mind about the Maeve and Sump era. Maeve loved candy, and she especially loved *Runts,* those little hard candies shaped like fruit. Sump had a thing for them too, especially the banana shaped and flavored ones. They would play together at the end of the day in Woodland's indoor arena. Maeve, with a box of *Runts* in her hands, would go hide behind a big barrel and call Sump. He would search earnestly at a trot until he found her and got his banana candy. It was hilarious. They would play hide and seek until all the banana *Runts* were in Sump's big spotted tummy.

One warm, summer afternoon Sump was totally sacked out in a Woodland Farm paddock, enjoying an all-out snooze in the warm sun. He looked like a spotted beached whale. One of Maeve's friends decided to sneak up on him. She was as stealthy as could be, but at the last second his radar detected her, and with a mighty, earth shaking leap he woke up and jumped to his feet, all sleepy and disoriented. Good thing she wasn't standing too close, or his great spotted mass would have knocked her silly! Poor old Sump, getting jolted out of such a lovely, deep nap. He didn't hold it against Maeve's friend though. I think he was hoping she was had *Runts* in her pocket.

That summer Maeve took Sump, I took Gracie, and Kate's now best pal Meredith took her pony Snapshot to the Vashon Island Pony Club Horse Trials. Meredith got so nervous in her dressage test that I stood by ringside pretending to smoke a great big "doobie." That put a smile on her face and a big sigh came forth. She finished the test in good shape. We were all in different divisions, and we each won first place. That was quite cool.

At the time I was reading *The Seven Secrets of Good Horsemanship* by Don Burt. He talked about how your horse and you were really made out of the very same stuff, the same elements, the same molecules that are floating around, and that there was always a molecular exchange going on. Therefore, since you and your horse were constantly in this molecular exchange, you were actually the same entity. Why couldn't the two of you exist in harmony? What a wonderful concept! That was a few years ago, but I see the message is back. And not just to horse people, either.

During Meredith's future dressage tests when I was still coaching her, I would pretend to take a big toke on the imaginary joint and silently mouth *"GOOD molecules"* as Meredith asked her horse for a free walk. It worked. Only her mom, my beloved Sistah Cayanna, could appreciate such unorthodox coaching. And maybe a few others. You know who you are.

Chapter Fifty-one

CALEB CAME HOME FROM ARBY'S® one evening and asked if I would like a puppy. "**Absolutely *not!*** " was the first thing to fly from my lips. One of his store managers had taken the little girl puppy from his sister in California, who had decided in short order that she just couldn't handle her. She had the pup flown up from California to her brother Eric in Washington. Eric was one of the Arby's® managers Caleb supervised. Eric lived in an apartment in West Seattle, about 15 or 20 miles from his store. Being single, he often went out and about after work. Whenever he was gone from the apartment, the puppy would have to stay in a crate. The puppy would howl and cry pitifully and LOUD for hours on end. The neighbors were complaining and Eric needed to find her a new home. Because we already had a dog and lived on 20 acres, he thought we would be the perfect new owners.

I surely didn't think so. Losing a grand old dog like Jim when she wasn't truly ready to go had been devastating. She hadn't been gone that long when the puppy issue came up. Hank was keeping me busy enough trying not to get tripped by his rope, untangling it and chasing him when he escaped. I thought the last thing we could possibly need was a puppy!

But I did ask Caleb two days later, in my smallest, quietest voice, "What *kind* of puppy? "A *beagle*", he replied, a silly, knowing grin on his face.

Caleb brought her to Sarah Anne's place where we were working the very next day. She was in her little crate, in a little Toyota we had bought for the kids from Caleb's bosses for when they were old enough to drive. Maeve, Ryan, Enya and I peered in through the car windows. I couldn't decide if she was terrified or wanted to bite our heads off. Caleb took her out of the crate and set her on the ground near the car. She cowered for a few moments and then threw herself into Maeve's arms, enthusiastically covering Maeve's face with little Beagle kisses. We named her Hallie, from *The Parent Trap* which had just been re-released. She has enthusiastically wriggled and kissed her way into our hearts ever since.

Summer meant camps at Woodland Farm. My kids had gotten old enough to be counselors. Most of the campers would progress from not riding at all to doing a musical drill ride set to a rock song … in one week. I did a Natural Horsemanship training camp for the more experienced kids. My friend Laurel let me use her 14 year old Arabian mare. That little mare was sweet but had never been sat on. She was living with my horses at the time, so everyday I would load her in the trailer and take her to "school". The campers and I got her started under saddle.

Another camp I taught had a medieval theme. A lot of boys had signed up, so I was in a bit of a panic. "What do you do with a bunch of *boys?*" I wondered. I was used to teaching girls and doing *girl* stuff. A mostly boy camp had me quite challenged. Thank God I had a boy who rode horses! Ryan and Maeve helped me brainstorm. We went to the thrift store and got material with which the campers made simple tunics. Ryan helped them fashion safe lances and swords out of PVC pipe and insulation. The campers covered their riding helmets with tin foil. Soon all the campers were knights in training. On the last day of camp we had a tournament with "medieval" mounted games. The camp counselors blew heralds and announced winners using orange traffic cones as trumpets.

At Woodland Farm's annual Halloween party and costume contest, Ryan was Harry Potter and Fire was his broomstick, *Firebolt*. The next year Ryan took Bob as the top NBA pick. Maeve and Sump were Priscilla and Elvis Presley. Enya was Dolly Parton, complete with a blonde wig and blown up balloons inside her shirt, and Fire was "Portly" Waggoner. Woodland Farm really did know how to have fun.

But eventually, inevitably, problems arose. I really didn't mind teaching at a hunter-jumper barn, but I was an eventer at heart. What I *didn't* realize was there was no regard for eventing at Woodland Farm. What I *didn't* realize was I was only there to teach "up-down" lessons. As soon as the owner's daughter saw one of my students become a pretty good rider, that student would mysteriously quit riding with me and mysteriously show up in her lessons. I was never told that's what I was hired to do. After it happened several times I confronted Fiona about it, but she denied it. When I asked the mothers of those same students, they told me how excited they were that they got invited to ride with the owner's daughter, who was the head instructor, as though it were a privilege and a big deal. But I had more education and experience than Fiona. She never told me I was there to prepare students for *her*. I thought we would each bring along groups of students and let them choose what type of competition they desired, or maybe even do both. Or none.

One of my young students had actually followed me from Pebble Creek to Bonnie Colson's to Woodland Farm, Gwen Johnston. She had become a terrific little rider so her parents decided it was time for her to have a pony of her own. We found her a beautiful POA gelding. He was about 13.3 and looked like a frosted pink cupcake. His mom was an Arabian, so he had a beautiful head, a full, gaily carried tail and excellent movement. He was also a good jumper. He was young, but I was able to coach Gwen through Northern's training. They did pretty well at the little local hunter-jumper shows. Her mom thought it would be cool for Gwen to show Northern at the Evergreen Classic in August. That's a prestigious, A-rated Hunter-Jumper Show that is held around here every summer. It's a fundraiser for some good charities, and is run very well. It is a big, beautiful show. I don't blame them at all for wanting to go.

I felt pretty intimidated at the thought of taking a student to the Evergreen Classic. In the A-System hunter-jumper world, I had been told one didn't waltz in and coach or show without a known trainer. You needed to have *connections*. I didn't think Gwen's pony was ready for a show of that caliber. He could jump, but he didn't have flying lead changes. I had been told if you are riding a hunter horse or pony and don't have flawless changes, you can forget about ribbons. Woodland Farm was taking a group to the Classic and Fiona would have been happy to board the pony and prepare him and Gwen, but her mom and I weren't terribly thrilled that if Gwen went to the Evergreen Classic they would be trained and coached by Fiona and not me.

So what did these girls do? We went to the hunter-jumper barn across the street for help with the pony's lead changes and to go to the show with them. They were an established A-system barn with a solid reputation. That did not please Fiona or her parents. Gwen did a fine job at the Classic with her little green pony, although she did accept help from an older Woodland student getting Northern around the course when he refused the first time. She won the under saddle class full of Woodland's students and that did not go over well with Fiona. The Evergreen Classic did not go over well with *me*. I saw so much wealth and so much waste. I saw rich kids mount their ponies (beautifully braided by a paid professional) after Hispanic grooms prepared the ponies for the show. I saw rich kids jump off after the class and hand their ponies back to the Hispanic grooms; rich kids of all ages and sizes.

The summer we went to Classic, Caleb got a huge promotion. He went from being an Arby's® restaurant manger to becoming the Area Supervisor of several stores. With the promotion came a company car and a big raise and big bonuses. It was the middle of the dot-com boom in the Pacific Northwest, and just about every business and everyone was benefiting, even us! Suddenly we could pay all the bills, feed the horses and feed ourselves. We weren't rich like the people I saw at the Evergreen Classic, but just like that we weren't poor anymore.

After the Classic I made arrangements to teach balanced seat on my own horses a few days a week at a different barn a few miles away, but still come teach "up-down" hunt seat lessons at Woodland Farm. Fiona seemed happy with that arrangement.

Colleen, now a college graduate from the University of North Carolina at Chapel Hill, was getting married Labor Day weekend in

Raleigh. We now had money to buy Colleen's wedding dress, fly out to the wedding and visit my family. We had a wonderful time visiting family and friends from our old church. I hadn't been home in thirteen years. My oldest sister let us stay in her beach condo for a couple of days. I was thrilled to introduce my kids to the wonders of Carolina Beach. All too soon it was time to kiss family goodbye and return home. The first full day back in Washington State, Woodland's owners called to tell me I was fired.

Chapter Fifty-two

I HAD TO GET A business running at the new barn a lot faster than I intended. When I first talked to the owner, I had told her it would be a very gradual and rather small enterprise, as I would be dividing my time between her place and Woodland Farm. All of a sudden I was going to board some horses and do *all* my teaching there! I rented three self-care stalls. One was for Bob and the other two were for the school ponies that lived at home but would be hauling over in the trailer. They would need a place to hang out in between lessons while they were there.

Wooden Nickel Stables wasn't a great place, but it was the closest, cheapest place I could find. The five acre property was right next to Highway 357, making it extremely noisy during commuter traffic in the afternoons, right when I usually taught after school lessons. Occasionally a very loud motorcycle would zip down the road and scare the horses. Occasionally a car or truck would backfire and scare the horses. The outdoor arena was nice enough, but it was only fenced on one side, had too much sand in it and no one ever ran a drag through it. The indoor arena was small, dark and narrow. Sometimes an Arabian stallion belonging to one of the boarders would rear in his stall and stick his head over the wall of the arena. A couple of my students got dumped because of that.

There were turn-out paddocks but not a blade of grass. There were lots of dangerous T-posts without caps. The owner had bought a house and 3 acres adjacent to Wooden Nickel and said we could put in a "cross-country course." She had a small shallow hole dug for a water jump. The dirt from the hole sort of made a bank and I put some barrels to jump out there. The kids thought it was fun and it gave them an introduction, *of sorts,* to cross-country jumping. We could also use it for limited grazing for the horses. You just had to make sure all the trash got picked up before hand. There was a lot of trash that kept surfacing, including broken glass and nails. It seemed like the land had been a dump site at some point.

The owner said I didn't need to give her a percentage of my lesson income until I got established. I thought that was very nice of her. I bought caps for all the T-posts and cleaned up the fence lines. I worked hard to make sure there was nothing dangerous in the "cross-country" field on a daily basis. I cleaned up the tack room. I regularly ran a piece of chain link fence across the arena with her little tractor. The owner bought rubber chips and I helped her put them in the indoor. My students' families helped repaint all the jumps.

My lessons started to pick up in the next few months and some of my students bought horses. Enya and Maeve had more or less stopped riding, but Ryan and I continued to ride and compete. The kids still attended Home-school Networks. Wooden Nickel was even closer to the campus than Woodland Farm.

Teagan Finch and her daughter Ciaran followed me from Woodland Farm to Wooden Nickel. I had been teaching Ciaran for a couple of years. Teagan and I had become fast friends. Teagan wanted to get a horse that Ciaran could ride and I could use for lessons. We would share the expenses. That way it would be less expensive for both of us, as I sort of needed another school horse. I had just left a place where I had access to several, and now only had access to my and my kids' horses. Fire and Sump were superb, but they didn't need to do *all* the lessons. Pete was retired and Bob was well, *Bob.* Gracie had issues with soundness and was "a lot of mare." It sounded like a pretty good plan to me.

Teagan embarked on the search with young Ciaran. I wasn't in a hurry because I didn't think I could afford to even *half* support another horse. I expected Teagan to look for a very long time, and I am not much of a shopper. Finally Teagan found one she thought I should see. She made an appointment for us to look at the horse, a small registered

Appaloosa-Colorado Rangerbred mare named I'm Misty's Shadow. She was at a family farm out near Lake Roesiger on the back way to Granite Falls. She belonged to a young girl who had outgrown her. The little mare had jumped, done gaming, and had a few foals. The family had one of her children on the farm; she looked just like her mom. The young girl rode Shadow and we were quite impressed with her movement and really impressed with her jumping ability. Ciaran was extremely tiny for her age, having been born prematurely. She got along very nicely with Shadow when she rode her. I was sold.

Equifriends, the therapeutic riding program that gave me Velvet, was ready to take Shadow on trial. Her price was a little high for Teagan, and we skipped all the sensible, normal things you do when you are horse shopping, like trying her a second time and scheduling a pre-purchase exam. It was a little out of character for me to be so hasty, but we did not want Shadow to slip away. Shadow became Ciaran's new first pony.

Even though Shadow was sixteen when the Finches purchased her, she ended up being quite a lot of pony for tiny Ciaran. She had tons of separation anxiety coupled by tons of energy, and occasionally only Ciaran's "magic bungee cord" would save Ciaran's tiny little bottom. Ciaran would fly so far out of the tack that only an invisible, magic bungee cord could have possibly snapped her right back to the middle of the saddle as it always seemed to do.

Looking back, now that I know Shadow so well, I'm sure those misbehaviors had to do with her feeling alone and vulnerable in a new place, missing her friends and children and her incredible maternal instincts. The first two behaviors have made Ciaran the fabulous rider she is today. The latter one shines through in her senior years.

Another young rider followed me from Woodland Farm, Amanda Dupree. Before long her mom told me she wanted to buy a horse for Amanda. I found one on an internet website that looked pretty good, and he was just a mile down the road at another barn. We went to try him. He was a tall handsome boy; an older bay thoroughbred gelding who had evented through Training Level. Ellie Simpson, the trainer who also owned the barn, said his owner had lost interest in him. He was excellent when Amanda rode him. They looked great together, as Amanda was as tall as Ciaran was tiny. My vet did a pre-purchase exam and he passed easily. We were very excited. Since I had met Ellie and it was an eventing barn, I made arrangements for Ryan and I to take lessons there.

A day or two after we brought her new boy Toby to Wooden Nickel Stables Amanda was having a lesson on him. He was good until she asked him to canter. He cantered nicely along the highway side of the outdoor arena. He cantered across the short end and picked up some speed down the other long side. Amanda was to trying to pull him up when he suddenly turned a hard right out of the arena, dumping Amanda on the gravel pathway. Her mom and I rushed to Amanda, who was not seriously hurt, but shaken and full of gravel shards. Then I went to find Toby who was peacefully grazing on the other side of the barn. I jumped on Toby and made him behave. Amanda rode a tiny bit more, then went home with her mom to pick the gravel shards out of her arm. Amanda eventually learned to keep Toby in the arena. He taught Amanda a *lot*.

Maeve had become a teenage girl with all the accompanying angst and drama. Getting her to ride Sump was a chore, much less showing him. Finally, we agreed that she could stop showing and even stop riding. It totally broke my heart, but I had sworn I would never force the kids to do horses against their will. Maeve followed other pursuits and Sump became a full time lesson horse, which he was very good at anyway.

In fact, Sump had gotten so confident (and *cheeky*) about jumping that I had to tell my students not to point him at any jump unless they were prepared to take it! A couple of times the kids were not steering as accurately as they could and accidentally pointed Sump at a jump in the arena. *You know what happened.* Whoops! Quickly his riders learned to pay attention and look where they wanted to go. Sump later earned the nickname "Flying Couch" from a girl who worked at the barn down the road where we found Toby. The nice thing about him being a flying couch was that even if a kid did get "jumped out of the tack" (meaning they fell off), it was not a big deal.

Firecracker kept right on chugging along from barn to barn with us, teaching all the kids who came for lessons. What a hard working boy he was. We probably asked way too much of him, but he was always a tryer. He was the first pony new kids rode. He was the pony timid kids rode. He was the first pony on whom kids learned to jump. Any kid who wanted to show took Fire to their first competition. Any kid who wanted to ride bareback rode Fire bareback first. Fire rarely dumped anyone. Occasionally he would hear a noise that scared him and he would bolt---for a few strides. A very new student was riding Fire in her second lesson. We were in the round pen at Wooden Nickel Stables when a car whizzing down 357 backfired loudly. Fire spooked and galloped halfway around the pen before my student fell off. She wasn't hurt, but scared enough that she didn't return after her pre-paid set of lessons was over.

What About Bob? was coming along nicely at Wooden Nickel. He and Ryan were good buddies. Ryan showed him successfully several times, and I showed him a couple of times myself when Gracie became unsound. I took him to a cross-country clinic south of Olympia given by Ellie Simpson. I took Bob, Teagan and Ciaran took their new pony Shadow, Gwen took her pretty pink pony whom she kept at her Grandma Stella's farm and hauled over for lessons. Another student who kept her mare at home came too. It was a wonderful clinic. Bob was tempted to be naughty but settled in to be a good boy. While there I met the animal communicator Fedora Gleason. I was curious but very wary of the whole animal communication thing---it sounded very New Age. I had been counseled for many years by well meaning Christians to stay away from that kind of stuff. Fedora was offering a inexpensive camp special fee and curiosity got the better of me. All of us ended up paying Fedora to have her "talk" to our horses. It was fascinating. The horses would come over to her and it seemed like they were really trying to connect. Fedora would listen quietly and write what she "heard" from each horse on a small tablet.

The results were incredible. We knew our horses pretty well. Fedora did not know them at all. The things she "heard" from all our horses confirmed what we knew and felt about them. The most amazing thing she told us was how much they loved us. I don't think any of us *really* believed that. We sure wanted too, but we doubted our horses could love us the way we loved them, or we felt we had done things to make them *not* like us. Fedora suggested that we give Bob a new name. She said "What About Bob?" was too ambiguous. He needed a name he could live up to. Then and there we renamed him *Gallant Rob.* The last day of the clinic we all rode a course like we were in a competition. I rode Bob like he *was* gallant, and he gallantly stepped right into his new name.

I had trained Gracie through Novice Level eventing and dabbled a bit with Training Level height fences. I took her to a winter schooling show at Reedy Creek Stables in Coleville. She was doing so well at Novice I signed up for a Training Level jumping round. On course she was cruising nicely, but when she jumped through the Triple Combination she took a misstep on the middle element and jumped it awkwardly, taking down a couple rails. She finished fine and didn't seem hurt. Looking back though, I think maybe she *did* get hurt. She never seemed quite right after that. She also came down with a horrible case of scratches on both hind legs. She had huge stubborn scabs from coronet to stifle. They were impossible to remove and caused Gracie a lot of pain when I tried to pick them off.

My vet at the time wanted me to try lots of different naturopathic treatments. I did but I was skeptical. It was hard to say if Gracie was lame because she had injured herself jumping, or if it was the scratches. My vet didn't want to ultrasound over the scabs, so we kept trying one thing after another. Nothing got rid of them. Finally, on a buying trip for a horse for some students of mine, the owner of the mare we were looking at told us that she had come down with terrible scratches moving from Eastern Washington to the Puget Sound area. "How did you get rid of them?" I wanted to know. She said the drug *Griseofulvin* had cleared up the scratches. I couldn't wait to talk to my vet. She knew about the drug, but didn't want to prescribe it because it was hard on horses' livers and required a liver function test halfway through treatment. I was so sick of the scratches and not knowing the whole story on Gracie, I begged her to order some and she reluctantly did so.

The drug worked. The scratches beat a hasty retreat. Gracie made it through fine. We did an ultra-sound and didn't find anything. I put Gracie back to work but she was on again, off again sound. When she was sound I shared her with my students and when she was lame she would have to rest.

Chapter Fifty-three

WOODEN NICKEL STABLES THOUGH SHABBY was in a good location. My business had started to grow and the barn the owner starting demanding money. She wanted a percentage of my lesson income along with the board. That was perfectly reasonable, but she approached me in a very aggressive way, as though I was trying to cheat her. She had told me not to pay her until I was established. I guess she thought I was established! When I pointed out the purchases I had made for her barn and the labor I had put in, she offered to reimburse me for the T-post caps. I didn't mind paying the percentage she wanted, because we had already discussed that, but I seemed to be the only one doing any work around the barn and everyone else were enjoying the benefits of my labors. I asked if I was going to have to keep doing all the work *and* pay a percentage as well.

The owner and her husband became hostile. A boarder at the barn who had aspirations of being a trainer complained bitterly to the owner about how busy I was. She said I was always in the arenas and my clients' cars filled up the parking lot. My horses and client's horses took up too many stalls and paddocks. She would come in during my lessons and wreak havoc with her crazy riding. The owner took her side even though the boarder's behavior was dangerous and immature. For some reason, even though I was making money for the owner and kept helping out around the farm, I became her #1 enemy. I had only been there a year, but clearly it was time to find yet *another* new barn.

Finding a new barn was not easy. I had a couple clients who had bought horses, but didn't have any that would pay higher boarding rates in that area. Wooden Nickle Stables was very inexpensive. They paid the barn owner for the stall and me for my cheap labor. The majority of my students rode my horses, which did not make me at all attractive to barn owners. They liked trainers who brought in lots of full-board paying clients. I could rent two or three stalls but I needed to pay self-care board prices.

Teagan Finch looked high and low, even for places that she and her husband could buy and let me run. It was fun to look and dream, but nothing ever came of it. In the meantime I just kept *gettin' it* up and down the roads and prayed for something to come up on the horizon.

Chapter Fifty-four

ONE DAY AS I WAS teaching in the indoor at Wooden Nickle Stables, a woman drove in, got out of her truck and abruptly interrupted my lesson. I thought, "Man, this lady is kind of *rude*." She wanted to know if I was May Dilles. *Yes.* Was I looking for a barn? *Yes.* "Well, I have one. Come see, then we'll talk." She left just as abruptly as she came.

I went to see her farm as soon as I could. What I discovered there was *Small World*. Caleb and I had looked at the place to possibly lease when things at Pebble Creek were falling apart. It was a 10 acre farm with a great barn, good fence, good loafing sheds and a double wide mobile home. No arenas, though it had been graded and corner foundations laid for a small indoor arena. We didn't know where we would get the money to buy it, much less finish it.

Lane and Mimi Andrews had bought it and done an excellent job of finishing it. Lane extended the arena perimeters to make it a large covered one. They also put in a nice outdoor arena right next to it. They took the front of the barn which had been a stallion showcase area and turned it into a darling little home for themselves and their little girl. It was a nice, sunny day when I went to look at it. The arena was painted light green, just like the color of the new spring leaves on the trees on one end of it and around the property. It was so beautiful it took my breath away. It was only 8 minutes from my house.

Mimi was very agreeable when we talked. It only took me a few minutes to make up my mind to move there, but I had to talk to my students and their parents. Nobody liked that it was 30 minutes farther North, but once they saw the place nearly everyone agreed to come with me. I gave notice to an irate Wooden Nickle Stables owner. We high-tailed it out of there as soon as we could.

I asked Mimi what she needed from us in terms of how to avoid conflict and confrontation. I was starting to get just as wary of moving to a new barn as I had become about going to a new church. All she said was, "*I want to be respected.*" Ah. She needed to know she *mattered*. I didn't think that would be too difficult, as she had once owned a barn with an Olympic 3-Day Team member, and had done way more eventing than I ever had. She had been through some difficulties at her barn with another trainer who had been there with some clients, and still was still leasing stalls to a difficult dressage trainer. She was hoping for an easier relationship with a new trainer and the boarders that came with her, and I was hoping for an easier relationship with a barn owner. I was amazed at this turn of events. God had heard me and answered my prayer most graciously.

Chapter Fifty-five

MOST OF MY STUDENTS ENDED up following me to the new barn, *Northwind Farm*, in Snohomish. Teagan and Ciaran brought Shadow. Amanda Dupree and her mom brought Toby. Vickie, the girl who worked at the barn in Woodinville where we found Toby, lived at Northwind Farm and also worked for the owner. *Small world.* That is where she christened Sump *The Flying Couch.* I rented three self-care stalls for my school horses to hang out in when I brought them up. Teagan Finch and Amanda's mom Marla rented full care stalls for their horses.

The only issues I had at first were dealing with the other trainer who was there. We rubbed elbows so much she finally left because of the friction. That is exactly what Mimi wanted, but I didn't know that when she invited me to her barn. With that trainer gone, things were pretty blissful. I had large indoor and outdoor arenas to ride and teach in. I only had to share them with Mimi and her boarders, and some of them were my students. It was nice and peaceful. Mimi wasn't the friendliest person in the world, but since she had invited me and my students over, I wasn't too worried about it.

Mimi had a couple of thoroughbred mares. She was breeding them to fancy warmblood stallions in hopes of making money selling the foals. That way she would have a steady string of nice young horses for her to bring along and show before they sold. The spring after we arrived, one of her mares foaled twin fillies. It was nip and tuck for both foals for several weeks. Just when it looked like the smaller, frailer twin was going to make it, she got kicked in the ribs by the nurse mare, as the real mom had rejected the smaller filly. The injured filly faded fast after having her ribs broken. Mimi and Lane were both exhausted from all the intensive care, and devastated at the loss of the filly.

My boarders and students' families, being the lovely people they are, showed Lane and Mimi great care and concern. It surprised Mimi, who hadn't had much experience with horse people who were loving and caring. After that she really lightened up.

I had relative ease and freedom at the new place. I slowly built my lesson program and took my students to local shows. Another girl and her mom had followed me from Woodland Farm to Wooden Nickle Stables to Northwind Farm. Marlie had moved from Fire, to Sump, to Gracie, but Gracie became consistently unsound enough to retire at the farm where we were living. I had always wanted to breed her mom Velvet to a fancy warmblood, but she had died before I could do that. I spoke to the vet that was managing Mimi's breeding program and had her look at Gracie to see if she was good breeding material. She seemed nice enough to me.

She wasn't. Her stifles and hocks were too straight and too weak, which may have contributed to her lameness. I had that vet ultrasound the left hock and stifle area with her better equipment and she discovered an old suspensory ligament injury. Gracie was destined to become a beautiful pasture ornament at eleven years old. She joined Bob who was about the same age, who had also more or less retired because of the bone spur that was finally giving him problems. As Ryan and I continued to ride Bob, we found it harder and harder to keep him sound. He would be okay preparing him for an event and even through it, but return home pretty sore. He would need a week or so off. Then it was enduring another week or so of rearing episodes until he settled enough to prepare for the next show. Finally, the periods of lameness outgrew the periods of soundness, and Bob wiled away his hours grazing away on the pastures of the farm where we lived.

The pastures were very rich; planted for dairy cows. One summer it looked like Gracie started to founder. I treated her with caution and care. I had learned my lesson after a terrible experience many years ago when I became the new barn manager at Potomac Horse Center. I kept her off grass and soaked her hay. She soon recovered, but I watched her like a hawk. Gracie sure hated a life of confinement with fresh grass in plain view.

One morning I went up to Northwind Farm to ride and teach. Ryan called me a short time later to tell me that Gracie was colicing. I dropped everything and rushed home. I called my vet and she came out to examine Gracie. She gave her pain meds and said to watch her and call if Gracie got worse, and she left to see other clients. All seemed well for a few hours and then Gracie took a turn for the worse. When my vet returned Gracie had collapsed and refused to get up. Both of us tried and tried and finally she made a huge effort to get to her feet. My vet palpated her again. She couldn't find a blockage, but everything was swollen inside. She recommended euthanasia. I couldn't afford colic surgery, anyway. There wasn't any room next to where Velvet was buried, so we took her to the back of the barn, as close to her mom as we could get. My vet gave the blue-colored injection. Gracie hit the ground so fast she exclaimed, "*Oh Gracie ...*" and then Gracie was gone.

I paid my landlord's son to dig a hole with his backhoe. He and a buddy helped me roll Gracie in the hole. Handling that much dead weight can be a harrowing experience. I think it was for my landlord's son; I *know* it was for his friend. Me? My feelings were numb.

All I could think was "**WHY?!?**" Gracie was young. She was beautiful. She hadn't gotten far out of the Start Box of Life. It seemed so unfair. I was angry at God, angry at my vet, and mostly angry at myself.

Why did God let this happen? Why didn't my vet handle her lameness and scratches better ... and why did it take so dang long to heal the scratches and come to a conclusion on the injury? Why didn't *she* find it? And I wondered if I had let the hay soak too long and caused it to ferment. Maybe *I* caused the colic. How could I be so stupid?

As the days went by, I began to wonder if Gracie didn't take herself out on purpose. I think she was done living on earth. She knew she was a crippled young horse, wasn't able to raise a child, and was going to be a very expensive, do-nothing horse that we couldn't afford for many years. She asked God to come home, and He said *yes*. That was *terrible* grace, but once more she lived up to her name.

Chapter Fifty-six

ANIMALS HAVE AN INCREDIBLY GRACIOUS way of getting *out* of the way for another animal to come in. Noble Valentine was a gorgeous bay thoroughbred gelding. Valentine's Day was his birthday. He was stunningly beautiful and also very kind. He was always the first horse you saw when you entered the barn. He sure got a lot of pats from me. And carrots. It didn't take me long to fall in love with him.

Mimi, his owner, put him on the market to sell. Sell him? I thought she was *crazy,* but Mimi was always buying and selling horses. I watched enviously while people came and tried him. His price tag was way over our heads so I didn't even consider it. Marlie and her mom became interested in buying him. They had bought a horse but he didn't stay sound long, and they were able to send him back. I thought it would be cool if they bought Valentine, but he seemed like a lot of horse for Marlie at the time. I got to I ride Valentine to see if I thought Marlie could manage him. We got along so well together, it was magic. He was a joy to ride. He flew over the jumps, and we jumped higher than I had in a long time. Mimi exclaimed "You ride him better than *I* do!"

It looked like Marlie would be getting Valentine, but Mimi approached me and asked if I would like to buy Valentine for about $1,000 less than she was asking, on interest-free monthly payments! She wanted to see Valentine go to me. For sure I wanted that as well, but I told her I'd have to ask Caleb. A few months ago it would have been out of the question, but with Caleb's latest promotion it just might be possible. I met him for lunch in Bellevue. I was very nervous about asking. I figured he'd say "NO WAY". But wonder of wonders, he said *"YES!"*

When Valentine became my boy, Marlie and her mom had hurt feelings. They felt like I bought Valentine right out from under them, and I suppose I did. They ended up being very gracious about it. I helped Marlie find a very nice experienced event horse, and I found a nice horse for her mom as well. I hope they have forgiven me for snagging Valentine.

I took him to the Area VII Adult Rider's spring clinic a week later. I excitedly told everyone he and I had just got married and that we were on our honeymoon!

Valentine and I got along pretty well for awhile. I didn't go out and win everything like I hoped and Mimi predicted. But hey, I was showing at USEA recognized events, and showing on a stunningly beautiful creature. Mimi suggested I ride with her trainer instead of my current one, so I did. Mimi made lots of suggestions and made lots of comments about my riding, my students' riding, and just about everything else. I listened because I was insecure and I respected her. After all, she used to own a barn with our area's own Equestrian Olympic star.

I took Valentine Novice level for a few events. My goal was to move up to Training Level before my 50th birthday. Back in the days of Potomac Horse Center I had gotten right to the edge of eventing at Training level. Twenty-two years and 3 kids later, I was *still* at the edge of Training level. I thought I finally had the horse to help me reach my goal.

Ciaran and Shadow progressed from local shows to local combined tests to out of town one-day horse trials and even some Recognized events that took up a weekend. At the horse trials the dressage rings were often set up on grass in the middle of the cross-country field or tucked away somewhere. Cross-country was tough as well, because Shadow had to put on her big girl pants and do it SOLO. Once they got going, everything would be (mostly) fine.

Shadow always warmed up fairly well as long as she was with other horses. Dressage was tricky, because that meant Shadow had to go in a ring ALONE. Ditto for stadium jumping, but that usually worked out because Shadow could be a little uptight and still jump extremely well. Good thing we didn't show hunters, where the horses' loose and relaxed jumping style is so important. At the little combined tests and horse trials we attended, it was all Ciaran could do to muscle Shadow through her dressage test, then hang on and steer while Shadow flew over everything in the stadium jumping ring or cross country course. Sometimes they managed to get a ribbon. But just like the Master Card commercials, at the end of the list of all the expenses of owning and showing a pony, came the words; "the experience of doing all the above: *priceless.*"

Mimi was currently competing her wonderful Selle Francais mare. We went to events and stabled together. Often Marlie would take her new horse to a combined test or horse trial; sometimes another student would go, so there would be a small group of us. That little girl who had gotten "Dexterized" back at Pebble Creek had grown into a lovely teen and was a very capable rider on her sturdy quarter horse. And always *Sump the Flying Couch* was ready to fill in for any capable student who found themselves horseless when an event rolled around.

In the fall I entered the Training Level section at Caber Farms Horse Trials in Onalaska, Washington. I had gone Novice the year before on a borrowed horse that my trainer in Woodinville had let me ride because Bob was lame and I had to withdraw him from the Event. I was so thankful to have a nice little horse to ride and I just went for it. He did really well and we had a blast. We came in 3rd! Later people told me how green he was and that his owner was having lots of problems with him. I didn't know that! I just thought he was a "been there, done that" horse---no big deal. He sure acted like I *thought*. My trainer let me show him a couple more times, but it was pretty disastrous. I wonder if we would have done so much better if I had remained blissfully ignorant? How our minds make trouble for us.

At the Caber Farm event, Valentine was a handful for dressage. There were too many spooky things to see, as the rings were tucked away in the woods. Then came cross-country. We rode in the rain on a very slippery, muddy, chewed-up course. My start time was held up by an accident at the optional corner jump. I opted out and did the option!

All in all, Valentine was really decent. Some of the jumps were intimidating to me (therefore to him, too) but we got over everything. Some were jumped more gracefully than others, but I was *thrilled*. It was 2 1/2 months before my 50th birthday!

Caber Farms was particularly challenging for Ciaran and Shadow, who were also competing. The start box was quite a long ways from the portable stabling and separated by a tree line. Many horses balked at leaving "home" to head out for parts unknown. When Ciaran and Shadow left the start box and cantered down to the first fence, Shadow's mind was back at the barn. To her, that jump was the dividing line between her horse buddies and the Twilight Zone. Not only did she refuse to jump, she dug in her hooves and refused to *move*. Ciaran, being young, inexperienced and sympathetically in love with Shadow, wasn't sure what to do, so she sat quietly on her back. I'm pretty sure there was some praying going on. Teagan and I watched all this from the start box area. We were afraid they would be disqualified right then and there for taking too long at the jump. I had a water bottle in my hands, and I started slapping it hard against my thigh like I was spanking a horse with a whip. People are not allowed to coach or offer help from the sidelines, but the rulebook doesn't say anything about body language. I finally caught Ciaran's eye. She got the message and gave Shadow a crack on her bum with her whip. Shadow got going, jumped Fence One and flew around the rest of the course and through the finish flags.

On the last day of the event, stadium jumping was the last thing to accomplish for Valentine and I. The jumps looked big. There was an ad banner over on the back side, tied on the fence. It flapped in a breeze and was spooking the horses. People were perched up above the ring by the barn, on a slope, staring at us! Mimi was there, warmed us up, and told me to just go out there, ride aggressively, and *make* him do it.

I rode aggressively. I rode badly too, and I *blew* it. It was very awkward to watch, I'm sure. Valentine was very distracted by all the stuff to look at and not real keen on jumping *anything*. We half-crawled over a big oxer on the back side, landed in a heap, then wobbled down to the last fence in the line, an airy vertical. I tried my best to shove my boy on over, but we were so poorly organized, he thought it was a *really* bad idea. Instead, he said, "You want to jump it *that* badly? Okay! Go over it without me!" He stopped just short of take off, fell on his knees and I landed *on* the jump. As we both leaped to our feet, I pulled the bridle off his head. He took off. We gave the spectators quite a show! After some nice folks caught him and we got the bridle back on, I walked him out of the ring, dying of embarrassment. Mimi had me get back on and jump a couple fences in the warm-up area. Of course he was good.

Back at home, Mimi said she would help me fix his stadium issues. Hmmmm, I wondered. Were they his issues or *mine*? Was he greener than Mimi had told me? One sunny day she had me school through a grid. He was doing great, and she kept raising the jumps higher. Then he came through, caught a foreleg on the middle jump's top rail, and fell. I rolled clear, and he got up and ran backwards at about 90 mph. That's when I saw blood gushing from his left elbow. A vet visit and several stitches later, he seemed okay, but I felt so badly that it had happened. *I* wasn't hurt. We missed the last event of our season.

That tumble seemed to leach the confidence right out of Valentine. All winter I schooled him at home and hauled out for lessons. His jumping was terrible. He stopped frequently. Sometimes he would put his front feet down in the middle of an oxer and send all the poles flying. It was not good.

As show season commenced that spring, I backed him down to Novice. He was fine, but I was bored. I wanted to move him up again. I went with Mimi, who was riding a young home-bred mare, and a couple of my students to Donida Farms down south of us to school cross-country. If it went well jumping the Training fences, I planned to take Valentine Training Level at the Whidbey Island Horse Trials in July.

The one fence that was our big bugaboo was *The Coffin*. Great name, huh? It's a jump, a stride or two to a ditch, then a stride or two to another jump. Now Valentine wasn't thrilled about jumping ditches anyway, but to have one come up on short notice after a jumping effort was even worse. The worst thing that could happen is that the horse could fall---on you---in the ditch. It rarely happens, but a Hairy Risk is there, lurking in the bushes. When a rider laughs at the Risk and tells it to scram the horse confidently jumps through like a little bunny rabbit.

After warming up and jumping a few things at Donida, it was time to tackle the coffin. Valentine did fabulously jumping it up a slight incline and I was ready to quit while we were ahead. But Mimi came riding over on her young mare to ask how it went.

When I told her she said, "Great! Did you jump it from the other direction?" That meant downhill, which is how it rode at Whidbey, which is how I should have jumped it, to be fully prepared. But the Risks were jiggling the bushes and sneering at us! When I told her, "*no*", she said I *had* to do it or we would have problems at the Event.

Logistically and legalistically she was correct, but my gut said "*No, don't push it.*" I told my gut, "Don't argue with Mimi! She has more experience than you!" So off I went on my beautiful bay boy, even though the Risks had started to bang drums!

We never made it over the log jump in, let alone the ditch. Valentine refused, even after several really hard smacks with my whip. The more I demanded, the more he shut down, until we were both sweating and exhausted. I broke his heart that day.

Mimi said, "You *have* to get him over!" but it was pointless. Loathing her and loathing my idiotic, spineless self, I left the course, cooled him out and loaded him in the trailer for the ride home.

I did take him to the Whidbey Event. He actually did pretty well until we came to the first ditch. Then he refused until we eliminated. We never even made it to the coffin. I opted out of Stadium Jumping the next day. The *Risks* and their cousins, *The Embarrassments*, had taunted me through the long night. Before I left the show grounds, one of them took human form in the person of a trainer I knew. She said, "You should *sell* Valentine! Mimi lied to you! He has big problems! You could be riding at the Preliminary level, but *never* on that horse!"

Well, my fragile ego jumped on the "*you could*" statement. Nobody had ever told me that. **WOW.** Even though my first trainer in Woodinville quietly told me she thought she could help me fix him, I listened to the other girl and my current coach, and I sadly put Valentine up for sale.

Quite a few people came to try him, but they weren't quite right for each other. One day a young girl came with her mom to try him. She was just learning dressage and thought she might like to jump a little. I knew of her trainer, who was a dressage judge I had ridden under a few times. She didn't come because she was bed-ridden with a sore back. She called me and told me not to let them jump at all, as the kid was too green. Green she may have been, but she was enormously talented raw material. Valentine said, *"This is the girl"*. They put a deposit on him, and we agreed that he would be vetted at her trainer's farm in Olympia.

I drove him down to Olympia with a very sad heart the following week. He passed the vet with flying colors. They wrote me a nice check and we said our goodbyes. This time *my* heart was broken. I cried all the way home.

Chapter Fifty-seven

DURING MY TIME WITH VALENTINE and after I sold him, many fun and wonderful things were happening with my students and horses and dogs. They didn't always start out or end that way, but the wonderful moments in between will always be cherished.

Fedora Gleason, the animal communicator, continued to pop up in my life. I was intrigued after she talked to our horses at that cross-country camp, but I was still a bit wary. She had come to Northwind Farm a time or two, and I had her talk to one or two of my guys. My students had her do the same. It always seemed to be very pertinent to whatever we were experiencing with a horse at the time. I really wanted to embrace the whole idea, but held back because of my Christian influence. That is, until the day our coonhound Hank disappeared.

I had Hank tethered out as usual on a hundred foot-long piece of climbing rope. When I went to move him, I saw that the rope had torn on the barbed-wire fence and Hank was gone, with a long section still snapped to his collar. Hank frequently escaped our house by diving through our legs out the door when we opened it, and we had learned that the harder we chased him, the harder he ran away. He would always return in his own sweet time after he had sniffed every inch of the neighborhood, raided neighbors' garbage cans and tracked coyotes. We didn't want to incur the wrath of the neighbors (whose cans he raided) or have him get hit by a car, so we always made an attempt to catch him. Caleb also very cleverly deduced that if he stood at the end of our driveway and popped a paper sack it would send Hank galloping home with his tail between his legs. It sounded just like a gun shot, which

Hank was deathly afraid of, which is why he ended up as a giveaway at the grocery store instead of up in the mountains hunting cougar.

But that day the paper sack trick failed to bring Hank home. I began to worry that the end of the rope still fastened to his collar had caught on something and held Hank prisoner in the woods near our house. When we had looked for hours and hadn't found him by late afternoon, I became quite anxious. I called Teagan Finch to tell her I couldn't teach Ciaran that afternoon, and why. I was going to keep scouring every inch of the woods until I found him.

Teagan called me back a short time later. Ciaran wanted to know if we had called Fedora. *Duh.* I hit my hand to my forehead. Fedora has helped so many people find lost pets! Fedora was currently living in Alabama, but could do work over the phone. It cost a lot more to do it that way, but I was feeling desperate. I called her. We also asked our friend Vickie who lived and worked at Northwind Farm. She had taken lots of Fedora's classes on animal communication. Both Fedora *and* my friend got mental pictures relating to Hank's whereabouts.

Vickie saw a gray building and tall, thin, cone-shaped trees. Fedora saw a chain-link fence; maybe a dog kennel, with Hank inside missing us and wishing to go home.

Laz Tool Shop was just down the road from us, surrounded by a chain link fence with tall, coned-shaped juniper trees in front. It was painted gray. Even though we had driven past it a couple of times that day and didn't see Hank, we thought we should go back. It was now after 5:00 p.m..

What was different this time as we slowly drove past was a large sign hanging on the fence. It read "Found: *hound dog*" and a number to call. I parked and ran into the shop. Everyone had gone home for the day but one guy. He said, "*Sure!* Your hound was here all day. He stayed under Susan's desk like a true gentleman. She took him home because she has a dog kennel. That's her number on the sign." I dialed Susan's number on my cell phone. Sure enough, the dog in her chain-link kennel fit my description of Hank perfectly. She offered to bring him back to the tool shop. Within 20 minutes Hank was joyously reunited with his relieved mom and family. Fedora didn't charge me a penny; neither did Vickie. Whatever doubts lingered in my mind about Fedora's abilities were gone for good. I wanted to believe before that, but I was too skeptical and wary. Finding Hank clinched it for me. I was now a true believer.

After that I made a habit of having Fedora talk to as many of my animals as I could afford when she came to Northwind Farm, or my house, or both. Because I had so many animals, Fedora always cheerfully gave me a nice discount.

One day she was at the farm where I lived, and she quickly did a "run through" of all the horses there, and the two dogs, Hallie and Hank. I loved getting a baseline on all the horses, just to see where they were at in their lives. I was always amazed and delighted to hear how much they loved us. It was great fun to hear from Hank and Hallie, who took their jobs of guarding the farm, sniffing every blade of grass and looking after us quite seriously. But the most interesting and surprising things came from my old retired thoroughbred, Pete.

Pete told Fedora he was a little bored and wished he could have some sort of a job. He thought he could teach students a few things, but he didn't think he could deal with beginners. I was floored. I would have never suspected he felt that way, *ever*.

I decided to take him seriously and started legging up this 26 year old thoroughbred. All that time off had been great for his "hitches" and he looked and felt sound. He ended up giving lessons to a few teenagers and adult intermediate riders for a couple of years. One young woman even took him to a dressage schooling show at Gold Creek Stables in Woodinville and Pete got good scores. He was wonderful and especially therapeutic for Amanda Dupree, who ended up giving her horse Toby away because he ended up being too much horse for her. That's because the people who took Toby discovered through their vet that he had fractured his pelvis years ago, way before Amanda owned him. No wonder he would run off. He was running away from pain!

Eventually Pete started showing me he was ready to retire again. I had Fedora out and she confirmed it. Pete had done such a good job teaching that his students' abilities outgrew his physical ability to do the dressage movements. We retired Pete for good at 29, and he was happy and peaceful. At the age of 33 he developed canker in his feet. I worked so hard with my vet to keep his feet clean and comfortable. Days and weeks of soaking and changing bandages was breaking me down but not helping Pete one bit. Finally I made the decision to send Pete on to his heavenly home. Like Jim, it took a lot of Phenobarbital to finally stop his heart. My heart almost stopped before Pete's did. I felt so guilty. I wished I had the money for a better barn, a dryer pasture, less mud, more vet care for Pete. I wished I had the energy to keep babying him along. But I didn't have any of those things.

Little Fire the wonder pony kept chugging away. Fire taught many more kids how to ride and no one fell off. On the same day Fedora was out listening to Pete, Fire told her that when he was young he had been a very naughty boy. As he got older he decided to be a good pony and had been good ever since. I said *Amen* to that! He told her that he could do lots of things. He could run and he could jump. He could also leave hoof prints of love on all our hearts.

I held a little show for my students and invited another trainer to bring hers. We did dressage tests and jumping. I had a very young beginner rider mounted on Fire for a dressage test. I knew she would not remember most of it even if I called the test for her, so I trotted the test on foot with Fire close at my heels. She had a very good time riding her test as Fire followed along perfectly behind me.

As the years rolled by, gray hairs showed up on his kind, wise face. He was getting a little stiff. It became hard for him to jump. It became hard for him to get up after rolling or taking a nap. He still patiently taught kids, but at a much slower pace, until he finally had to stop altogether. Sometimes it took two of us to help Fire get up. Then the day arrived when he couldn't get up *or* down. His hind legs started to swell. We held a vigil for two days with Fire, comforting him, praying for him, and thanking him for all his years of wonderful service. Then I called my vet. We laid him to rest with Velvet, Pete, Gracie, Jim, Hank and some of our beloved cats in our animal cemetery on the farm where we lived, our own little "Rest Haven."

Fire the wonder pony. Absolutely the most wonderful pony ever born.

Then of course there was Sump---a hunka-hunka *burnin'* Sump. The next big era in Sump's life and career was when my first group of seriously good riders started to event. When I was teaching at Woodland Farm Sump had been diagnosed with uveitis, a chronic eye disease. It's also called Periodic Opthalmia or Moon Blindness. It's an auto-immune reaction to a foreign body or virus that causes anti-bodies in the horse's body to attack its' eyes, as though they were the enemy. Apparently Sump had uveitis for many years and we didn't recognize the very mild signs until they became more pronounced. There is a regular inflammatory episode with swelling, pain and tearing once a month, seemingly in conjunction with the phases of the moon; at least that was what the old timers thought. We began to treat his eyes with a steroidal anti-biotic ointment to keep the inflammation under control, as it was quite painful for Sump. If he did have an acute response at any time, I was supposed to immediately stop the steroidal ointment and switch to a plain antibiotic one, as the steroids could cause serious damage.

One of my seriously good students, Abelie DeFranco, was a teeny-tiny little thing (she still is, in her twenties). She had progressed from riding Little Fire to mighty Sump. It was a personal triumph for her. Even though Sump was only three inches taller than Fire, she looked like a little peanut on him, overshadowed by his huge, cresty neck. One time during Abelie's early cross-country jumping experiences, we were schooling down at Camas Meadows. Every thing was going "swimmingly" 'till we asked him to trot off a bank into the water. He thought running through the water was fun, but *jump* in? Hmmmmn ... it took some coaxing. When he finally took a gigantic Sump-like leap in, Abelie took a leap off Sump into the drink! We all tried to be polite and not laugh, but Sump had a way of making even a mishap funny. Abelie was fine, just soaked, and she ended up laughing too.

After a while her parents purchased her first steed. He was a 13.2 h.h. Pony of the Americas. They named him Paco, a Native American word for golden eagle. Maybe his named should have been *Bucko*. Paco was an amazing jumper, but he also turned out to be an amazing bucker.

While Abelie was learning to ride those bucks and prevent them from happening, if possible, she continued to ride and show Sump. They were quite a team. I don't know who adored him more, Abelie or her mom, Celia. She would spend hours brushing him. He would love it and nibble her thighs in gratitude. Abelie, now a young adult, has a gorgeous leopard Appaloosa of her own. Sump started a legacy.

Sump's eye condition deteriorated to the point where he couldn't see well on bright, sunny days. That very much affected his confidence. He couldn't see the jumps well enough to judge takeoff. When it was overcast, he was fine. We had to pick shows according to the cloud cover. In early spring and fall it was a go, but late summer was nip and tuck. It really depended on time of day as well. One August at Donida Farms down in Auburn, Washington, Abelie and Sump's cross country ride time was in the late afternoon. That might have been a disaster had the sun been glaring as it usually does in August, but just as Sump took off out of the start box, clouds rolled in. They rolled back out as he finished. It's great to have heavenly connections.

One early fall day Abelie was going to have a lesson on Sump. After she tacked him up it became apparent that there was something very wrong. Sump was not his usual blustery self. He was very tentative and did not want to go forward. There were jump poles on the ground and he tripped over them. He was very tentative and unsure of himself. I called my vet and she came right out.

Sump was having a very severe episode of inflammation. His eyes developed lesions and they were leaking corneal fluid. In a couple more days Sump was completely blind. It took a while to get an appointment with the crackerjack animal eye specialist, Dr. O'Meara. It was too late to save Sump's eyesight. He probably wouldn't have been able to anyway, even if he was able to see Sump right away. Needless to say I died a thousand deaths, right along with Sump's beautiful eyes. What made it even more painful were Celia and Abelie's heartbreaks and feeling that they were judging me for not working hard enough or fast enough to save his sight.

Once Sump's eyesight was gone, so was the pain. His eyes had been painful for several years; the steroidal ointment helped a lot with the pressure and inflammation caused by the uveitis. Now that most of his corneal fluid had leaked out there was no more pressure or pain! What a tradeoff. But Sump was comfortable and relieved, and I was to a point, except I always wondered if I could have prevented Sump's blindness by handling his medications more carefully. Guilt was the gift that kept on giving.

Over the next days and weeks I had to come to terms with the fact that my wonderful Sump's career as a fabulous school and show horse had come to an end. I was angry because I thought it took too long to get an appointment with Dr. O'Meara. I was angry at Celia because I thought she was angry at me because getting him seen by Dr. O'Meara took so long it was somehow my fault. *I* was angry at me. I felt I should have managed Sump's medications better. I was also angry at God. I felt He could have prevented this disaster. How could we let this happen to Sump?

It was really hard to look at Sump, whose eyes had become so disfigured. They had always been so bright, so happy, and so full of mischief. It was hard to help him find his way around the barn, paddock and field as a blind horse, especially thinking I had possibly contributed to it. We took steps to make a very safe area for Sump in the pasture. We made the fencing a lot safer and showed him where the boundaries were. We walked him back and forth from the stall area to the paddock. Abelie even tried riding him again. He did fine, but he was worried about where he was in relationship to the arena fence. He couldn't exactly practice a dressage test, and he certainly couldn't jump.

Within a short time Sump adjusted incredibly well to being blind and retired. Soon he was going back and forth from barn to pasture as though he still had sight. It was great to see him pain-free. My other horses looked after Sump in their own horsey ways. We kept a fly mask on Sump to protect his eyes and to protect us from looking at the holes where his eyes once were. Over time we got used to it. Sump's personality was too big to go away just because his eyes were gone. He still sparkled and shone; his wonderful energy manifested itself in other ways.

Shadow's anxiety at the shows mostly kept Ciaran out of the ribbons, but Shadow could surely jump. We jumped higher and higher at home. One evening close to Halloween I was teaching Ciaran, Abelie and Vickie's daughter Jennifer. I set up the *Great Pumpkin Jump-Off*. I set three small pumpkins, stems intact, on top of a vertical jump pole. Ciaran was riding Shadow, Abelie was riding Sump, and Jennifer was on Squeaky Pony, a medium-sized pony she was leasing. The jump got higher and higher and Squeaky Pony had to bow out. At around 3'6," Sump cleared the jump but one of his back hooves neatly clipped the stem off the pumpkin. The pumpkin didn't budge off the top rail. Shadow sailed over the pumpkins with air to spare. We got to the last jump cup hole at the top of the standard when I declared Shadow the winner, because I couldn't stand watching Ciaran and Shadow jump any higher!

Shadow jumped cleanly and quickly at Novice (2'11" height) at the Gold Creek Stables combined tests. After the Great Pumpkin Jump off victory, we thought we'd try Shadow at Training Level (3'3"). At one of the Gold Creek shows in late winter/early spring, Ciaran started her Training level jump round. It was absolutely brilliant until Shadow galloped down to an oxer off a curve. Shadow took off long, caught her front legs on the top rail, and crashed on the other side. The magic bungee cord ripped; no doubt it was for the best. Ciaran rolled clear, muddy and shaken, but otherwise unhurt. Shadow seemed okay too.

I think Teagan was the most shaken up of the three. It was just so unlike Shadow to do anything like that. It was so unlike Ciaran's Magic Bungee cord to fail. Teagan had our vet check Shadow over. Shadow seemed okay, especially for an older gal, but what the vet did discover was cataracts in both of Shadow's eyes. The vet said Shadow could still see, but her eyesight was diminished, which probably led to her misjudging the take off to that jump. No more big jumps for Miss Shadow.

One gift that Shadow gave Ciaran, if you want to call it a gift, was the ability to persevere through two hour *(plus)* dressage lessons, where I tried to teach Ciaran how to put Shadow on the bit. Ciaran need the strength of a lumber jack to supple Shadow's extremely set jaw and poll, and I needed the patience of a saint with both Shadow *and* Ciaran. In the end, Ciaran got stronger arms and more of an education in how to supple a very inflexible and *unwilling* mare. Shadow got a little more supple, and I think I got a little more patient.

Chapter Fifty-eight

With Valentine's money burning a hole in my pocket, I started shopping for a new horse. Wow, I actually had money to buy a new horse! At least *some* money. I had sold Valentine for $8,500.00. At the time, a stellar event horse was going for thirty, forty, or even more than fifty thousand dollars. I was going to have to buy a prospect, but I didn't mind. Training them yourself was half the fun, especially if you had great support from a mentor-trainer, and I was pretty happy with mine.

I traveled to look at a few horses and soon realized how time consuming it was. First, it took time to look up a horse on the internet or call around, or look through magazines. Then there was the time spent making arrangements to go see the horse. Then there was the time spent driving to see the horse. Then time spent watching the horse being ridden, riding the horse yourself, then jawing with the owners for a long time, who of course thought their horse was *the* horse for me!

Caleb and I spent 6 hours round trip driving one day to see a horse that looked great on-line and sounded really terrific when I called, but was lame when we finally got to see him. He was in a nasty pasture and couldn't be ridden because his feet were unshod, cracked, and sore. Even if he was sound, there was nowhere to ride him. I started to rethink the whole shopping thing.

I kept thinking about a horse that had caught my eye on a website I had looked up when I had just begun to shop. Hopper's Appaloosa Sport Horses in Emmet, Idaho, stood a beautiful Appy sport horse at stud, *HAS Hoppin' Hunkie.* I'd had my eye on him for years, dreaming of owning one of his babies. I have had a soft spot in my heart for

Appaloosas ever since Potomac Horse Center. There was a really cool Thoroughbred-Appaloosa cross boarded at Pebble Creek Stables, and ever since then I had wanted an Appaloosa Sport Horse. I called Fred and Kylie Hopper and they sent me a CD with their sale prospects on it. Excitedly I took it out of its' mailer and sat down to look. Hunk's babies were cute, but not spectacular. They were small and not exactly what I was dreaming of, 'till I came to the very last horse. Then, **WOW.**

What a *head*-turner. He was jet black with a blaze and three white stockings. He had beautiful snowy white hindquarters with big black spots. He was only three and only green broke, but he was *beautiful!* His breeder's comments on the CD said "should mature to 16 hands". He was a Thoroughbred-Appaloosa-Trakhener cross. His name was *HAS All That Jazzy.* I showed his picture to Mimi. She thought he was cute, but wasn't all that impressed. Lots of people are prejudiced against Appaloosas. After all, they are *horses of color.* Since he was the very first horse I picked out, I put the thought of him aside and tried to look for other horses that would fit the bill. I found quite a few on the web, but they were either too expensive, too far away, or not quite right.

Fall was approaching, and I didn't want to "winter over" without a horse. I kept looking at Jazz's picture on the sales CD. I had them send me a video of Kylie longeing Jazz over a jump. He jumped really well. After that I couldn't get him out of my mind. Finally I called his owners and set a date for Caleb and I to go to Idaho to look at Jazz. *With* the horse trailer.

We left in early October. It was a very long drive through very barren countryside. It was Eastern Washington plus several hundred more miles of sand, volcanic rock, and tumbleweed. There were strange clouds, high winds and snow flurries in the eastern Washington/ Oregon/ Idaho mountain passes. We saw parts of the old Oregon Trail. I don't know how *anyone* survived.

We finally made it to Emmet, which was in the middle of Nowhere. Kylie and Fred Hopper's farm was on a barren hilltop just outside of Nowhere. My '95 Ford Turbo Diesel straight drive threatened to overheat as it lugged my nice big gooseneck trailer I had acquired from a fellow eventer up a steep dirt road. We pulled into Fred and Kylie's driveway with the radiator hissing and the transmission smelling hot. Kylie met us at the door with her arm in a cast. I flippantly asked, "Oh, did *Jazzy* do that to you?" Her reply was a sheepish "Yes." Apparently Jazz had caught his tail on a loose nail in a homemade wood mounting block. It had frightened him with the end result of Kylie getting dumped and breaking her arm. *Oh boy.* A foreshadowing of things to come.

We caught all 15 hands of him and took him to the barn to groom and tack. In the cross-ties he pulled back out of his halter. Kylie said it was because he didn't know me. *Oh Boy.* We took him down to the ring to ride. She had me longe him first, because she hadn't been able to ride him for about three weeks. When we got down there, he started snorting at my rig in the driveway. When I sent him out on the longe line, he proceeded to tear around at the end of it at Mach 10, blowing and snorting, with his tail up over his back. He did that a very long time.

When he finally settled down and I got on he felt amazing. Everybody said he was brilliant. He showed us all his qualities. Caleb videotaped our ride. Later on when we watched it I was really pleased how nice Jazz looked, but he also looked so *small*. I called Mimi back in Snohomish for advice, but she wasn't much help at all. I watched the video a couple more times, full of doubts about myself picking the right horse, but still really liking Jazz's looks. We slept on it, in a little Emmet motel. The next morning we said *yes*. We took him for a vet pre-purchase examination; only $150.00 slightly northeast of Nowhere. Jazz passed with flying colors. The vet said he was one of the most correctly built horses he had ever seen, and he should stay sound a very long time. Fred even came down $500 on Jazz's price. We shook hands and signed the papers.

We loaded him up along with a big good looking Appaloosa gelding Fred and Kylie had also bred. He had been sold, experienced some trauma, and Fred and Kylie had taken him back. Kylie said if I could fix him, I could have him. I liked his size, about 16.1 hands high. I was still thinking Jazz was tiny, and at least it gave Jazz a traveling companion for the long ride home.

Since we didn't leave until after two in the afternoon, we didn't get home till after two in the morning. There we were, unloading horses in Mimi's driveway at two in the morning. The bigger gelding jumped right out. Jazz did not. He couldn't figure out how to walk down a ramp. His owner's trailer was a step up. Our ramp was a steep, skinny one to boot. He wouldn't back out or turn around and walk out. We were stuck there for about an hour, coaxing, pushing and spanking Jazz until he finally decided to jump the ramp out of the trailer. After we made sure that they were both settled in, we went home for a few hours sleep.

A couple days later I rode Jazz. He was a bit "looky-loo" at his new surroundings, but pretty good otherwise. He seemed a bit lazy the next couple of rides. I put on little blunt spurs. I got really tired of him leaning on my right leg, so I gave him a little kick that meant *please get off my leg.* He answered with a big buckaroo that set me sailing through the air. He sure got off my leg all right and my leg flew off him! Jazz was like a Blue Angel screaming over the 520 bridge across Lake Washington in July.

Lesson learned: you put a quarter in, you might get back $500.00. *On fire.* I put the spurs away till much later in our relationship. I didn't waste any time taking him over to my trainer. She thought I was pretty crazy to get a three year old, and a spotted one at that. Maybe, just maybe she liked him a teeny-tiny bit. My teacher was a pretty rare Appy lovin' eventing trainer herself. She had had one as a Young Rider that carried her pretty far. She also owned one of the most beautiful leopard Appaloosas I had ever seen. He was almost as spectacular as Sump.

I first introduced Jazz to jumps on the longe line. His form was beautiful. When I brought out blue plastic barrels, he thought they were blue fire-breathing dragons! But *boy* was he a stylist; he sure didn't want any dragon breath licking his heels! He was tight as a tick front and back.

After Jazz learned that scary looking jumps could be negotiated on the longe line without attacking him, I would jump him under saddle. Little by little progress was made. When we went over to my trainer's place for lessons, he learned to jump painted cow barrels and a blue plastic Liverpool, which was filled with water. My trainer also had some little cross country-type jumps around the outside of her outdoor arena. At first he was highly suspicious and doubtful, but once he checked them out he was fine. He slowly got to where he would be a good boy and jump everything the first time. He was uptight but obedient.

I took him cross-country schooling all over the place. After the initial excitement of the new place and wide open fields, he would settle down and jump a little, instead of buck a lot and gallop fast. By that time show season was underway and I was able to take him to a couple of recognized shows just to hang out and see the sights while I coached my students.

Toward the end of August and the end of the show season, I took him to another recognized event at Donida Farm. He seemed quite relaxed, so I rode him in their nice outdoor arena. He was a good boy. I went to the show office to see if they had room for any more entries, and they did. Pretty soon Jazz and I were signed up for the Beginner Novice Division.

Our dressage test was fairly respectable. Then came the cross-country phase. Low and behold, Jazzy jumped everything except an imposing looking bench jump near the end of the course. But just one refusal; he jumped it the second try. Glory, glory! Was I ever proud of my boy. My trainer just shook her head and gave me a hard time about bringing him out too soon. No doubt there was wisdom in her thinking, but I was too excited to care. We were in the game!

The next day we jerked and jolted our way through stadium jumping. Jazz jumped over an oxer that lots of horses had refused, and I was thrilled. There was a two- stride combination that got us in the end. Jazzy jumped in, then said, "*Whoa!* What's that other jump doing there parked so close to the first one?!?" He ducked to the side. I got him over the second time. According to my trainer if I had taken the first one at a trot he would have made it all the way through on the first go. My bad! I *am* a little impulsive sometimes. I was absolutely thrilled down to my toes that my squirrelly little baby Appaloosa put on his big boy pants that weekend. I could hardly wait for the next show!

That meant waiting for early summer, *next* year. In the Pacific Northwest, even shows in May can be w-e-t and freezing; in June as well! We kept on training. Jazz got a little better, a little braver. My trainer had several dogs that followed her everywhere. If you were jumping and your horse (or you) made a mistake, she would growl loud instructions. Her dogs loved to jump in and growl their own loud instructions, even to the point of chasing after you, to make sure you got the message. That could be pretty unnerving sometimes, especially on a quick-trigger pony like Jazz. Sometime her pups would stand defiantly in your path and my trainer would yell, *"Just keep coming. Just run over them!"* Which of course I didn't want to do. They always moved at the last minute. Looking back, I sometimes wish I had her pups with me on most of my cross-country courses to aid and assist when things got tough!

Chapter Fifty-nine

MIMI WAS ALWAYS LOOKING FOR a way to make a buck selling horses. She noticed draft-crosses starting to appear at events. Lots of farms were using draft mares to make synthetic estrogen for drug companies. They used it in the relief of menopausal symptoms. The farmers had to breed the mares, collect the urine, then sell it to the drug companies who made the product. Soon the horse market was flooded with weanling draft crosses. Depending on who and what the stallion was, some of the weanlings were really nice. The best prospects for eventing and jumping were draft/thoroughbred crosses. They were big and athletic. Mimi thought there would be an excellent market for these weanlings when they were older and started under saddle. She contacted a woman in Virginia who was getting draft-cross weanlings from Canada. Mimi and her husband took their trailer out there on a buying trip. She came back with three really nice young horses; two three-year olds and one two year old. None of them had much handling at all. They had grown up on the plains of central Canada wild and free.

Mimi had her husband gentle the big boys. He was very patient and kind. It took a really long time for them to accept a saddle and bridle. Mimi had planned on starting them, but was having second thoughts. I offered to help. I told her I had started several horses using Natural Horsemanship techniques. I told her about taking Gracie to that amazing horse whispering wizard. Mimi agreed that it might be a good idea, and that she would pay me when she sold the youngsters. That sounded great to me.

We made a round pen in her indoor arena out of jump standards and poles. That worked well until the draft-crosses neatly jumped over the round pen poles. Sometimes they continued on and jumped over the arena gates as well! At least they were showing their abilities. It got to where some of us would have to stand outside the round pen and the arena gates to make sure the horses would stay put. That worked, and finally they were ready to be ridden.

I took my time swinging a leg over their backs. The horses were so scared. Once up Mimi would lead me around both ways and sometimes she would ask them to trot a few steps along with her. It was such a relief when I finally felt like we could all relax and get down to business. They all developed into very nice prospects and sold easily, so Mimi got a few more. Only one of them proved to be very difficult. He was a big, stout, gorgeous boy. He wasn't any harder than the others to handle before I got on, so we proceeded as usual. I think I rode him once or twice at the walk, but on the first trot he came unglued. He tore out of Mimi's hand and proceeded to buck like a bronc in a rodeo. I went sailing through the air and landed squarely on my head. I heard a loud crack as I hit the ground. As I lay face down in the arena sand, I wondered if I had broken my neck. I was still breathing. *Check.* I could wiggle my fingers and toes. *Check, check.* I could sit up. *Check.* My shoulder ached and pain shot up and down my arm, but I had full range of motion. *Check.* Finally I got to my feet, walked out of the arena, and laid on the mattress in the gooseneck of my trailer. I don't remember the rest of the day, and I don't remember Mimi catching her horse and taking him to the barn. I must have ridden more or taught lessons. I drove the trailer home and was back at it the next day. I never went to the doctor, but I was sure sore and shook up for several days. I had to tell Mimi I was too scared to ride that horse again. She ended up taking him to a natural horsemanship guy, who did an excellent job with him, although the horse would still pull stuff and needed a tranquilizer sometimes. After he came home I did get on him once or twice more in a little pen, but I was very scared. Mimi managed to sell him anyway, even letting people know he had issues. Amazing.

One of my lovely students, Meribeth, the one who had been "Dexterized" as a little girl in Pebble Creek's dusty indoor arena, bought one of the draft crosses that had come from Virginia. She was going to be a high-school senior, and wanted to train him as her Senior Project. She asked if I would please be her mentor on the project. I thought that was really cool. Her new horse turned out to be such a nice guy that she did most of the training herself, with me supervising. It was really fun.

Ciaran Lynch got the golden opportunity to lease the most wonderful horse with whom she did very well. Sump had become blind and little Fire had gone to Glory, so I asked Keagan and Ciaran if I could care-lease Shadow. I wasn't sure if she would make the ideal school horse, as her trot could become very large, her canter was bumpy, and she could very quickly turn into a "*lot of pony*" if something in her world was not to her liking. Good ponies were extremely hard to find and I didn't have the money to buy a new school pony. Besides, Ciaran and Keagan loved Shadow and didn't want to sell her.

Lo and behold, Shadow fit seamlessly into my program like she was made for it. It was amazing. She seemed relieved to be able to baby-sit kids instead of being Ciaran's show pony. She was quite the gentle caregiver; the younger the child, the more gentle she was. Shadow would even put her head down to nuzzle the little kids affectionately.

Chapter Sixty

MIMI TALKED ME INTO GOING with her to our local racetrack, *Meadow Downs,* to look at thoroughbreds that weren't winning for their owners and were for sale. It was a good place to buy an eventing prospect inexpensively. I didn't really need a horse, but Mimi thought I might find something cheap and be able to make a little money once I got it going and sold it. She had done that several times; a lot of event trainers did that. Some even made a living at it.

A beautiful black horse looked at me over the stall grate. His eyes seemed to say, *get me out of here.* I had the trainer bring him out. He was tall, black and gorgeous. He had fractured a sesamoid bone and could no longer race. He might be able to do other things; only time would tell. His price was only five hundred dollars. Mimi thought he might be worth a five hundred dollar risk. I went home and talked to Caleb. The next weekend I bought him and brought him home.

He was still on stall rest and hand walking. As I walked and cared for him I got attached to the pretty gelding. When it got close to the time when I thought he could be ridden, I had my vet out. She did x-rays and announced that he had fractured sesamoids on both front legs and it was doubtful he would ever be sound again. Her eyes were both sad and kind. She knew I had been taken for a sucker. Mimi offered to help me sell him. I wonder if she felt responsible, as she thought I should buy him too. I ended up selling him to someone in Oregon as a trail horse. I hope he stayed sound and had a decent life. I wasn't at all sure when I dropped him off at his new home. It really bothered me. At least I got my money back, but I felt miserable.

I tried buying prospects a couple more times. I got a thoroughbred from a racehorse trainer's home on trial. He had raced but retired. He was a big beautiful bay gelding. I rode him for about a month, but his feet hurt, even with shoes on, so I took him back to his owners. I also took a young Connemara on trial. If he worked out I was going to train him and split the sale profits with his owner. My vet said *forget it, he's not sound either.* His owner came to get him. What a shame I didn't know the Trinity Farrier school people at the time. After that I gave up. *Kind* of.

Mimi had started showing me pictures of Danish Knabstruppers when I became interested in buying Jazz. What an amazing breed; they are warm bloods of color. They look and move like a warm blood, have beautiful tales, and can have lots have gorgeous spots like an Appaloosa! At the time there was only a handful in the United States. I drooled over stallions on the web, learned a lot about the art of genetically producing spots, and dreamed of having one of my own. Not that I didn't have a nice spotted boy, but he was a little Appaloosa. Mimi thought I should have something a little more competitive as warm blood-thoroughbred crosses were starting to dominate the eventing scene.

To have a Knabstrupper, I would either have to buy one or breed one. The ones in Europe and the United States were out of my price range, which wasn't enough to buy even a Knabstupper's *leg.* Mimi suggested breeding one. I liked that idea, but I didn't have a broodmare. Mimi had sold one of her broodmares and her other one was getting old to have more foals. Besides, she was a chestnut and I was thinking dark bay or black. My old vet had a bay mare she would give me if I kept her forever. She had already had a couple of foals, but she had a slight club foot. Mimi advised against it; my new vet too, so I turned down the offer.

Mimi, her husband, Caleb and I ended up going to a Winter Mix Sale in early March at Meadow Downs. Mimi was casually looking herself, and was there to help me pick out a potential broodmare. We looked at lots and lots of them and narrowed it down to six or so. We kept getting outbid. Finally one of our picks came in. Caleb sat right up as they trotted her in hand. She was black. She was beautiful. Mimi said *no*, she was too much on her forehand. *I* didn't think so. The bidding started. Caleb bid on her. A couple others bid too, but we ended up with *Go Congo*, in foal, for $350.00.

Mimi thought we were stupid, but we were thrilled. We had brought the trailer, and she loaded right up after we paid for her. We brought her to the barn and settled her in, while visions of Knabstrupper babies danced in my head.

The plan was to foal out *Go Congo* the following January when she was due, breed her in the spring, then sell her current foal as a weanling, as it was "just" a thoroughbred. Its' sire was a chestnut stallion whose color or conformation didn't appeal to me in the least.

Show season arrived. Meribeth and Crispin were doing great. Ciaran was mounted on a tried and true campaigner. Marlie had put in a couple of good years on her elegant and stoic campaigner, then he started having soundness issues. Her mom found a lovely warm blood mare on-line and they went to try her. They liked her and bought her. Gwen Johnston had graduated from her pretty pink POA pony to an older, experienced thoroughbred that her wonderful grandmother Stella had bought for her. I had a nice little group of really nice young riders that could *ride like stink* mounted on nice horses. My squirrelly little Appaloosa Sport Horse was coming along nicely. Jazz was a pretty good boy. He held a lot of tension in his body but he put in respectable dressage tests. He didn't dump me or jump out of the dressage arena. In cross-country he was quite a good boy though he did like to put his head down suddenly over every jump to get a good look at what he was jumping! Jazz liked to give a little signature "buck" as an exclamation point when he finished stadium jumping. Our scores sometimes put us in 5th or 6th place. I was pleased, but of course I wanted to *win*.

Some of my students wanted to go to an Event at Rebecca Farms in Montana that summer, so we did. It was a long, hot drive. We had a bad blowout on the way, resulting in some body damage to my brand new Chevy Silverado, but we made it. It was surely worth it; what a gorgeous place! It was done right. The staff made you feel special. That was refreshing, especially the free ice! The cross-country course was pretty big and I was a bit scared. When I asked my trainer for advice, she just barked at me which made me feel very alone. I was mad because I didn't know what I had done to upset her. I made up my mind to *ride like stink.*

Believe it or not, Jazz was a good boy. We only had one refusal at a table jump shaded by trees. Jazz said, "Yikes! What's in the shadows? That's really scary!" I did get him over the second try. After Montana, feeling a bit over-confident, I set my sights on Training Level. There I am, being impulsive again.

We did a Training Level at a One Day at Lincoln Creek late that summer. Jazz was quite difficult to get over most of the jumps, but somehow we did it. A short time later we did a half-star, which was the original long format version of a Training Level event. It had the steeplechase, roads and tracks, vet box, and pre-stadium jog out inspection. It was really premature to bite that off, but it was actually very good for Jazzy. All the extra activities helped settle him down. He was the most fit horse in the vet box! I had a blast. We had enough bloopers at fences to eliminate, but I was still very proud of my boy.

Next, I took a Training Level clinic sponsored by Equestrian's Institute at Donida Farm. Jazz started out hot and spooky, but the excellent clinician really helped me settle him down. Jazz was turned into a super star. It seemed reasonable that I should go Training Level at the event Equestrian's Institute ran at Donida that September, so I entered Jazz in it.

When we arrived and I walked the course, I found it rearranged and ramped up. After all, events get more challenging as the season goes by. It looked plenty challenging to me, all right.

The next morning Jazz did his best dressage test ever, and we stood in second place. Our cross country ride time that afternoon was late, just before sunset. The first jump, a big decorated log, was right out of the start box. Jazz refused. I got him over the next time in a heap. The next three jumps went pretty well. There was a big table jump coming up next. Jazz jumped it like a good boy, but I could tell the width of it unnerved him. He almost put his feet down on top of it. I rode him hard up to the next fence, flew over, and then it was time for the big Training ditch. Jazz said "NO WAY!" at first, but I finally got him over.

The next jump was a parallel oxer made of telephone poles. The sun was directly behind it, turning it black. It was also shining directly in our faces. I steeled up for it and Jazz obediently took off. As he was sailing over, he saw the second pole, and went *"WHOA!!* What is *that* doing there?" Down went his front legs neatly between the first and second poles. He quickly scrambled out, and after seeing that he was okay. I tried again. And again. We eliminated.

Chapter Sixty-One

I RODE OFF THE COURSE in humiliation, dismounted and made sure that Jazz wasn't visibly hurt. Over the next few days, he seemed none the worse for the wear. Jazz is an amazingly sound spotted pony; a tribute to his breed, and the Native Americans who bred his forefathers. Early on in his jump training with me, I approached the blue dragon horse-eating barrels exactly the way (I interpreted) my trainer told me to approach any scary jump that I thought Jazz might refuse. *I* was to be scarier than any jump. I scared Jazz so badly he tried to bolt out from under me. Then he bucked me off. He proceeded to tear around the arena at Mach 10. In that process my girth loosened and the saddle slipped all the way under his belly. That scared him even more and so he ran harder. He could not get rid of the Appy-eating saddle, so he decided to strike out to parts unknown, away from certain death and destruction, right over a four foot metal gate. He would have cleared it beautifully if my saddle wasn't hanging under his belly. The saddle caught the top rung and flipped Jazz over neatly. He landed on his upper neck, then his shoulders, and finally the rest of him. Then he jumped up and took off down to the barn, where we found him trembling in fear next to his stall, my saddle still threatening to eat him belly-first. Other than a very slight sprain above his right hock and the bumps and bruises of a nasty fall, he was okay. It was a BIG lesson in not taking my trainer so literally. Jazz healed quickly, and I soon put him back to work.

After the event at Donida Farm, Jazz didn't seem to have any physical trauma, but I wondered about psychological damage. Show season was over and I needed help. Selby Fischer, with whom I had a wonderful lesson on Valentine at the Adult Rider's clinic right after I bought him, had recently moved back to our area after having lived back east for awhile. She and her husband Grant had bought a 450 acre dairy farm about a half-hour north of us and had recently opened their beautiful facility. I went out, visited her, and was amazed. The barns were nicer than any house I had lived in, for sure. There were acres of well-fenced pasture and a cross country course in progress. I hoped Selby could help us, and having access to all that pasture, trails and cross-country practice would be great for Jazzy. I dreamed of boarding him there.

That fall things really changed. Gwen Johnston, whose parents had purchased a young warm blood mare for her, was accepted into the local Olympic rider's training program. Marlie got her driver's license. Her mom wanted the horses closer to where they lived, about an hour south of Northwind, so Marlie could drive to the barn and back without the worries of such a long commute in heavy traffic. They moved their horses a short time after Gwen left. Meribeth was struggling with young adult issues and moved Crispin to a pasture board situation she could afford. The DeFrancos had moved to Sequim a while back, taking their pony with them. That left Teagan, Ciaran, and a few beginner students. I strongly encouraged the Finches to go find another trainer. I wasn't going to be able to afford to show without more students to pay my way, and I wasn't sure if Jazz was going to be up for it. Teagan and Ciaran would have stayed on forever it seemed, loyal friends as they were. It did not seem fair to let them do so. I nearly had to push them out the barn door. Finally they found an instructor they thought they could get along with.

Feeling like a total failure as a rider, trainer and mentor, I thought about what to do next. I wanted to take Jazz to Selby's farm. I had promised him that someday I would get him out of the dinky run he was in at Northwind and find him a place with lovely pasture turnout. I wanted Jazz to have lots and lots of exposure to cross country jumps. I wanted lots and lots of lessons with Selby. I had to figure out a way to pay for his board there. It was expensive, but I felt sure it would be worth it. I had a trainer friend from my Woodland Farm days who worked at a Starbuck's near my home. She helped me get a job there. Between working there and teaching what students I had, I figured I could afford to move Jazz. I made arrangements with Selby and soon had him settled in his glorious new digs. I left Shadow and Go Congo at Northwind.

Things didn't go exactly as I hoped. Working at Starbucks was really stressful. I would get up at 3:00 a.m. to be at work by 4:00 a.m.. I never was quite fast enough to suit my boss or the young women I worked with. I would get off and make the trek out to see Jazz, often having to pull over for a cat-nap along the way. Afterward I would head back to Snohomish to take care of the horses at Mimi's, teach or ride a couple of horses that I was training.

My biological clock was ticking. I was no spring chicken. I wanted to fix Jazz *right now*. Selby was a bit taken aback over my intensity, and Jazz was more than a bit put off.

One day I was out riding him on the cross country field. Jazz was always a handful out there, but we were managing to get over whatever I pointed him at. I dropped down over a little bank with him. Jazz was good; we were just trotting, but it wasn't as graceful as it could be. Jazz landed with a big grunt. "*Geeze, I* thought, better cut back on all those lattes I was drinking at Starbucks! "Then I picked up a canter and circled back to jump it again. It never happened.

Jazz cantered up to the edge of the bank, slammed on the brakes, and said "*no way*." I tried being nice several times. "*No Way!*" I got tougher. "*NO WAY!!!!*" I got *really* tough; Jazz got tougher. I dragged him back to the barn and got my longe line and longe whip. I tried longing him off the bank. Still, he said "***NO!***" As I was engaged in WWIII with Jazz, Selby came flying out in her golf cart. She asked, "*What on earth are you doing!?!*" She saw rather quickly that we were going nowhere fast. I was like an enraged Killer Zombie. Somehow Selby got me to stop trying to annihilate Jazz and bring him back to the barn. She stayed in the stall with me as I put Jazz away (probably so I wouldn't finish him off). She pointed out that he was still showing his love for me even though I had just beaten the the tar out of him.

I broke down sobbing. My heart ached for Jazz. I was full of disgust for myself.

Selby was in tune with Jazz, but unfortunately, I wasn't. I did slow down a bit, but not enough. I was determined to keep going. I wanted to move up to Training Level before I got too old. It seemed like it was taking forever! Geeze, it was only Training Level. What about Preliminary and beyond? I was an eventing trainer, for Christ's sake! Or at least I was *trying* to become one.

I evented Jazz one more time in the fall, dropping down to Novice. Jazz was pretty decent except for the down bank, of course, where we had one stop. At Selby's we kept working on Training Level jump questions. After a bad crash on the up-bank side of the Training level water jump question, Selby told me I should NOT ride Jazz at Training Level, because when it got too demanding his brain would freeze, followed by his body. She kept saying, "We need a Parelli Person to help us!"

After that it seemed pointless to stay at Selby's barn. I was killing myself getting up early and driving to Selby's and driving back to Northwind, and it looked like Jazz might finish me off. I moved Jazz back to Mimi's barn. I had Fedora Gleason come out and have a talk with Jazz. It was like he was on a psychoanalyst's couch. He seemed so relieved to be able to pour his guts out to someone who would listen and not judge. He told her that things had been going pretty well at first, and he was having fun, but then I started putting a whole lot of pressure on him, and he started freaking out. He felt frazzled and overwhelmed by my demands. He knew I was disappointed in him, and he was sorry he let me down. He still loved me in spite of everything.

As Joan was relaying this information to me, I gasped. Jazz felt exactly how I felt at Starbucks!! I wanted to do so well there, but I couldn't take the pressure. The worse the pressure, the more I flubbed up. I felt incredibly disappointed in the job, in my boss, in myself. Jazz and I were going through the same thing!! I broke down in big sobs. I cried and cried. I hugged Jazz and hugged Fedora. I apologized to Jazz, *and* to God, for being such a driven idiot! At that point I knew I should back off on Jazz's training and let our relationship heal.

So what did this girl do? Frantically look around for another horse to make my Training Level dreams come true. I just didn't know when to stop! Mimi had an older chestnut Thoroughbred mare that she had taken to Intermediate once or twice. Then the mare had gotten busy having babies. Now her uterus was worn out and it was too much trouble and expense to get her in foal again. Mimi said I could lease her and see if I could get her going again. I jumped at the chance. It went okay for awhile. My farrier obligingly put shoes on her, even though the sight and smell of him made her come into estrus immediately. It was tough (and messy!) to shoe her. The first few rides went pretty well. I even took her up to Selby's for a lesson, which was interesting. She then kicked like crazy in my trailer as soon as we got back in Mimi's driveway. I am lucky she didn't kick my trailer to bits along with my head as I unloaded her. Over the next three weeks she degenerated into an insane, frantic, and *angry* chestnut mare. I couldn't get anywhere with her. Mimi tried, thinking she could ride her better, but no luck. I ended the lease.

Meribeth called to let me know she needed to sell Crispin. I asked Caleb if we could buy him. Caleb warily said *yes*, bud didn't know where we would get the money. As soon as Mimi found out he was for sale *she* bought Crispin back from Meribeth. Three weeks later she doubled her money selling him to a Pony Club kid from up north. At least he got a good home.

I struck out trying to find a horse to go Training Level on. I struck out at Starbucks, where I felt like a dismal failure. All I could do was get up in the morning, breathe in and out, and get on with the day. My prayers amounted to whispered cries of ***HELP!***

On a brighter note Caleb and I renamed Go Congo or at least gave her a barn name; *Mamu,* which is Congolese for mamma. Mamu hated being turned out alone and would frantically pace the fence line. We ended up handwalking her for exercise a lot. Sometimes Caleb would come up and walk Mamu. He liked her; she was a nice mare. They walked and walked while Mamu got wider and wider.

Chapter Sixty-Two

CIARAN FINCH WAS NOW RIDING with a trainer who operated out of the local Olympic eventing team person's headquarters. Ciaran's mom Teagan told me her trainer was looking for a working student. Teagan was singing her praises. I contacted the trainer and got the position. I thought I might as well go see life at the top of the sport for myself.

Shortly after the trainer hired me she took off to have a vacation in Mexico. It snowed here. A lot. I very carefully drove to Duvall every other day on snow and ice. It took a very long time to get there and back. I was driving south storing up credit for lessons with the trainer, driving back north to work for Starbucks, driving a few miles to Northwind to teach, ride and care for my horses there, driving back south to a client's barn to ride her horses, then north again and home to care for my horses. It was insane.

Mamu's due date came and went right out the window. Several weeks went by. Five whole weeks, to be exact, and no foal. All this time I had been sleeping on a cot in the barn tackroom and setting my phone alarm for every hour, and finally every half-hour. That was insane, too. It was late January, and it was cold. Thank God there was a plug-in for the space heater Mimi let me borrow. I called the breeding farm to check on the cover dates; no mistakes there! She was hauled in, bred once, and hauled home. I had my vet check her again. Everything was fine except the "oven" was turned on "low," so her foal wasn't quite done "baking." Mamu wasn't exactly sporting a dial I could turn up, either. Caleb and I walked and walked and walked her daily, but that didn't jar her foal loose. Finally March 5th, 2007, at 2 p.m., he made his appearance. I have to laugh, or maybe cry, when I think of getting up all those nights and how careful I was not to disturb Mamu. Let's just foal in broad daylight so *everyone* can participate!! Mamu labored quietly. The forelegs slithered out up to the knees, then slithered back. When he tried to come out for good, the foal's toes got stuck in the edges of Mamu's vagina. I shuddered, as I feared she would tear horribly. I was just about to intervene when Mamu backed up to the stall wall, rubbed her "privates" against it, and fixed the problem. A few minutes later her little colt was delivered.

He was on the small side, dark brown; no markings except a tiny white spot on the bottom of his upper lip. His ears seemed *huge.* As I dried him with a big towel, I looked in his eyes. I saw a very old soul in there. He just looked like a *Gus,* so that became his name. He took his sweet time getting up. He took his time nursing too, but otherwise seemed okay. When my vet came out to check him, she said that he was almost a *"dummy"* foal, one that has not thrived properly in the womb. Mamu's afterbirth was not very healthy and was full of scar tissue. *Oh dear.* Gus didn't "cook" properly, and that is why he took so long to be born. That was hard for me to accept, because he looked just fine. He passed his first stool, the *meconium,* then he lay back down to sleep. So did I. I slept another night in the tackroom, as Teresa said Gus would need monitoring that night and for the next few days. I was so sleep deprived, I overslept instead of getting up to make sure Gus nursed. By morning Gus was dehydrated and colicky. I had to have my vet back out to oil him up. To be sure I did not oversleep the next two nights. By the third day Gus was racing around his stall like a whirling dervish and rearing up on Mamu and me. I guess he rallied, all right!

Soon Gus turned into a holy terror. When I would open the door to Gus and Mamu's stall Gus was right there ready to play. That meant rearing up and boxing at me with his hard little feet. A couple of times he bopped my nose so hard it bled. Once he split my lip. I started carrying a dressage whip with me when ever I had to go into his stall or turn him out with Mamu. I halter broke him right away. Whenever I had someone to lead his momma I would bring Gus rearing and plunging to turnout. When I didn't have help and had to lead Mamu with Gus supposedly following her, he was likely to strike off for parts unknown to explore. When I would go into the paddock to feed Mamu lunch or catch her to bring them in, Gus would come bounding up, ready to pounce right on my head. Good thing I had my dressage whip ready to whack him and make him back off! I don't know what kind of mom Mamu was before I bought her, but she did not seem interested in protecting Gus the way most mares do. She nursed him and did show *some* motherly qualities, but she did not hover or obsess over Gus like most mares with foals. At noon I would go out to the paddock with Mamu's lunch, and there she would be, peacefully grazing, but Gus was nowhere to be found. *"Mamu!"* I would say rather sternly. *"Where is your child?"* A search around the paddock usually found Gus far away, talking with butterflies! They weren't nearly as concerned as I was.

I ended up calling Mamu *Trailer Trash Mom* because if she was a human, she would be in her trailer watching T.V. talk shows and eating junk food, while Gus was out playing and getting a street education. Maybe Gus was just too much baby horse to keep up with and discipline. As a result, Gus is very confident and pretty fearless. He did not learn much in the way of social skills, however. That is where we tend to butt heads, both literally and figuratively. Underneath the street tough and goofiness though, he is just a little boy longing for attention and love. He needs to know he *matters*.

Soon it was time to breed Mamu. I sold a saddle on EBay to pay for the frozen semen I ordered from the owners of that beautiful, 100% color producing Knabstrupper stallion from Denmark. Since Artificial Insemination with frozen semen was a delicate procedure, I had to take her up to my vets' clinic to be bred. Gus jumped right in the trailer, happy to have an adventure. He was a wild child at the clinic, making friends with the barn help by kicking him in a very tender area. On Mamu's second unsuccessful trip to the clinic, they decided to turn Mamu and Gus out in a nice little paddock so he could run off some steam.

Unfortunately Mamu did not get in foal. My vet said her uterus did not like the material the frozen semen was floating around in.

And to think she had gotten pregnant with Gus on one trip to Gus's daddy! I looked at other local stallions with whom she could be bred using live semen, as the vet said that might work better than frozen. Nothing really caught my eye, and I was out of money anyway. The Knabstrupper babies of my dreams flew out my ears and galloped away.

Chapter Sixty-three

IT WAS TOUGH BEING A working student at that barn. And seeing life at the top of my sport? I *saw* it, all right. What I saw, heard, and *felt* was a bunch of very immature, competitive bullies who spent their days gossiping about everyone else. What a bunch of backbiters. They did take excellent physical care of the horses, in the sense that they looked after them as the valuable athletes that they were. At least I was working for Ciaran's trainer and not the Olympic team member. Ciaran's trainer was intense and wound up, but she didn't gossip. She just kept her head down and worked at a furious pace so she could get out of there as quickly as possible. She was impossible to please, no matter how hard I tried. She complained about how slow I was, even though if I went any faster I would upset the horses or I would have had to run everywhere I went, like a Les Schwab employee!

An old client called me one day and asked if I was interested in returning to her farm to help with her horses. I was surprised she called me. I had started her huge gorgeous Percheron gelding, an absolutely beautiful Percheron-Warmblood cross and her small Akal-Teke. They were quite diverse, but everything went fine. When I went to her barn I had to go catch the horses in the pasture, groom and tack them up myself. Often they were wet and muddy. It took so much time that I excused myself from coming back as graciously as possible. I thought she was mad at me. Maybe she was a year ago, but now she wanted me to come back and start another draft-cross youngster and keep working with her two big boys. She had sold her Akal Teke.

I thought hard about it. Maybe I could quit Starbucks. That job was driving me crazy. My boss had sent me off to a quieter store to get more experience at a less frantic pace. That was kind of him, but it humiliated me. In a little while he loaned me out to another Starbucks to fill in some holes. I absolutely hated it there. I didn't think the other girls liked me very much. I had been so excited when I got hired, but I felt awful that I couldn't get the hang of it and settle into a rhythm. I was harder on myself than my boss and co-workers ever were. They were trying to help me, but I felt too ashamed that I was too slow and made too many mistakes. I wanted to be the *best*, of course.

When it came time for me to go back to the original store that hired me, I did not feel welcome there at all. It seemed as if they didn't want me back. I quit Starbucks and went back to work for the lady with the draft horses.

I enjoyed riding her horses very much. I started her young horse, a lovely Percheron-Thoroughbred cross from Cancaid Farm up in Saskatchewan, Canada, and put her other two back to work. I took her beautiful Percheron-Warmblood cross to the trainer I was working for a couple of times. He was awesome to ride in lessons. I loved riding her huge black full Percheron. I decided I really was meant to be in the horse business. Starbucks was so disappointing; I felt like a huge failure, but at least it showed me that I needed to stick with riding and teaching. I had considered leaving the horse business for awhile.

Jazz did *not* get any better. I learned to ride with very heavy aids. Jazz *hated* it. By the end of a dressage lesson he felt pretty amazing, but I was exhausted. The jumping didn't improve at all. Riding became all about strength and dominance; it was making me very sore and tired. I became too heavy with my hands. My client's horses were practically impossible for me to ride that way. They were huge and incredibly strong. I had been traveling to a client's barn to ride her horses, but she fired me for making bit rubs on one of her young horse's mouths.

It took me awhile to get the picture, but I *finally* began to see. When a client's horse viciously bit the trainer on her side as she rushed in impatiently to fix some tack she thought I was putting on incorrectly,

I knew I had to get out of there. Shortly thereafter I got a call from the agitated woman, and we both agreed that I should quit. That's when I thought I should quit *life*, period. I had no seriously good students anymore; not very many students at *all*. Jazz wouldn't event, my marriage was old ashes, and I felt distant from my kids. I didn't understand God at all. I wanted to kill myself. I wasn't particularly worried about going to hell; life as I knew it was hellish enough. I hoped death was a relief.

Chapter Sixty-four

I took Jazz to my favorite place to ride, Bridle Trails, one last time. After that I was gonna figure out how to do myself in. I wanted one last ride on my horse in the beautiful green forest. When I got done with my ride and I was untacking Jazz back at my trailer I ran into a friend from my old Equifriends days. She told me about a Parelli-educated trainer who was looking for someone to help her who had experience with Eventing. She asked me for my phone number and I gave it to her, thinking I' be dead before the trainer called, *if* she called. But early the next morning I got a call from her, wanting to know if I could come to her barn. That afternoon. I was surprised and said okay. I hadn't yet figured out how I wanted to "off" myself yet anyway.

After a barn tour and chatting a bit, the trainer let me know she was a Christian believer. We had an awful lot in common. One of her goals was to have an at-risk program. I hadn't forgotten about my dreams for the same thing since my experience at the Evergreen Classic. I burst into tears. We sat on the tailgate of my truck and talked for a couple of hours. I ended up running headfirst into God during our visit. While talking with this amazing woman I had a vision. I saw myself as a sport-horse type mare turned out in a beautiful pasture. It had perfect grass, perfect shelter and shade trees, ample clear water and was surrounded by perfect ultra-safe horse fence. I knew I had sustained a serious injury, like a bowed tendon or torn suspensory ligament. I had been turned out for a long time to rest and heal. I was content in that lovely place, but somehow I knew I had more to do. Then Jesus showed up with a halter and lead rope. He opened the gate. I went to Him, so happy to see Him. He very lovingly put the halter on my lowered head. "Time to go back to work," said Jesus. And we walked through the gate together. End of vision.

Obviously God did *not* want me to kill myself. For six months I worked for this wonderful woman who embraced my wounded soul and tried to teach me the Parelli method; I was lousy with the carrot stick. I taught some lessons for her and rode some of the horses there. She also helped me with Jazz a little bit. I continued working at my client's place. I was being loved and healed by my Heavenly Daddy. I rode the horses with much lighter aids. My poor arms recovered, and so did the horses' mouths. My heart recovered and returned to God. I was amazed at the turn of events; that He had intervened in such a powerful way. I apologized profusely for feeding my ego with the money Caleb was making. I was using it to try to get a toehold on the competitive horse show world. I had turned from resting and trusting in Him and forged out on my own, trusting in the power of money. You cannot serve both.

Chapter Sixty-five

BACK AT NORTHWIND FARM, GUS was steadily growing and learning a few manners. He learned not to punch me in the face with his forefeet, and how to behave on a halter and lead. He learned to have his face clipped. In fact, he loved the hum and vibration of the motor so much he would extend his neck so I would clip his under jaw. He still does that, funny boy that he is. In early fall it would be time to wean him. Mimi asked me if I wanted her to sell Mamu for me because she was seventeen and barren. She knew I hated selling horses, and she was much better at it than I. I told Mimi *yes, please do.*

Mimi had purchased 6 draft-cross weanlings from Cancaid Farm. The Canadian farm had shipped a lot of their young stock down from Saskatchewan to Indiana to be sold at an Amish horse and buggy auction. They could be purchased at the sale or online. Mimi bought them on-line from her computer. Most of them were purchased for around five hundred dollars, and a few for three hundred. They were nice weanlings. Some were half thoroughbred, half-draft, and some were three-quarter Thoroughbred, one fourth draft. Mimi went for the extra thoroughbred blood, as they were more refined. After the auction Mimi and her husband headed to Indiana with their big trailer. Once there they stuffed all their new weanlings in it and hauled them back to Washington. These babies got named as Sean and Mimi drove through different states and cities on the way back to the Pacific Northwest. Memphis got named as they drove through Tennessee. Roslyn, a beautiful bay filly, got named for a little town in the Cascade Mountains of Washington State.

They more or less fell out of Sean and Mimi's trailer when they got back and we herded them into a small, safe paddock for a few days. Then it was time to move them into a pasture with a loafing shed, where they would live until they were sold or ready to be started under saddle. We had to figure out the best way to do it. None were trained to be led, and most wouldn't let you anywhere near them. They all wore mangy rope halters with a little snub of a rope dangling from the end so at least you could *try* to grab one. Three or four of us herded them out the paddock gate to the indoor arena, through a gate to the outdoor arena, then through another gate to the pasture. There's an old cowboy song that goes, *"they were wild and wooly and full of fleas"* … which best describes the scenario. Memphis was the only one that let us catch him, and hanging on to him fell to me. His huge dark eyes were full of fear, but he was very calm in the midst of chaos. Right then and there I decided if I were ever able to buy one of those weanlings, I would choose Memphis.

All those babies grew into sturdy yearlings. Memphis ended up being the runt of the litter and last in the pecking order. He looked pretty disheveled and sad most of the time. He also reminded me of *Eeyore* a little bit, like Dexter did. I felt sorry for him.

Gus, on the other hand, was looking truly gorgeous. He was built like his mamma. I loved his look and the fact the he was pretty fearless. Even though my vet had predicted he would be small, he was a big boy for a six month old colt. I decided to keep him.

Mimi sold Mamu to a very nice woman in Eastern Washington who was going to pasture breed her. She had several stallions of different breeds. She had seen a picture of Gus alongside Mamu and bought her based on Gus's good looks. Mimi doubled my money and earned herself a small commission.

I didn't want to wean Gus alone. Mimi had not had any foals born that year for Gus to possibly hang out with. I had seen what happens when you take away a baby from its momma and it has to be alone. They don't do well at all. I needed a buddy for Gus. I contemplated Mimi's draft-cross yearlings. I had a bit of credit with Mimi for starting some of her other youngsters. Memphis was the smallest and the cheapest. The others seemed too huge to put with a weanling and they were more expensive. Besides, I had always been partial to him since the day I led him from paddock to pasture.

Caleb said we could pay the remainder of his price tag after Mimi deducted what she owed me. Shy, pot-bellied, scruffy little Memphis became my new baby boy.

Mamu's new owner came to pick her up. She waited patiently while I tried to catch Memphis for about an hour. Once I finally got him, Memphis let me lead him to the barn. Mamu left Gus without a backward glance or even a nicker and hopped into the trailer. I slipped Memphis in with Gus, and they were too busy checking each other out for Gus to worry about his mama leaving.

Those two young boys got along really well. Soon I moved them over to my friend Stella Fenwick's farm so that they could have plenty of turnout space to play and graze. Stella is the grandma of two of my past students. Gwen is now a college graduate and a beautiful upper level event rider. Her plucky cousin Raina took lessons when she wasn't busy with basketball, soccer, softball, and who knows what else. Stella had a few fenced acres and a nice little barn. She and her husband, God rest his soul, had trained Morgan horses in their younger days. Her pretty little farm was perfect for the boys to just be boys and hang out for a year or two. Gus hopped right in my trailer with a *let's go!* look on his face. Memphis was hesitant, but since his pal Gus was so confident, eventually he got in, too.

I would go out to Stella's every few days to check on them and deliver hay and grain. At least once a week I would groom them and take them for walks around the pasture. They learned to tie, have their feet picked up, and get clipped. Gus still loved the hum and feel of the clipper vibration. Memphis was really good about it too, but you couldn't get the clippers near the front of his muzzle. Everywhere else was fine, but that place was off limits! I wonder if it was really tickly, or some trauma had occurred in that area. There were no scars or disfigurement, so who knows? *Only God.* I am happy to report that as I write this Memphis lets me clip his muzzle without a fuss.

They stayed at Stella's for about a year, where they had the pleasure of becoming geldings. I moved them to my draft horse client's farm so I could handle them more and eventually start them under saddle, as she had decent facilities including a pretty nice round pen. Stella had been an entirely sweet and gracious host, and I didn't want to take advantage of her. I also wanted to consolidate my horses and stop spending so much time driving from place to place. Her neighbors had a nice round pen, and they were open to the idea of me using it, but I couldn't figure out the logistics of going over there without someone to help me. It would not do to separate those two buddies and take one to a strange place and expect him to concentrate on work, especially in sight of his best and only pal!

It was manageable working at Mimi's, the Parelli trainer's and my client's for awhile. It seemed a lot less crazy than working for Starbucks, driving to Duvall to work for the eventing trainer and working out of Northwind Farm. It was still a lot of driving around, but a lot less stressful. Gus and Memphis loved being at their new place. The grass in their large paddock was about three feet tall. They could go in and out of their stalls at will. They were both growing into very attractive young men. I started calling them *Punk Boys,* because their swaggering attitude reminded me of the teenage boys I saw sauntering around town near the high school with their baseball caps on backwards and their baggy pants hanging halfway down their behinds.

I asked my client if she would ever consider opening up her barn to the public again. She had done that at one time, but dealing with her boarders had driven her crazy. I told her I would cover her back and help her run her barn as an experienced horse person who had been in the business for awhile. She was tentative, but said yes. I told her what she needed to do to get her barn and arenas useable and safe, and offered to help with the work. My plan was to bring Jazz and Shadow over to join the young boys when it was ready.

My client and I worked everything out on paper regarding the trade.

It seemed pretty good. That winter, with all the snow, the roof for the stabling on one side of the arena collapsed. Thank God it was not the side my boys were on! My landlord's construction company, needing work, came to replace they roof, but they were so ridiculously expensive my client found another company a whole lot cheaper, and they did a great job.

She removed the old dirt in the indoor and I helped her pay for new sand. It was a huge improvement though neither arena was truly level. I cleaned up my side of the arena where my horses had their stalls. I brought in tons of gravel to keep their adjoining paddock free of mud. I bought and hauled in sand in for the round pen; at least around the edges so we could work horses without them slipping and falling. I cleaned out the sheds on both ends of the arena. I cleaned out and painted the tackroom. Caleb and I bought lots of electric fencing and helped fix the paddocks for our horses and future boarders.

Around January, things were more or less ready, and I brought over Shadow and Jazz. Shortly thereafter, my friends who used to board at Mimi's decided to bring their three horses over to board and take lessons. *Wa-la!* Instant business for both of us. Most of my students, what few I had at the time, came to continue lessons.

I started taking Centered Riding lessons from a lovely woman who was teaching one of my client's neighbors in the farm owner's arena. I learned to sit Jazz's trot a whole lot better. Not only did my sitting trot improve, my whole outlook did as well. I learned a ton from that wonderful instructor. She was, and is, a beacon of light and an unsung hero in the murky world of competitive horsemanship. I am sure all the horses I ride appreciate the gifts she gave me. They got ridden much more carefully and thoughtfully.

I also started riding with Sonya Masterton, a dressage instructor and advanced Certified N.A.R.A.H. instructor. I had been teaching her daughter how to ride for several months. We had been trading barn work for lessons, and now we were trading lessons for lessons. Even though I had my doubts that Sonya could help us much, she was magic for me and Jazz. She had a pretty strong dressage background; also what she had learned as a therapeutic instructor was invaluable help to loosen up my very tight muscles. We "got" each other. Sometimes we would hit snags, but I could actually talk to Sonya, and she always took time to listen. After that, our lesson would take on a "magical" feel. We began to progress nicely in dressage. I jumped Jazz a little bit just to keep him in the game. I wasn't sure exactly where we would end up as dance partners. I didn't want to sell him, especially with the economy in a huge slump. It didn't look like eventing was going to agree with Jazz, but I couldn't see how a little Appaloosa could possibly compete against those big, elegant warm bloods in dressage competitions.

In early summer I took Jazz to a little one-day event down at Northwest Equestrian Center in Rainier, Washington. I hadn't been down there in about three years. I entered "not to be judged" because I didn't know how things would go, and I really wanted a no-pressure, schooling type of situation.

His dressage test was so-so; a little tight and tense as usual. It didn't help that the rings were set up next to the cross-country warm up area and next to a dense tree-line. On the other side of the trees was a walking and biking trail that was spooking horses as people strolled or jogged or whizzed by on their bikes.

Later, as I walked the cross country course, I decided to ride the Novice course instead of Beginner Novice. Jazz had jumped those jumps so many times. Since I was schooling, I could pick and choose anyway. So could Jazz.

He was pretty bug-eyed in anticipation as we walked to the start box. But he jumped the first fence, and the second, and the third! He went in the water fine, but for some reason didn't want to jump the log out. He did on the next try, then we cantered over the path and down the hill to the next section of the course.

That's when trouble started. Jazz could see the stalls and horse trailers. He wanted to go get in his trailer and go home to his little herd. He started leaping in the air and bucking to get his point across. I abandoned all thought of jumping and make a concerted effort to stay on and get him galloping away from the trailers. We hopped, skipped, bucked, leaped, neighed, and galloped our way down the big hill to the second water complex. It took some coaxing to get him in the water but after that he jumped out fine and suddenly realized we were headed back to the stalls. He settled into a lovely gallop rhythm and jumped everything else beautifully. I was too blind to see it back then, but now I know Jazz just wanted to get back to his herd; his *family*. To do dressage alone away from home and to jump alone away from home causes major separation anxiety in Jazz. In addition to being such a handful on the cross-country course, he was a basket case in stadium jumping. He was such a handful I forgot the jump order and we disqualified. I gave up the idea of ever having a decent go on him again at an event. I couldn't bear the thought of selling my beautiful boy, though. I just kept on with lessons from Sonya and my Centered Riding instructor and told the Lord he would have to send me the perfect person who totally fell in love with Jazz. They would have to beg me to buy him for me to even consider it.

Chapter Sixty-six

MY FRIENDS BOARDING THREE HORSES at my client's farm ended up leaving at the end of summer, probably to avoid the inevitable mud that was coming with the fall rain. Two new boarders came, then a third, fourth and a fifth. I kept training all the farm owner's horses. I got my Punk Boys started under saddle. Memphis was three and I started Gus in the summer of his two year old year. That is young for a dressage or event horse, but everyone thought I should do him early before he got even bigger for his britches. The idea was to get him *started* under saddle, then give him six months off to grow and develop.

Memphis was such a good boy it didn't take long at all to get him going under saddle. When he was just shy of three years old I would throw my students up on him bareback for a few minutes. They were thrilled and Memphis didn't care. When it was time to start him more formally he and I started off in the round pen, then moved to the indoor. The only slightly naughty thing he ever did was push into me when I was standing on the mounting block preparing to mount. It was almost like he was trying to push me off! I had to nip that in the bud, but it showed up later in a comical sort of way.

Gus didn't take long at all to join up when I worked him at liberty. After all, I was his two-legged mom. He thought it was mostly play time anyway, and I finally figured out how to handle a carrot stick. Use it to whack Gus hard whenever he tried to crowd me! Actually he was pretty good except for trying to steal anything left hanging on the arena walls, especially blankets. Those were his favorites. I am lucky he didn't trash any blankets that weren't mine! Gus learned to wear a surcingle and a bridle. He learned to longe and long-line.

The bridling part was pretty interesting. Gus *hates* having his face held for any reason. One time I had the bridle nearly on when Gus whirled away and went bucking around the arena. The reins got tangled around his front legs. Gus kept bucking with his head held fast by the reins. Eventually stitches and studs started to pop and pieces of the bridle flew through the air. Finally his head was freed and he came to a stop with what was left of the bridle hanging lopsided on his head. He thought that whole episode was *awesome*. Fortunately it was an old bridle, and I was able to get the broken pieces fixed. I swear I could hear Gus laughing as I walked around the arena picking up the far-flung leather straps. So much for John Lyons, Pat Parrelli, or any of the other "Natural Horsemanship" gurus! Or traditional horsemanship, for that matter. Gus had his *own* brand of training. It was "One-*up*-man-ship".

I did get to the point where I thought I could get on Gus and survive … maybe. *So what did this girl do?*

One night, I just did it. I got a wild hair up my backside and just got on with a Parelli halter and lead---bareback. It just seemed like the time was right. I didn't have an agenda or anything; I didn't care whether he was tacked up or not. I have a great mounting box Rachel's dad built for me back in the Pebble Creek days. It is sturdy and tall and square, for all the little kids who needed a big boost. I brought Gus to it and he stood quietly chewing on the leather popper of the Parelli lead while I jumped up and down on the box. That didn't faze Gus. I leaned on him. No problem. I swung a leg over. He chewed a little harder. I sat there. He just stood there, enjoying his chew.

We repeated that over the next few days with the same results. Gus was a whole lot more interested in chewing the lead rope than whether or not I was on his back. In fact, it took some doing to get him to move out! He was way more interested in munching the end of the lead rope or the toe of my boot than working. I had to spank him to get him to go. He was offended, but he never tried to dump me. Gus mostly tried to grab the whip from my hand! He would have spanked me back, if he had gotten hold of it, no doubt. He was such a goofy and silly boy. It's just that he weighed around 1,000 lbs. and had a big bony head, very active teeth, and four hard hooves that were prone to invade my personal space.

I must have ridden him at least ten times bareback in the Parelli halter. We did our first couple of canters that way. About the third time Gus said, *Wheee!* and crow-hopped a little. It was time to ride him in a saddle. He had already gotten used to wearing one, but he was so comfortable to ride bareback I hadn't bothered. It was easier to bail too, if necessary, without a saddle. I started riding him with a bridle, although it was so much easier to slip a halter on. Sometimes we were both worn out before I ever got on. One thing about Gus: all the horsemanship books written, all the chapters about safety---they were written with a horse like Gus in mind. Gus makes you tow the line. With my other horses you can cheat a little; bend or even break the rules. Not so with Gus. I think maybe he has created a few *new* rules.

I ended up riding Gus lightly for a couple of more months, progressing to the outdoor arena and even the hacking track that circled the farm. The first time I got three-quarters of the way around before I had to bail because Gus threw a hissy fit. The second time I made it all the way around with an exciting interlude, but staying on. The third time was a charm. His canter work also improved drastically. He never reared or bucked; he never dumped me, although it seemed the thought was often in his lil' punkin' head. Soon it was time to give him another six months off, which is what you do when you start babies so young. About two months into Gus's sabbatical came *The Great Head Bonk*. Gus ended up having an extended vacation.

I started Memphis over fences and he was amazing. Memphis had put his big boy pants on so easily that I felt he was ready to go try a show. Some of my students were riding him in lessons without much fuss. Abelie DeFranco had come from Sequim to hang out for a week and jumped him beautifully. In June I took him to the Vashon Island Horse Trials along with Jazz. He was terrified but made it through.

In July I called Tiffani Loy. She was an Energy Healer highly recommended to me by Fedora Gleason, my animal communicator friend and author. I had been thinking for a very, *very* long time that I needed help; a life coach or shrink or something.

I wasn't quite sure what Energy Healing was, and I was a little leery of it because my Judeo-Christian background had trained me to be wary of such things, but I felt very strongly that I should go. Fedora had given me Tiffani's number a year ago and amazingly I ran across it one day while cleaning up clutter. I called and made an appointment. She worked out of her house, about an hour south from mine. I asked God if I was making a serious mistake to please give me a flat tire so I would miss my appointment, but I made it to Issaquah just fine.

Tiffani asked me if I had any questions. Boy did I *ever*. I confessed my doubts and apprehensions about receiving this kind of treatment, especially if it was in conflict with my beliefs. Tiffani was very gentle and patiently explained that Energy Healing *was* God, because He *is* energy. He is in all things, in fact He *is* all things! She asked me what I hoped to get out of the healing sessions. I told her that I felt like my legs were stuck in concrete blocks and I couldn't get anywhere. I felt particularly stuck in my relation-ship to God, my relationship to Caleb, and in my business. None of them were going anywhere.

The session we had was very simple and restful, with me laying on a massage table listening to lovely music. Tiffani said my chakras went easily back into place. I didn't even know what chakras were back then, but I do now. I asked her if I needed to come back, and she smiled and said "you'll know if you need too."

Right away my business started to pick up. A few weeks later, August 7th to be exact, came "The Great Head Bonk." The rest is history. *His* story.

PART TWO

Dreams Really Do
Come True

Chapter Sixty-seven

AROUND THE TIME I STARTED riding again and going up to Trinity Farrier School, I drove my truck to Murphy to do a little shopping. That was the farthest I'd driven so far, and it was the first time back in traffic. I was a little nervous. It meant I had to drive East on U.S. 2, which is a dangerous two-lane highway, and negotiate a busy business section with lots of cars and lots of interesting and challenging turning lanes even for drivers without a head injury.

I got in my truck, buckled up and turned out of our driveway. I prayed non-stop the whole way to town. I pulled into the Fred Meyer parking lot and breathed a prayer of thanksgiving. Then I had to go to the bathroom really badly. I wasn't too far from the store doors so I thought I could make it to their restrooms. As I got out of my truck I suddenly had to squat and wiggle to keep from wetting my pants. I had been incontinent when I was in the hospital, but I was slowly getting back to normal. Not normal enough to go to Murphy, I guess! As I sat there wiggling and praying for grace, I looked up and saw a big crow on top of a light post looking back at me. Crows are so very common in store parking lots, but this one seemed significant. It seemed I had a visitation from this crow. We held each other's gazes for a few moments. Then I recovered enough to walk into the store. I made it to the restroom.

I hadn't been in a Fred Meyer or any type of store in so long, I decided to look around a bit. While in the ladies clothing section, I got a call on my cell phone. It was my old friend Kerry Westfield from my Pebble Creek Stables days. She lived across the road from Pebble Creek and her daughter had taken lessons from me and was in the Pony Club, so we went way back. We had kept in touch over the years. She had been out to the house and met all my horses a time or two.

She was calling to offer me a horse. Not just *any* horse, but a draft-cross filly from Cancaid Farm in Saskatchewan, Canada. She said she had one too many horses and this filly seemed more of an event type horse than a dressage prospect, which was her passion. She had met Memphis and knew he was from the same farm. She knew how much I liked him and all the Cancaid farm youngsters I had worked with. Would I like to have the filly, for free?

Would I? I started bubbling and squeaking all over the place. I tried to keep it together so I hid myself a little in the clothing racks. Kerry asked in a concerned voice, "Are you alright?" When I could talk, I told her about my dream of having a filly from Cancaid Farm, as they bred such nice, beautiful horses. When I was still at my draft horse client's we used to talk about going up to Saskatchewan to have a look at Cancaid Farm's current foal crop. We talked about how wonderful it would be to buy a filly or two we could breed when they were old enough. Cancaid Farm had a nice website where you could go and look at videos of all their horses. My client and I would both look on it from time to time and dream, but the last time I went on-line to look their website said they had gone out of business! My client and I were devastated. But here was Kerry offering me a Cancaid Farm filly! For free! *Would* I?

By the grace of God I did not wet my pants right then and there in the ladies section of Fred Meyer, but tears of joy fell on some of the clothing. Somehow I made it back to the truck, still bubbling and squeaking and praising God. My last challenge before heading home was to park at a local gas station to get some gas. I had whacky concerns of running into a gas pump and causing a huge explosion. It was quite a busy place with cars constantly coming in and out. I seldom went there because my truck was hard to maneuver in the tight gas pump area. I think I went there just to see if I could do it. I pulled up to the pumps without a hitch and made sure it was diesel I was pumping and not gasoline. I had made that sorry mistake before in my old Ford. After I got the fuel going I looked up to see a Chevy Silverado that looked just like mine except for the color. It was the same year, slightly banged up, and missing its tail gate, just like mine. I looked at the guy pumping diesel into it. He was a big guy with long hair and overalls. Was it God in a different Bad Out-*Fit?* Our eyes met. I so wanted to say something and I got ready to do it, but the guy seemed shy and looked away. It didn't matter. I knew.

I drove home very exhilarated and excited. Not only had I successfully driven to town, but I didn't wet my pants! I had been visited by a mysterious crow! I had been given a Cancaid Farm filly! I had seen God in one of His Bad Out-*Fits!* I looked up crows on a website about animal totems. After I read about them I knew I was not imagining things about the crow in the Fred Meyer parking lot. I don't think I imagined what I saw at the gas pump either. Whew. Going to Murphy that day was *A Magical Mystery Tour.*

A few days later I went to Kerry's house to meet my new filly. *What* a cutie. She also looked like a pretty pink cupcake, like Gwen's old pony, and she had a beautiful, almost Arabian-shaped head like him too. She was ¼ Percheron, ¾ Thoroughbred like Memphis. Her dad, Khatef, who traces back to Man O' War, was one of the new young stallion prospects standing at Cancaid Farm. If she is any indication of the quality foals he sires, whoever has him now should be very pleased with the children he sires.

We had a full house at our barn at home, and our landlords had told us *no more horses unless you pay more money,* so I didn't bring her home right away. Kerry was very gracious to hang on to her and I told her we might start looking for a different place to live and keep the horses. I helped with the filly's feed bill whenever I could. When Kerry gave me the filly's registration papers I was absolutely thrilled to see that she was related to both Memphis and Gus through Mr. Prospector. What fun! I had a little blood-related horse family! Those three were first and second cousins. Kerry had named her Cara Mia, but I wanted a different name; something Irish, even though her recent thoroughbred ancestry was thoroughly American, and Percherons originated in France.

A beautiful book we have on Irish myths and legends, *The Names Upon the Harp* written by Marie Heaney and illustrated by P.J. Lynch, showed up in the bathroom one day. Caleb or one of the kids must have uncovered it in the clutter and put in the "potty reading" stack. One day I read the story of the Children of Lir, from the Mythological Cycle. Lir was a king from the north and had four children whom he dearly loved; Fionnualla, Aed, Conn, and Fiacra. Fionnualla was his oldest; a daughter, and she looked after her younger brothers, for their mother had died when the children were very young.

After a time king Lir remarried. His new wife Aoife became very jealous of Lir's love for his children. With a druid's wand she turned them all into beautiful white swans with amazing singing voices. Fionnuala begged Aoife for mercy; particularly that she and her brothers be released from the enchantment at some point before they died. Aoife condemned them to 900 years of being swans, migrating every 300 years to different bodies of water. At the end of that time a king from the north would marry a queen from the south, a bell would ring out a new era of faith, and their exile would be over.

The swan children bore out their long imprisonment with stoic patience and endurance. Their story became legend. St. Patrick came and spread Christianity over Ireland, replacing the old mythological religions. A hermit monk named Mochaomhog knew the swans' legend and realized that the time of their exile would soon be over. He came to the island of Inish Glora, near the swans' final destination in a quiet cove off the Atlantic sea, and built a church. Mochaomhog prayed every morning and rang a bronze bell, hoping the swans would hear and respond. Fionnuala heard the bell and began to sing for joy, for she new that the pealing of the bell signaled the end of the 900 year enchantment.

Mochaomhog heard her singing and went down to the water's edge. He called to the swans to come and shelter with him. They trustingly approached the shore and went to live with Mochaomhog in his hut. He put silver chains around their necks, linking them together so that they would never again be parted.

Soon a king from the north married a queen from the south, King Lairgren sent a soldier to Inish Glora to fetch the swans as a wedding gift for his new queen. Mochaomhog refused to let them go, so the soldier tried to drag the terrified swans from the hut by the silver chain. In the ensuing struggle the swan plumage fell away and there laid four very frail old people. At the end of their 900 year enchantment and exile, they had returned to who they really were.

Mochaomhog rushed to comfort them. Even though they were soon to cross over, they were deeply happy and content. Fionnuala asked that their kind friend bury them when they had departed. Mochaomhog did as Fionnuala requested, and raised a large stone over their grave.

So now you know how Fionnuala got her name. We call her Finny for short. Or Filly. Have she and her brothers returned as *horses?* Am I their Mochaomhog? For sure as the days are long and the Puget Sound area is wet, they can stay with me as long as they like.

Chapter Sixty-eight

When I began driving back and forth from Trinity Farrier School a 10 acre piece of property just below it came on the real estate market. My ears pricked and my heart beat faster when I saw the For Sale sign. I had always liked that property and thought it would be so neat to live there. Part of its pasture fence line bordered Trinity, and it had that same, majestic view of the Snohomish River Valley and the Olympic Mountain range. It came with a nice house, a nice outdoor arena, and a separate 5-bay garage that could easily be converted into a stable.

We had tried to buy horse property a few years after Caleb got his promotions at Arby's®. We found a couple places we liked a lot; we actually qualified to buy them, but the real estate market was so hot we kept getting outbid. It was crazy. People were fighting over property like little kids over toys. Discouraged, we quit looking and wondered if maybe God did not want us to be home owners. Many years ago it seemed like God had shown me a scripture in Leviticus about the priests of Israel who were not allowed to own property. (Leviticus 18; 20-23 NASB) Was God reminding us about that scripture now? We somehow had never gotten around to acting very priestly.

The guy who owned the property on the way to Trinity Farrier School was someone I had known since our Pebble Creek Stables days, as he and his wife had boarded their horses there. I *just happened* to run into him at the hardware store and asked him about it. He was super nice, super friendly, and super spiritual. I didn't know that about him. I knew he had been through an unpleasant divorce. I wonder if he hadn't found Jesus through it all, or if he'd always been a believer.

He gave me the lowdown on the land. He had spent a lot of money refurbishing the house and putting in a professional quality arena with proper drainage and footing. Then the recession hit. His roofing business wasn't making enough money to cover his payments, as this property was in addition to his very nice property right next door, where his ex-wife still lived. His parting words to me were, "Hey, if it's meant to be, you'll get it!" My feelings *exactly*. He also told us to use Owen Flanders as our real estate agent. I had never met Owen, but his office is right on the corner of where Highway 2 meets our road. Caleb felt God say "**YES**" when I told him about Owen---and away we went. I walked down to his office one day and introduced myself. I told him what we wanted to do and had no idea if we could buy the property or not. With Owen's help we looked into pre-qualifying for it, and wonder of wonders, we did.

The now-depressed real estate market was definitely in our favor. That and the fact that Caleb had held a steady job with a good income for some time. That, and the fact that I worked really hard to fix our credit, even though at times it seemed like a lost cause. I used to say to myself, "We need to fix this in case we ever *do* get to buy a farm." That and the voice of my momma in my head about the need to have good credit and how to manage it wisely.

My heart starting beating a ***Va-va voom! Hooty-hoo! Lub-Dub.***

But we didn't get that property. There were two other offers in line ahead of us. Sale of the property had come to a halt, as work on the septic needed to be done before the sale could go through. Caleb and I thought God was stalling the sale long enough for us to get our ducks in a row. But just a few days before Christmas, the sign came down and the new owners moved right in.

Needless to say, we were taken aback. Lots of thoughts bombarded my head---was I *really* hearing from God? Was I so head-injured that I was imagining His voice, His leading? Was I *crazy*? Was I just supposed to work at Trinity, and were we supposed to stay where we were renting? Was the verse in Leviticus showing up again?

I was thoroughly "under the pile." It's when you are just kind of sad and depressed; maybe a little angry and stressed. But I didn't feel *too* bad. I didn't come completely unraveled the way I used to.

Owen kept telling us we needed to go see this other place outside Murphy, but we weren't that interested. We just weren't thrilled with Murphy. It just seemed so right to stay near our current place where God let me off the train, near Trinity Farrier School, with that fabulous view. There was a 6-acre property on the northeast side of Trinity's driveway that was for sale. I can't tell you how many times I had driven past it; close to a thousand probably, because it was on the way to Northern Lights Farm. It was also on the way to shopping in Murphy. It also on the way to Evergreen State Fairgrounds, where the kids showed their horses in 4-H when they were younger. We went every year to the Evergreen Fair in the fall. Colleen Maera came with the grandkids to go to Fair the when I ended up in the hospital. I didn't get to go that year, but I did get to go on a really cool train ride.

I was drawn to those 6 acres. In days past when I drove by, there would often be a little girl lying on the back of her old gray Arabian while he munched grass or snoozed in the sun. Though I had never met the little girl, I *loved* her for the way she obviously loved her horse. I wished I could give her riding lessons. I just *knew* she was a kindred soul. I passed that scene for a few years and watched the girl grow bigger and her horse grow older. They still had quiet times together in the pasture. I often thought about stopping by to speak with her parents about teaching her. I was a chicken, so I never did. Her horse got older and older and over time became frail and very thin, and then he was gone. After a while the family was gone too, and the blackberries took over the pasture and the house fell into disrepair. I always wondered what had become of them.

Owen took us up to look at that property. It had that same amazing view. The house was now condemned. It had belonged to the little girl's grandparents who had gone on the train to heaven. The girl's mom had lived there for awhile and then left in a hurry, leaving her stuff and trash everywhere. The house and the little barn would have to be torn down and new ones built. The pasture would have to be restored and new fencing put up. Soon the city of Murphy would annex it into its city limits, and we weren't sure what restrictions on livestock would come with the annexation. We sadly turned away from it.

Owen finally succeeded in taking us to the place he really wanted us to see southeast of Murphy. It was in a floodplain near the Snoqualmie River. It was just down the street from a dairy farm, which can smell very ripe at times, but it was a lovely. It was on the backside of Lord Hill, with an awesome view of the Cascades to the east. You could see this little knobby mini-mountain that was unique and we all had fallen in love with over the years right out the kitchen and living room windows. We have always called it *Knob Hill*. It was easy access for us to get to other places, like Seattle, and for potential customers to get to us.

The house was beautiful, huge and built to last forever. The land was perfect for livestock keeping and growing stuff. The house was elevated above the floodplain enough to not require insurance. However, it was priced higher than what we qualified for and we would have to bring in lots of fill dirt to build a barn. Not only build a barn but fence the whole property, *and* put in an arena. Hmmm.

So what did this girl do? I contacted my dear friend Cayanna who had been steadfastly at my side during my long stay in the hospital. She had been tragically widowed a few years ago. Her wonderful husband and father of their beautiful children died while waiting for a second liver transplant. His own liver had contracted Hepatitis C from a dirty needle in a vaccination gun when Edward was a young man in the Merchant Marines.

Cayanna had her own health issues that made her more than a little fragile. I wanted to look after her. We had talked with her about renting the mother-in-law apartment of the first place we tried to buy south of Trinity, and eventually letting her buy a little piece of the property and building a house. She'd been renting a little house ever since Edward died, as she had to sell their house to pay astronomical hospital and doctor bills for both of them *and* their daughter Meredith, who had diabetes. Her kids wanted to use some of their money they inherited from their grandma to help Cayanna buy her own home. We asked her if she wanted to go property shopping with us.

She said "*Yep!,* I'm game". Not only did we take her to see the place I just mentioned, we took her all over! We spent the whole day with Cayanna and Owen traipsing around mid-Snohomish County looking at property. Here was this woman who has been near death's door several times with severe respiratory problems, who had been chronically lame, who had three major joint replacements because all the prednisone she took for her breathing issues ate up her joints … and who has had her heart so dashed on the rocky coast of life because of losing her wonderful Edward. Here was his beloved wife, cheerfully hobbling around, climbing up and down stairs, over rough ground, around and over peoples' messes they had left behind. Cayanna is an *extraordinary* example of God's healing and restoration.

In the midst of looking at all these properties, Caleb thought it would be a good idea for him to get back into organic farming. He only had a couple more years until he could retire from Arby's®. Since we had dabbled in it before up in Maine, he thought he might as well get back into it seeing as we were going to be living on a farm. That made me so very happy, as he hadn't been that excited about buying a place when I started talking about it. He was thinking he would spend the next two years working and building up the farm on his days off. It sounded like a great plan to me.

We looked at lots of pretty cool places. They were all nearly perfect, but each of them was missing something or had something that wasn't quite right. Either the house was great or the land was great, or both were great but the location wasn't.

We looked at this one place that seemed magically absurd but magically wonderful at the same time. The house looked like a huge barn; more like Noah's ark. The house was 7,500 square feet! Caleb and I, Cayanna, our kids, her kids, and all our combined pets could easily fit with room for more. It was so big we thought we would need an intercom or at least walkie-talkies to find each other and not get lost. There was room after room after room, including two bedroom lofts up flights of stairs. They each had great big windows looking out on absolutely amazing mountain views. To top it off, it was on twenty acres with access to 4,500 acres of DNR land; trail riding heaven.

When Owen looked at the house with us, he kept exclaiming *bizarre!* under his big mustache. Caleb, Cayanna and I kept exclaiming *cool!* I kept thinking of how much fun our kids would have had growing up in this house of many rooms and hidden passageways and stairways to heaven. What I thought was *truly* bizarre was that two years ago it was appraised at over $800,000.00, but now it was down to $550,000.00. Too expensive for Caleb and I, but doable if Cayanna partnered with us. It was an awful lot of work, because the house wasn't finished and the land was raw and mostly wooded. It didn't seem very practical, especially for old duffers like us.

I finished the day with my head brimming with all the properties we had looked at. It seemed we hadn't seen "the one" yet. I was wondering if we weren't on some time-consuming wild goose chase. After all, that property near our house that came up for sale didn't require hoofing all over looking at property like "normal" people! I felt like God was going to give it to us in His own unique way, not by looking, and looking, and looking, and looking. I hate shopping, anyway.

I put the whole idea to rest for a few days. I got very busy taking care of the horses, riding, and teaching, but every morning when I woke up that big, crazy Noah's Ark house kept popping into my head. One day I drove out with Maeve just to show her the outside of the house. I got Owen to show us the inside again a few days later. Maeve fell in love with it and so did I. I spent the next few days visualizing all the ways it *could* work.

Finally I arranged with Owen for Cayanna to bring her kids out. Caleb and I brought Enya and Ryan. Maeve drove in with a friend. They all loved it, even Enya, who was diametrically opposed to moving anywhere. She fell in love with a purple bedroom and said *fine by me*! Maeve and her friend walked around all starry-eyed. We spent about 3 hours there dreaming and planning. Cayanna's kids seemed okay with the idea. Now it seemed like maybe this place *was* The One.

I pondered God's plans. What was He up to now? Very early that morning I had a vision of me being a small child and walking with God as He held my hand to make sure I wouldn't trip over stuff and fall and skin my knee. I felt very small and stayed quiet all day as I thought of that vision.

When we spent that one day property shopping with Owen, we looked at a place up in Sultan, about 20 minutes east of Snohomish. I thought it was kind of silly to go out there as it was too far out in the boonies to attract customers, both for a CSA and to ride. Most people in that area grew their own livestock and vegetables, and they "grew their own" as well! If they liked horses, they tended to keep one in their backyard and ride Western in the nearby Cascade foothills, not learn what they considered stuffy English style riding in an arena.

That property was nice and had some decent features, but we knew it wasn't *The One*. As we were leaving I looked out the kitchen window and started to bubble and squeak. Through the window I saw the exact same mountain scene I viewed as I sat on my new horse Velvet in the outdoor arena of Equifriends twenty years ago. I was riding her outside for the first time on a sunny summer day. I was so overwhelmed with joy and thanksgiving I had to stop riding and worship God as I looked at the gorgeous snow capped mountains. It was that very same scene I was looking at now. Psalm 121 says, *"I will lift up my eyes to the mountains, from where does my help come? My help comes from the Lord, who made heaven and earth. He will not allow your foot to slip; he who keeps you will not slumber."* I had set it to music many years ago. I sang that Psalm to the Lord over and over as I sat on my beautiful mare that God gave me. I wept with utter gratitude. It was one of the biggest "God moments" of my life. As I looked through the kitchen window of that house in Sultan, I felt again the wonder and joy of that summer afternoon.

Chapter Sixty-nine

WE DECIDED TO PURSUE BUYING "Noah's Ark". Owen advised all three of us to find a good lawyer. We needed a contract and an LLC with a good exit strategy drawn up in case human nature took over or something drastic happened, because it does, you know. We also had to meet with the neighbors to find out if our plans for a small farm and riding school fit in with the neighborhood covenant. I was ready to get on with things full speed ahead. I called Cayanna just to make sure she and her kids were fully ready to proceed, all flags flying.

They weren't. The whole vastness of it had given them cold feet. The Ark was too big, too unfinished and the land too raw. That was all perfectly true and all their decisions were perfectly practical, but oh *man*, was I in for some more burying. I felt so sure that that place was IT. I said *"okay"* in a frail little voice, and promised to keep in touch.

Oy Vey. Major Ferklumpedness!

Was I totally missing God? *No, I knew I wasn't.* Did I want to feel a little frustrated with Cayanna's kids and their decision? Sure! *But I knew I shouldn't.* Like an injured dog I curled up to rest and lick my wounds for a few days. That's what I told Owen when he called wondering what he should do next. After a few days of licking my soul wounds and God pouring His healing balm on them, I recovered.

That Sunday Len went to Owen's office and they did internet search for properties. I contacted two more families, the Finches and DeFrancos, whom I had reunited with in a very warm, strong way after my head bonk.

I have always said that if "the balloon goes up" the people I most wanted with me in the trenches were Teagan and Celia. We were such good friends and spiritual "sistahs" back in the Woodland Farm, Wooden Nickel Farm, and Northern Lights Farm days. Those two women had followed me loyally through all the good and bad times of being at those barns. I adored their horse crazy children. They were good friends of Cayanna too, and had always been generous when I tried to raise money for the Cayanna's family's' health issues and resulting financial struggles. Teagan told me that as she was in church praying one day she saw a vision of her, Cayanna, and me together. That was around the same time Caleb and I started looking earnestly for a farm. Neither the Finches nor the DeFrancos were in a position to buy a farm with us, but it was fun to reconnect over it.

I had a dream about God throwing a ball for his buds, which happened to be a bunch of golden retrievers. God was having a great time and so were his furry friends. I saw Him throw the ball with that same easy grace and amazing strength that I saw on the train. The pups joyfully took turns fetching the ball; then they would all galumph back to God and lay it at His feet. Over and over they played the game, with joy and zeal and love.

Suddenly I realized that the dream was about our farm-hunting adventure! The pack of retrievers represented all the folks God has connected and reconnected in this epic adventure. Somehow I think we *will* be reconnected as this exciting drama plays out. Not only did God have a ball to throw to his faithful companions, He also had one up his sleeve! *Heh, heh, heh.*

Stay tuned.

There will no doubt be a sequel to this book.

Before long I was rested up and ready for God to throw the ball again. He threw it to an absolutely amazing place. One chilly winter Saturday Owen took us to look at several properties an hour north and northeast of us in incredibly beautiful country. It seems to me the farther away you live from the Seattle area, the more beautiful and peaceful it becomes. The people are nicer, too. Could it be to do with the fact that they have to work hard to earn a buck and they have less money than their neighbors to the south? It could be to do with the fact that there is less traffic, less noise, less pressure. Who knows? *Only God knows.*

We started an hour northeast and worked our way back south. We looked at so-so houses and barns with interesting land, interesting homes with so-so barns and land, and everything in between. It got to be late afternoon and I was getting cold and tired. Our last stop was an abandoned equestrian center in bankruptcy court. It had a tiny but darling cedar home, a huge indoor arena with 42 stalls, a huge outdoor arena, and a stallion barn with 12 stalls. There was a studio apartment with a big window looking over the indoor arena and another window to look over the barn aisle. There was a cozy viewing room for parents and owners. There were men's and lady's bathrooms with showers. There was a horse laundry room with a washer and dryer. There was a barn kitchen. There was a wonderful grooming, tacking, and bathing area. There were two offices. There were lots of interesting outbuildings. It was on nearly 10 acres of nice pasture.

There was trash and stuff and junk everywhere, as if the people had left in a huge hurry. Some meth-heads had vandalized the barn and house to steal the copper wiring and pipes for drug money. There were huge holes ripped everywhere in the walls and of course, no water or electricity.

As I looked it over, my first reaction was, "Oh boy, this *was* a fancy horse place. I thought maybe it had been a really fancy hunter-jumper or dressage barn. I suddenly wanted to get out of there fast. I was feeling like it was *too* fancy, *too* nice, for losers like us, even though it needed a lot of repairs and TLC. I put it out of my head. I was thinking we were not good enough for a fancy place like that.

The next day, Sunday, Caleb was off and he wanted to go back out and look at a place we didn't get to the day before. I felt rested and refreshed, and the weather was a little nicer, so off we went. The property we went to see was mediocre. It was abandoned, run down, and had power lines running through the front of the pasture. We decided to go have another look at the equestrian center in North Lake Stevens. The front gate was locked but by climbing over a big rock we got in. We gave it a more thorough looking over, as we weren't so cold and tired.

The place seemed totally different that day. I didn't feel like leaving; in fact, I was getting such good vibes I started to bubble and squeak! We both felt like "*this* is the one." We zeroed in on getting *that* place. We found out that it used to belong to a dressage trainer I was familiar with who was once short-listed for the Olympic dressage team. It had been *her* dream farm. Something had happened to cause them to give it up. I heard lots of different stories about why they sold it, who bought the place, and why it was now abandoned.

One story was that the new owner had fallen from a ladder and sustained a Traumatic Head Injury. While he was in the hospital not knowing whether he would recover fully, his wife left him. That made *her* sound like a horrible person. I could sure relate to the poor head-bonked guy! Since then I have heard things a little differently from a person who knew the woman well. She said not to assume the woman was in error at all; that the husband was a total jerk. I don't know if he fell off the roof or not, but the man can't be found; he's completely disappeared. The farm is in bankruptcy and with all the damages, extremely hard to finance. About the only way you could buy it is with cold, hard cash. We had hit a dead-end. It was time for me to curl up and lick my wounds again. They kept re-opening.

In the meantime, God threw the ball to a farm in Granite Falls.

Owen, who was also the seller's agent for the farm, had taken Caleb to see it one day when I was still feeling really sad about the impossibility of financing the North Lake Stevens property. Caleb brought home lots of pictures to show me, but I wasn't impressed. It was the middle of winter and the place looked rundown and dreary. I was so in love with the equestrian center in Lake Stevens I had eyes for nothing else. When we went to look at it in late spring, my eyes saw it differently.

It was nearly 40 acres at the end of a majestically treed rural road, about 3 miles east of the town of Granite Falls. There was a 60' x 120' indoor arena adjoining a barn with 14 stalls. It was not amazing like the other place, but decent and sturdy. I thought we could build a big outdoor arena later. There were several pastures, and woods with overgrown trails through them.

The *house* was amazing. Originally it was a two story log cabin, built in 1874. It was still there, in all its' ancient glory. It had a huge u-shaped addition around the sides and back. Wood, wood, wood was *everywhere!* Wood trim inside around the windows. Wood floors. Huge timbers for the log cabin. Most of the walls and ceilings in the additions were cedar. There were so many windows and skylights.

It had a big river rock fireplace in one of the rooms, and on the outside of the house there was a barbeque grill built into the chimney. In the yard stood a huge, ancient black walnut tree. Around the house were lots of old cedars, pines, firs, and hemlocks. Far below a steep cliff ran the Pilchuck River. You could see the snow capped peak of Mount Pilchuck out the kitchen windows and off the deck. It was breathtakingly beautiful.

I hadn't dreamt much about having a nice house. Really cool barns, *yes*; really cool houses, no. I'd just as soon live in a barn. When Caleb and I were newlyweds, we had some friends who lived in a Christian Community, *Sunshine Farm*. It was just outside of Danville, Virginia. We would go to Sunshine Farm for spiritual retreats. They had great guest speakers and awesome music. Families in the community were buying some of the 100 donated acres and building homes.

One of the married couples became our friends. They built their amazing dream home with lots and lots of found materials they had collected for many years. It was truly one of the most unique and beautiful homes I had ever seen. If we were ever going to own a home, it would be like *that*.

Caleb and I started a folder back then for our ideas. It was called *"Our House"* after the Crosby, Stills, and Nash song that Graham Nash had penned for Joni Mitchell when they lived in Laurel Canyon, California. The place we were looking at now even had a sink in one of the bedrooms that had been thrown on a potter's wheel. That was something I had put in the folder. The sink was brown too, just like I wanted. We had abandoned the folder long ago when life got way too hard to dream of *anything*. As I walked through the majesty of that old cabin and the beautiful additions, I thought of *"Our House."* So did Caleb.

Bubble and squeak time!

Our house,
Is a very, very, very fine house
With two cats in the yard,
Life used to be so hard,
Now everything is easy
*'Cause of **You**. (Crosby. Stills & Nash)*

Chapter Seventy

WE KNEW WE COULDN'T BUY a forty acre farm by ourselves. What to do next? Pray. Trust. Wait.

Two of the golden retrievers turn out to be Caleb's mom and step-dad. They had been snowbirds for 14 years; summering at campgrounds in the Puget Sound area and wintering in Yuma, Arizona. Caleb's step-dad Rafe was a retired truck driver as was his mom, Evie. They met driving for a boat manufacturing company. It was nothing for Rafe to take their huge 5th wheel down to Arizona every fall.

However, that spring down in Yuma Rafe had emergency open heart surgery. He had to have the mitral valve in his heart replaced. Caleb flew to Yuma for three weeks to look after his mom and help get Rafe to his follow-up appointments. Then Caleb flew home and one of Rafe's relatives came down and drove their motor home back to Washington with Evie and Rafe. It looked like their snowbird days were over. While in Yuma Caleb talked with them about the North Lake Stevens horse farm. He asked them if they might want to help us buy it and live in the little house while we lived in the barn apartment. They were sad about not going to Yuma every fall, but also excited about the idea of living on a farm. Rafe thought of lots of ways to contribute. So did Evie. They said *yes* to the Lake Stevens property, and when that didn't work out, yes to the Granite Falls farm. Caleb and Rafe were both U.S. Army veterans, so they began the process of seeing if they could get a double Veterans home loan. That took some time.

Months and seasons came and went. If you've ever watched *Field of Dreams*, and watched Kevin Costner stare out the window at his baseball field as the seasons changed, you know how I felt. Caleb and Rafe got qualified trough the VA. We made an offer on the Granite Falls farm; it got rejected. We made another offer. It got rejected. All this took a tremendous amount of time. Pray more. Trust more. Wait more.

So what did this girl do in the meantime? Sit around and twiddle her thumbs?

Nope. My old dear friend Danae McManus from my Equifriends days asked me to haul one of her horses to Oregon to give to one of her young relatives. I was not sure if I could do it, but I'd driven my truck and trailer down there before to an event, and I was driving back and forth from Mission, so I thought I could pull it off. By God's grace I drove just fine even through heavy rain, only dinging a running board on a light post in a parking lot. Nothing unusual there. Danae and I had a wonderful time catching up on the long drive. Her horse was delivered safely to the sweetest young girl with the nicest parents, and I got a huge confidence boost. *Thanks,* Abba.

Gus's six month sabbatical had turned into nine. I finally started working with him again, and he was terrific. He remembered all his lessons from before and seemed quite happy to go back to work. He was difficult to get groomed and tacked up, especially the bridle, but now I see that I should have done it in the round pen like I did when I started him, instead of just forcing the issue. I would take him to Mission and tie him to the arena wall to groom and tack up. He wasn't used to the place or being tied for a long time, and he was quite challenging. But once the tack was on, he was quite good. I even had Ciaran Finch jump on for a little ride one night when they were up visiting. The only naughty thing he did was kick out lazily at her leg aids when she asked him for canter, but he finally did it.

I had started taking Memphis back to my current coach for jump lessons, but one day it was easier to catch Gus than Memphis. It seemed like Gus wanted to go, so I took him instead. He was pretty excited to be in a new place. Tacking him up, even inside the trailer, was pretty tough. Finally he was ready, even though I was sweaty and a bit disheveled. With a short longe he was ready to ride. What a good boy he was! He liked checking out the fascinating new surroundings. There wasn't much steering, and he quickly tired. But all in all, he got an A-plus that day.

I took him back a couple more times mostly just to get him out and about. I tried jumping him a teeny bit. He was pretty good but he tired out quickly. I tried to tell my coach how tired he felt, and that was probably why he resisted cantering, but she dismissed me with *"AWWW!* He's a big strapping thoroughbred! He can do it! He's just calling your bluff! Looks like he's got your number!" So, I pressed Gus to keep going. That's when he started to contemplate rearing. Sometimes a horse has to shout before he's heard. Sometimes their deaf and dumb, too intimidated by their trainer, too busy, too egocentric *people* don't hear them whispering.

Spring had almost arrived and my coach was having her cross-country camp again. I had taken Jazz and Memphis last year and really liked it. Jazz had been very difficult at first, but found his groove on the last day. Young and green Memphis learned a ton and was quite good. I wanted to go again. This time I thought I would take Memphis and Gus. Memphis could stretch his wings and show his potential, and Gus could have the same "newbie" outing that Memphis had last year. Jazz had shown me the previous summer that eventing rattled his nerves way too much so we were just going to stick to dressage.

I had John and his students put Gus and Memphis' first shoes on in preparation for camp. I wanted to use studs to avoid any more spills! I had always worried about putting shoes on Gus. I knew my current farriers were not looking forward to it. I didn't think Memphis would be too bad, but he was big and strong. I wanted it to be a positive situation for both horse *and* human. Because I had been riding and teaching at Trinity for a few months, I had gotten a really good sense of how John does things and teaches his students to do them as well. It made perfect sense to have John and his students work on my Punk Boys.

Shoeing Gus was like putting shoes on the month of March. It started off with a roar. Gus did not want anything to do with John or his students or the shoes! He proceeded to rear, buck, fire both hinds at

John and plunge around the round pen. He looked a little dangerous, especially now that he was a big, strapping boy. John kept sending Gus away and calmly teaching his class. Gus eventually joined up with John and totally submitted to the shoes. If he were a kitten, he would have been purring loudly. He stood like a lamb.

I invited Teagan and Ciaran to come with me to camp. I thought it would be good for Ciaran to ride with my coach and they could help pay for gas, which had gotten sky-high. Ciaran brought a cute little mare she borrowed named Grenache. We made it over Snoqualmie Pass in spite of avalanche warnings and the threat of the roads being closed for several hours. To tell you the truth, I had a check in my spirit about that whole trip and camp; a warning that I shouldn't go. I didn't listen. I should have.

Both boys and Grenache settled in fine. I had a lesson on Memphis that afternoon, and he was great. I longed Gus a little; he was great as well. I had to be careful about separating them so that neither one of them would have a hissy fit and try to jump out of the paddock. That is what Memphis did last year when I rode off on Jazz. He jumped right over a four-foot metal gate, bent it in half in the process, and I had to buy a new one. It was good that Grenache made a threesome, as there was always a buddy to keep the one left behind company.

Ciaran and Grenache had a lesson the next morning with my coach, and then it was my turn. I thought I would let Ciaran ride Memphis while I rode Gus. I would just kind of tag along with the lesson group on Gus, while Ciaran got a lesson on Memphis. I thought I was doing something nice for Ciaran. I guess Teagan and Ciaran thought they were doing something nice for me.

When it became time to get the two horses ready, including putting in studs, I assumed Teagan and Ciaran would show up to help. My friend Cayanna has a little saying about assuming she likes to pull out for these situations. I did not plan enough time to get both horses ready alone, and my coach was a big stickler for showing up on time. I used round pen techniques on both boys to get them cooperative for putting in the studs, and that went well. Gus actually seemed sleepy.

I was late for my lesson. My classmates were already riding out to warm up. Finally Teagan and Ciaran showed up. By then my coach was hollering at us "*Hurry up!*" I grabbed Gus and took him over to the stool I had for a mounting block. No sooner then I had swung my leg over did he rear. He reared sky high several times. My backside hit the hard ground with a thud. I got back on. He starting rearing again. I was hanging on for dear life, but the more he went up the more people were yelling at me to bail, so I did. *Thud* number two. I got a lecture from camp participant about how naughty Gus was. I was in a lot of pain, so I thought longeing him and walking him around the cross-country course in hand while Ciaran rode Memphis would keep me loosened up. I longed a lazy Gus while Ciaran walked around on Memphis.

"Why isn't she warming up?" I thought to myself. The class had commenced a while ago. I hadn't taught Ciaran for a few years; I wasn't in teacher mode, and she was not riding with her regular coach. I encouraged Ciaran to get going and the coach yelled something to her also. The rest of the class had come to a series of ditches. My coach asked Ciaran if she would like to jump Memphis over a Novice-size ditch. Ciaran hesitated, but I said to go for it because I knew Memphis would jump it. He jumped it the first time beautifully. Ciaran stayed with him over the ditch and through his "that was exciting! I need to hooty-hoo a little bit!" with his head down between his knees. That brought them to an old rubber tire covering an irrigation sprinkler. Memphis had been so busy shimmy-shaking he didn't see it. He came to a halt right next to it then shied away from it. That was enough to dislodge Ciaran, whose position was already somewhat compromised. She was wearing one of those new-fangled air vests which promptly inflated. Ciaran was unhurt, just shaken up a bit. Teagan could not find another CO_2 canister to put back on the vest, so she did not let Ciaran get back on Memphis. By this time I was really frustrated. We led both horses back to the paddocks. I put Gus away and then *I* got on Memphis. I rode back to where my coach was teaching but she ignored me completely. I didn't think it was very productive to stand around, so I rode off. I found a line of small ditches that I thought I should pop

Memphis over. But Memphis didn't want to, poor guy. He was still shaken up that his slip and fall last summer had put me in intensive care. Now he had caused a young girl to hit the dust! "Nothing doing!" he said. "I am not going to hurt you again."

Some other riders from a different visiting group came over with their trainer and asked if I wanted help to get Memphis over. I said, "Sure!" They gave him a million leads over a couple of tiny ditches until he finally jumped over. I thanked them profusely until I heard my coach yelling for me to come where she was. When I got there she told me in no uncertain terms that I was *not* to ride off on my own and jump anything, nor receive help from anyone but her. Liability and all that, you know. Then she turned her attention to her other students. I sat for awhile doing nothing. Then I said *"Forget this!"* to myself and headed back to the paddocks, jumping the tiny ditch on the way back.

I didn't ride the rest of camp. I was in tremendous pain from falling off Gus. I wondered if I hadn't hairline fractured my pelvis. One of my truck tires had gone flat after we arrived at Tulip Springs and I spent most of Sunday morning going around trying to find a place to get it fixed. A very nice dad put my spare tire on so I could get to town. By the time I got back it was time to load up and go home. And least I got some of my camp fees back, along with a bonus lecture from my coach about how I should have longed the snot out of Gus before I rode instead of the Natural Horsemanship I was doing while putting his studs in.

It was a good three weeks before I could ride anybody. I was in a quandary. I was lucky I didn't get hurt worse. I was lucky I didn't bonk my head and die. One of my neurologists had said, "Don't ride anymore." When I started to turn blue he said, "Okay you can ride but don't fall off! I must have freaked out everyone at camp. Gus certainly didn't score any brownie points. I haven't been back to ride with that coach since. I would have, but soon an Equine Herpes outbreak was in full swing, and her barn got quarantined. I figured it was just as well to stay away, but I was in a quandary. I didn't know where to go for help. I had already ridden with all the eventing trainers in our area. I tried to contact Selby; no luck there. I approached Ellie Simpson, who had helped Ryan and I with Bob. She was so swamped being a birthing center for mares I didn't even get to tell her what I needed. If anyone could help me and understand Gus, I thought it would be her.

I asked God for help and insight. He reminded me that Ryan and I had fixed Bob's rearing issue and reminded me how we did it. We hit the dirt a lot, yes, but eventually we stayed on and figured out how to keep Bob from going sky-high. Gus's rears where similar but not nearly as big as Bob's, but I *hated* rearing. It made me want to puke. I was determined to keep riding Gus, so I started from the beginning. I just prayed my way into it, asking Abba for help in every step. I prayed *especially* hard when I got back on Gus in the round pen. He didn't rear right away, and when he did it was pretty half-hearted so I stayed on. I rode him several more times in the round pen. Then we progressed to starting in the round pen but opening the gate and going around the indoor a couple of times. Eventually we progressed from starting in the indoor and finishing in the outdoor.

I took him up to Sunset Park in Blaine with Memphis and Ticket. I didn't feel comfortable riding him, but I longed him in the sand arena and over jumps and took him into the water jump with my rubber wellies on. That was *after* he pulled and bucked so hard on the longe line that I got yanked right off my feet and had to let go. Gus just squealed and bucked his way back to his buds who were busy mowing the tall grass in the paddocks.

One day up at Trinity Farrier School, Gus was trying his very hardest *not* to be a good boy and do the work I was requiring of him. I wanted him go forward in a nice, calm manner and jump a tiny crossrail on the longe line. Of course Gus knew how to do this perfectly well, and he wasn't concerned about jumping. He just did not feel like doing it at the time. He exerted a tremendous amount of energy trying *not* to jump the jump. He bucked and he squealed. He would bolt off at a gallop, then randomly and abruptly stop and turn around. He pulled the line out of my hands a few times, then calmly stopped to eat the grass growing on the edges of the outdoor arena.

I had a longeing cavesson on him, which is sturdy and *most* horses really respect it. One great thing about it is that you hook the longe line to a ring on the cavesson, which rests on the bridge of the horse's nose. If they turn around, the longe line neatly swivels on the nose ring instead on getting tangled around the horse. Gus turned around at least ten times and thought himself very clever to do so. But the longe cavesson design was even cleverer than Gus, so each time he swiveled *it* swiveled. Regardless of the direction he ended up in, I sent him forward with the longe whip.

When he discovered that he could not end his workout that way he tried to dive out the arena gates. I shut them. He tried diving into the cattle holding area, sometimes going forward, sometimes backwards. Each act of rebellion was met with a calm but determined response from me: "Gus, go *forward*. You choose which way. If you want to back up, go ahead. You will back yourself right into a corner. If you try to run over me to escape, I will bonk you as hard as I can with the end of this whip. I am not going away, and you need to jump that tiny jump in a nice calm, workmanlike manner a few times. *Then* I will let you rest. But if you keep insisting that you can't or won't, it's another trip around the circle to the jump."

The lesson went on and on. We were both sweaty and breathing hard. We were both getting tired. Finally, Gus changed gears. The look in his eye changed and became thoughtful instead of obstinate. He settled into a nice, rhythmical hand gallop. He took *himself* over the jump several times. He even jumped a little brush box I had brought out "just in case" we could get that far. At that point I let him stop. We walked to cool out and go find a carrot. I was very, *very* grateful to God that I had the skill, balance and stamina to see the lesson through.

Gus was a little humbled. In that gnarly process his sensitive thoroughbred feet took a little beating on the pebbles that arenas always seem to grow like weeds in a beautiful garden. He got a nasty stone bruise which became an abscess. There was a waiting and rest period so his foot could recover. I noticed he kept himself out of the mealtime fray like Gandalf does. He was more fragile with a sore foot, so he felt more vulnerable. I brought dinner to him in a quiet place, away from the group, and he was grateful.

Once Gus's abscess was healed and I started riding him, he managed to dump me about three more times by rearing, but I kept right on working with Gus. I worked with him in the round pen and I longed him too. I asked God to show me what I needed to see. I kept carrots in my pocket to reward Gus when he did the right things on the longe line, the round pen, arenas and in the stall during grooming and tacking. God *did* show me what I needed to see.

I don't know how many people would have given up on Gus, or tried to manhandle him into submission. He has been a very feisty, very unique individual since the day he was born. He came into this world small and frail and weak, but no more. He was no longer small. He was 16.2 hands high. He was fairly sturdy for a thoroughbred, and hardly weak. He had some moves that knocked me right off my feet. I was the small, weak, frail one. I often had to remind Gus about that. Gus thinks I should play rough and rowdy horse games like him and Memphis.

Lots of well-meaning friends and acquaintances have given me advice on what to do with Gus:

Sell him.
Dump that one.
Get rid of him!

Later on, when it became clear I was keeping him, it was:
Better geld that boy as early as possible.

When I started bringing Gus to Trinity Farrier School and John Roderman got to know Gus from shoeing him, it was:

Put some manners on that boy before he hurts you.
Don't longe Gus. That's a stupid waste of time and it's unproductive.

From my coach at camp it was:
Longe that boy! He's not a little quarter horse!

At Trinity it was:
Don't feed carrots.

All my English riding friends said,
Of course it's okay to feed carrots.

I ended up doing what I felt *God* was leading me to do; what works best for Gus. I gelded him when he was nearly a year old. I longe *and* I do Natural Horsemanship. I do natural horsemanship *on* the longe line. I longe in the round pen. I feed carrots, but Gus is not allowed to be rude or aggressive about it. Gus works hard for those carrots. They cured him from throwing me to the ground while I was bridling him to opening his mouth politely for the bit because he knows he will get a carrot. I give Gus carrots to reward him. I give Gus carrots to reassure him. I give Gus carrots because I *love* him.

Gus hasn't dumped me in a long time on *purpose,* at this writing. The only time I have fallen off him was when we was doing a lively trot on the trail at Lord Hill. A jogger came around the bend also doing a lively trot. He scared Gus's big boy pants right down around his fetlocks. As Gus was trying hard not to trip over them I came off. This time Gus was totally repentant. His beautiful face said, "Oh, Mom! I am *so* sorry! All those other times I *meant* to dump you, but not this time! It was an accident, I swear!"

He changed from rearing sky-high repeatedly until I fell off to considering it, with lots of warning signs, but choosing the better way. Aside from Gandalf, Gus was now the most well mannered horse I had. That was because he required *all* of the above methods *all* of the time, A rather remarkable transformation took place in Gus. He was starting to *get it.* He was a whole lot more settled, more gentle, more loving. He had gotten a pretty good grip on what was okay and what wasn't. He knew he should not bite, kick, gallop over, rear at, or shove into me. He knew he should stand quietly to be groomed, blanketed, saddled, bridled, and mounted. He knew he should show restraint under saddle. He knew to move away from pressure rather than into it. He knew not to use Sump as a punching bag. I am not saying that Gus was perfect. He often yielded to temptation in all those areas. But now he *knew*, whereas before he was totally clueless. That's *huge*. Not only that, but he actually started to enjoy being good both on the ground and under saddle. That's not just huge, that's huge-*mongous*!

One day I was longeing Gus over 3 cavaletti raised about 3 inches off the ground. Finny had kicked Gus in the hock and it was blown up like a dirigible. No doubt she got her point across! He healed up fine, but that day the joint was still pretty stiff and swollen, so I was using the trot poles as physical therapy, requiring Gus to bend that hock, but he really didn't want to. He was trying to avoid them altogether, or jump them. It took some coaxing. He finally did it correctly, so I stopped him and gave him a carrot and praise. He loved that. I asked him to go the other way. After a couple of false starts and "do I *have* to's?" he went over, but it was half-assed and he knew it. The look on his face said, "Messed up. Gotta make it better!" Then Gus took himself around the circle again while I just held the longe line in wonder. He trotted the cavaletti perfectly, then stopped and looked at me. Of *course* he got a carrot and a scratch. In fact, he got several of each!

Even though Gus could be quite exasperating, one thing about him that thrilled me was the fact that he was pretty fearless and quite independent. I had to thank his "trailer trash" mamma for that, as she constantly let him go play farther and farther down the street. Gus got excited about new situations, but he didn't become anxious. He thought it was intriguing. Everything was a grand adventure.

Lisa and John liked "Cowboy Mounted Shooting." That's a Western riding activity when you gallop around and shoot balloons with a pistol. You needed a steady horse and a steady hand. They practiced shooting a lot. Lisa had asked me not to teach anyone while they practice so they didn't have to worry about getting sued if anyone got dumped from the noise of the pistols while they shot. It was okay for me to ride, though. I guess they weren't worried about me suing them.

I could ride Gus during the shooting practice! The first time I had him on the longe line warming him up I wasn't sure if I would get to ride or not. I was cantering Gus and working on him getting the correct lead, as he usually didn't going to the right. He was cantering to the right on his left lead when he heard the first shots fire. He neatly did a beautiful flying change. *Good boy.* That's all the concerned he got about the noise. The whole inside of the indoor arena would vibrate with the sounds of the pistol firing. Gus's ears would swivel and he would lengthen a couple strides, but then canter calmly around. I ended up riding him. He was *terrific*.

Another evening when I brought Gus to Trinity there was a crew of people fixing the electricity in the tack room on the other side of the barn. They had flashlights on their heads and were tromping around on the tack room roof, banging hammers and running an electric staple gun. Usually that kind of visual and auditory stimulus would cause most horses, *especially* thoroughbreds, to throw a major hissy fit. Gus hardly batted an eye. We did lots of 20 meter circles on the end of the arena way from the commotion, so Gus could see it well. He never once spooked or jumped. *Good boy!*

I believed Gus was destined for greatness. He *would* live up to the name one of my students gave him, *Gus the Great.* When I first came home from the hospital, the Lord spoke to me about Gus one afternoon down at the barn. "There's greatness in him," I heard Him say. There had always been something about Gus that confirmed those words. At the time I didn't yet know if I would be able to ride or compete, so I thought Gus might be for Ciaran Finch. But since then she has found a special mare. I think Gus is for me.

Chapter Seventy-One

PRAY. TRUST. WAIT. THE DAYS and weeks went by. God continued to love, heal and bless me with His presence and guidance. A boarder at Trinity, a lovely young girl I mentioned earlier, gave me her gorgeous gray thoroughbred gelding. When I first saw her horse, Scout, I thought *WOW*. How beautiful he was! John Roderman had saved his life by shoeing him therapeutically and was given Scout by his owners who had sought out John's help. John helped Scout so much he was able to sell him to the Hoffman family for their daughter Augusta. He proceeded to win many blue ribbons and championships in 4-H, but now she needed a younger dance partner. Scout, now twenty years old, was having trouble staying sound enough to jump and do dressage as much as his girl wanted him to do. I felt about taking Scout the way I felt about taking George; it was meant to be. John Roderman cautioned me about taking on an older horse with soundness issues. In spite of the wisdom in that thinking I took him anyway. Scout needed to be shod by John the Master with special shoes. *Expensive.* I took him anyway.

His board was paid at Trinity till the end of the month, but after that I took him home. Our board went up for the additional horse. I took him home anyway. Scout settled in quite well. I was very careful with him, though. Sump needed companionship and Scout didn't like the hustle and jostle of herd life, so most of the time Scout had turnout with Sump only. Scout was a wonderful caregiver for my old blind Appaloosa. Sometimes he would let me know he was tired of babysitting and want to go out with the rest of the gang, and that worked out pretty well too. Sump would go in a big stall to rest and eat, and Scout would go have social time---at a respectful distance. Often he would return to the stabling area and keep Sump company.

The funniest thing happened one morning when I was down at the barn. Our landlords were keeping five heifer cows in the shed right next to where our horses lived. It was mostly cold and rainy, so often the heifers would be in the shed eating hay or laying around in the deep straw chewing their cuds. I left one of the paddock gates open to bring Sump through from his stall in the aisle to a bigger stall in the other horse's paddock area for the day. Scout slipped through the open gate and went in to have a visit with the cows. It was a happy little visit and amusing to see a very tall white horse among little black and brown cows. The Hoffmans had just left on a Mission trip to India. They were very attractive tall white people. I imagined them hanging out with little brown East Indians. At one point the cows acted like they were going to go out to the pasture and Scout was going with them. I did not want that, as that pasture could be dangerous. All I could do was yell, "Scout! No! Stay here!" He stopped, turned around and came back doing a beautiful floating trot. He was surrounded by all the little trundling cows. To me it was a picture of the Holy Spirit floating amongst little earthbound people. It was quite the picture.

Scout was fairly sound when I took him home, and he stayed that way. I started to bring him up for lessons. He became a huge hit with my students. I nursed and babied him along, made sure his feet stayed pretty dry and didn't over use him. I had long talks with him about his new career---a lesson horse. He had been such a big winner as an event horse in his younger days and as a 4-H horse as he got older. He was extremely well trained. I didn't want him to feel slighted.

He did so very well in his new career I felt he needed a new name. Being a huge *Lord of the Rings* fan, it seemed exactly right to rename him *Gandalf.* He was tall and white and ageless, and he was truly a wizard.

Chapter Seventy-two

KERRY WESTFIELD CALLED TO SEE if I could bring Finny home any time soon. She needed her stall for one of her other horses that was coming home from a training barn. When she called I didn't have room because I had taken Gandalf, but within a few days I did. Ryan's retired warm blood *What About Bob* came up lame just after Ryan and I decided to take him up to Mission to get shod, so that Ryan could trail ride him a little bit. My vet discovered a small but deep puncture wound in his left front heel area. She ultra-sounded it and left me some antibiotics. Later she called to encourage me to have a new plasma-rich treatment done to Bob's wound to speed up and guarantee healing. Otherwise she said it may not ever heal, or take a very long time. The treatment was very expensive, so again I asked God to show me through Caleb. He said to go ahead and do it.

I hauled Bob up to the clinic for his treatment. A short time later my vet called to say the wound was worse then she thought. She didn't think the treatment would do much good. I told her to go ahead and clean it out really well and do what she could. We would hope for the best. After a while she called me back and said that Bob was not coming out of the general anesthesia very well at all. At that point she was thinking euthanasia. I said *oh no*, please give him a little more time. The thought of Bob dying alone at the clinic was more than I could bear. We had always been with our horses when it was their time to go, and they were all buried at the farm except for Dexter. She said okay and we hung up.

A couple hours later the clinic secretary called me. She said Bob was no better. He hadn't gotten up and it was time to let him go. I couldn't exactly go bring him home to bury him in his current condition. It was agonizing to agree to end his life at the clinic, and more so to arrange for the disposal of his body, but I didn't have a choice.

We were left with a big vet bill, sad hearts and an empty stall. I called Kerry to tell her we had room now for Finny. It was almost as if Bob had gotten out of the way so she could come. I hitched up my trailer, loaded a friend for Finny to ride home with, and headed over to the Westfield's. It only took a little coaxing to get Finny in my nice extra tall and wide trailer. She rode home like a champ, and once more we introduced a new member into our herd.

At first I was really reluctant to bring a yearling filly home to barb-wire fences with all my Punk Boys and a Dragon Lady pony, but now somehow I knew she would be okay. First I put her out with Gandalf and Sump. I knew the three of them would get along beautifully, and they did. Gradually I introduced her to the boys and finally Shadow. Mares don't mess around; if they decide they don't like you, they just turn around and kick the daylights out of you. For several days things seem to go very well. Then one day I came home from teaching and found Finny standing quietly in the hall of the barn. She was quite happy to see me. What on *earth?*

I checked the fence lines. Everything was okay. I checked the gates; all were shut. I guess I never will know what happened, but it is very possible Shadow cornered Finny and she jumped over the concrete wall that divides the stabling area from the barn hallway. It's an old dairy barn with thick concrete walls, and pipe stanchions lining those walls inside each aisle. A heavy wire runs along the top of the stanchions. It was really scary to think of Finny jumping over that wall, because she could have flipped over the wire and broken her neck, or her back, or a leg or two. All she did was injure a hind leg a little bit. My vet came out and ultra-sounded her leg. She had dislodged her splint bone on that leg, but no fracture. My vet prescribed SMZ's and Bute for pain and swelling. Finny wasn't even that lame. I poulticed her leg and kept her in a few days and soon she was good as new. I put her back in with gentle Gandalf and geriatric Sump, just to be on the safe side. Gradually she was integrated back into the whole herd. She and Shadow reached an understanding, even though Jazz now favored Finny over Shadow. I am pretty sure that is why Shadow kicked her bottom, if that is what sent Finny over the wall. But *hey*, that means she could jump! Her cousin Memphis sure could.

Finny soon learned to hold her own with every horse in the herd. She kicked Jazz in the chest, Ticket in the forearm, Memphis on a hind cannon, and I'm pretty sure she is the one who left her signature on Gus's hock. She kicked just hard enough for them to be slightly injured but not maimed. *Hmmmmm.* I checked to see if the imprint left by her hoof on the Punk Boy's body parts was in the shape of an F.

She didn't suffer anymore at the hooves of *anyone.* She loved Gandalf and I saw them playing quite a bit. She liked Jazz and he liked her. It is pretty amazing that he let her share a stall, *especially* at mealtimes. Of course I didn't ever shut the door. The amazing thing was when the weather was particularly brutal, I put her and Gandalf together in the biggest stall with the door shut. That way they were safe from the Punk Boys and the Dragon Lady. They kept each other warm. Gandalf said it was okay but he didn't want me to make a habit of it.

The other amazing thing I saw her do was protect Sump. When the three of them were out in the pasture and Sump got anxious on occasion, he would whinny pitifully and blunder headfirst into a fence post or the barbed wire, which could have been disastrous. Gandalf very calmly put himself between Sump and the fence. I have seen Finny do that as well. I was very touched to see Gandalf do that, but totally amazed that a youngster would follow suit. No wonder Kerry called her an *old soul.* I am sure I had divine guidance in naming her.

Chapter Seventy-three

When I was making arrangements with Kerry to bring Finny home, I talked to her about our farm search. When I told her about the place in Granite Falls she said the executrix of the estate, Elaine, was her horses' massage therapist. Elaine had grown up there and really loved the place. She had talked to Kerry a lot about how hard it was for her to sell it. I told Kerry it was certainly hard to buy it as well. Kerry said, "That place may come back to you!"

The estate had lots and lots of red tape surrounding it, choking up closing the sale. Elaine didn't want it to sell, but it *was* for sale, which is why we were trying to buy it! My in-laws were not looking forward to spending the winter up in the Puget Sound area in their fifth wheel. I was not looking forward to another winter at the farm we were renting. I didn't want to spend more any money for gravel for someone else's place. I missed George. I was getting tired of hauling the horses up to Trinity. It was costing a good bit of money to work out of there and I couldn't teach when they had other activities going on, which was often, especially when good weather rolled around. I could never leave jumps up in either arena. I needed my own place.

In my early morning quiet times with Abba, I felt for sure that He had told me *Yes* on the Granite Falls farm but nothing was moving forward. As the days and weeks went by I would get so discouraged. As I cried my eyes out before Abba, it seemed he would take my chin lovingly in his hands and have me look into his eyes, like on my train trip to heaven, His eyes said "I know you. I love you, and I know the outcome of *everything*."

It was so hard not to give up, but I knew we must not. I *know* I heard right. And when my heavenly Father took me by the chin and looked into my eyes, I couldn't help but completely trust him. In the past, so many times I felt like I heard from the Lord. Things didn't work out right away so I started believing I did not hear Him at all. That put me on the road to despair.

There is the hearing of God's voice, then there is the hard part. We work out our salvation with fear and trembling; maybe fear that we didn't really hear and trembling at the thought of being able *to* hear. I probably *did* hear God all those other times but I just gave up and gave in to my doubts all too quickly. It is easy to do, especially when you are not getting your spiritual batteries charged; not getting the garbage cleaned out. My current big question was: "How many more times will You throw that ball, Abba? I'm *panting*, see?"

Abba threw the ball once again and He had another one up His sleeve.

This time the ball landed in east Arlington, about an hour north of Snohomish. It was way, way out in the boondocks, but it was lovely. The property was twenty acres with the potential to buy more. It had a double-wide manufactured home that was clean and nice, a cute three bedroom chalet, and a really cool shotgun style guest house. There was a freshly painted red barn and a big pasture with a couple of loafing sheds. There was a lovely bubbling stream running through it. Five hundred acres of DNR land bordered it. The mountain views were tremendous. A lovely older widower owned it. It seemed liked an uncomplicated deal. We thought hard about trying to buy it. It was time to take a deep breath, then gallop back to Abba with the ball. We would see if He threw it again or put it, and *us*, in his pocket.

On the way home from looking at that farm we were both really hungry, so we looked for a place to eat in nearby Arlington. I spied the *Mirkwood and Shire Café*. It was straight from the *Lord of the Rings*. In the same building were *Rivendell Hair* and *Mordor Tattoo*. No hobbits served us, but come to think of it, that would be *us*, the ordinary folks who just want to live peacefully. We just want to have a little pipe and a little fun. I began to contemplate that. It seems that we are gearing up for major battle in this era, with us being the Shire folk and Mordor and Sauron being big companies who have industrialized farming to the point it is criminal. Criminal to the animals kept in horrid, close confinement and then butchered without honor, if they even live that long. Criminal against the people who eat that meat, because it is not nutritious and can be downright hazardous. Then there are genetically engineered seeds and all the processed foods with high fructose corn syrup. It's a dishonor to the land, the plants and the animals, us included. On top of that it is a dishonor to God who made it all and is in it all.

Within a week Len, Owen, my in-laws and myself went back to see the farm in Arlington. The night before I was in a serious funk worrying about finding the money to buy it, much less build an outdoor arena, as there was no place to ride except in the pasture or on nearby trails. The next morning *the Funks* raised their ugly heads as soon as I woke up. I practically ran into the Lord's arms in a bit of a panic. My amazing daily devotional's (*God Calling*) message for that day was all about praise regardless of what one saw or what the circumstances were. I started singing to Abba. In a moment all anxiety washed away, taking the Funks with them. It was just like the scene in the *Fellowship of the Ring* where Arwen called the river to come and overcome the Black Riders. In the Funks' place the Joy family stopped by for a happy visit.

My in-laws fell in love with the place. There wasn't much *not* to love. To wake up every morning with a towering mountain in your face would be pretty sweet. We went back to look at it again with Evie and Rafe. It *was* so beautiful, but so far out of the way, and no arena. I was still struggling with how we were going to be able to afford to build one, as an outdoor costs around fifty thousand dollars. We were having a hard time coming up with earnest money! Caleb said, "Well, when we first started this adventure we were over $50,000.00 dollars in debt, but the Lord provided, didn't he?" Well yes, He sure did. Out of the blue my dear friend Sissy gave us a large financial gift. My good old momma gave us a loan. Lack of faith would have been totally stupid.

I didn't have a consistently steady place to work horses or teach lessons and yet we were getting ready to make an offer on a place way out in the sticks with no place to teach *or* ride. We did not have the money to build an arena, but as my friend Sissy loved to say, *"It all comes out in the wash"*.

Chapter Seventy-four

GOD DID NOT THROW THE ball He had in His hands again, but He pulled the other one out from his sleeve.

Things got really interesting. Caleb and I had a big rift. It was the very same entrenched pattern that we both had experienced way too much in our 32 years of married life. We had never been able to talk things out to a peaceful solution/conclusion. I always wanted a resolution on the spot; Len wanted to avoid. Therefore, whenever there was a problem which I thought required discussion and resolution, Caleb went into his "cave," leaving me outside to have a full-blown Hissy Fit. The longer he stayed in his cave, the longer and louder I yelled. It used to be that way frequently, including a couple of times where we came to blows. Over the years we had learned how to avoid taking things that far, thank God. We had yet to learn the fine art of resolution. I was pretty sure that is what God was putting his finger on.

This fight was about Caleb coming home from work and ending that portion of the day by settling in with a glass of wine or Scotch to read books or do research on the internet. Ryan was visiting a friend in Colorado, so that week I had my usual long day plus the chores that Ryan does, which are cleaning the stalls, stall maintenance, cleaning the paddock, and watering. That took at least an hour. Feeding the horses and putting them to bed took another half-hour. Often I was in the barn till eight or nine in the evening, especially when Ryan was gone. You would think (at least *I* would think) that Caleb would change out of his work clothes and come help me finish up so that I could relax a little too. But he didn't see it that way. He thought because I love what

I do, and because it usually shows a loss on the tax forms, that it didn't count as work. His job *was* work, because:

A. He hated it.
B. He made more money than I did.

Hmmmm … I thought that argument was centuries old. What about being a stay-at-home Mom? That is a ton of work and responsibility without pay. Men and women have been fighting long and hard over that one for many years. Had Caleb forgotten about the 60's feminist movement? In college he seemed pretty pro-feminist. To me, taking care of the horses was no different than being a Mom. At least they paid for themselves some years, and even have turned a profit once or twice. When that happened we had to pay taxes, when it didn't we got a refund. What about that?

Caleb's perspective was "the horses are *your* thing, not mine. Why should I help you with them?" If that's the case, why should *I* pay the bills, keep all our activities organized, do dishes, laundry, or anything else that is "not my thing?" It seemed ridiculous to me that we were thinking about having a farm and be farmers, yet I wouldn't help Caleb and he wouldn't help me. That seemed incredibly *stupid*. In my mind I was thinking that if Caleb cared about me at all he would come down and help because it would go a lot faster and then we *both* could rest from our laborious day. Caleb's job was an emotional sucker-punch; my day was mostly physically demanding. What Caleb didn't know or realize is that the horse work that I wanted him to help me with would actually be more restorative and healing than his nightly glass of Scotch, and the act of him helping me would be restorative and healing to *me*.

Chapter Seventy-five

THEN I BECAME AWARE OF *The Great Reversal*. I was reading in Matthew early one morning when it hit me. "This is the Great Reversal: many of the first ending up last, and the last first." *Matthew 19:30 The Message* There was an awful lot of that going on. I thought of Ireland's troubled history and how they called it "A Terrible Beauty." We were in a period of a Terrible Beauty all over the world, affecting all things great and small. There were a lot of wonderful and terrible things happening, from the biggest leader down to the tiniest child. Thank God he has given many of his children eyes to see, ears to hear, and hearts to feel and discern. I got a lot of stuff on my email because I was plugged into *Neale Donald Walsh's* website. I saw it in stuff on the news, and I talked about it amongst my friends and family. There was a movie called *I Am* that came out earlier that year. Subtitle: *"When the Shift Hits the Fan."* It was incredible. There were a lot of gatherings worldwide to discuss the coming Shift. Much of it God had already showed me as I curled up Baxter-like on the couch with him in the morning hush. All the stuff that was coming forth in the media was confirmation.

Caleb and I jokingly called it *The Gweat Rewversal* after a scene in an animated children's movie made several years ago called *An American Tail*.

Some mouse immigrants got together to take a stand against the fat cats who were oppressively ruling the city where they lived. They built a *Secret Weapon* which was a giant mouse statue sitting on a stick of dynamite mounted on a wagon. It would be released to run amok amongst the cats with fireworks shooting out of its' mouth; pretty terrifying! One of the mouse leaders was a rotund lady mouse who spoke with a lisp. She called out "WE-WEASE DE SECWET WEAPON!" at the appointed time. The poor little mice overcame the rich and powerful fat cats, which is exactly what is starting to happen all over the world right now. God is our *Secwet Weapon*. He cares about the Fat Cats too, but He wants everyone to *love* one another. He is raising up the oppressed, not to win over the Fat Cats and in turn oppress *them*, but as an example of his love, faithfulness, power and sovereignty. Not so that the newly freed from oppression can turn around and do the same thing the Fat Cats have been doing to them, but for them to show the Way of Grace. Talk about terrible. Terribly *exciting!* And terribly beautiful.

Just to show you that it trickles down to the most insignificant households, *The Gweat Reversal* came to our house. Caleb and I discussed our *issues*. We talked it all out civilly, without it breaking down into a finger-pointing, name-calling disaster, as what usually happened. We were able to get to the bottom of 32 years of garbage. We put the shovel to it and cleaned it out. The very next day I came home from teaching and riding completely exhausted and not looking forward to cleaning the barn. I didn't even think I had the strength to do it. I came home to find it done! *Beautifully.* I let out great sobs of relief, gratitude, and pure joy. God *is* our Secwet Weapon. Yeth. He is.

Chapter Seventy-six

ON THE HEELS OF THAT epic "Shift" came another "Gweat Reversal". We got another shot at the Granite Falls Place! After my Sunday jump lesson up at Selby's farm, I stopped at Owen's office, with my good boy Memphis in the trailer. I was going to sign the papers on the East Arlington offer. Before I put my John Henry on the line Owen asked me how I *really* felt about the place, compared to the farm in Granite Falls. I said, "Well, I really loved the farm in Granite Falls; the house was amazing; it was 39 acres, and it had a barn and an indoor!" Owen wondered why we weren't counter offering. "Because Caleb told me we couldn't, and I thought you felt the same way." Arnie talked about how the Granite Falls property had much more value in it than the East Arlington place. I said Caleb didn't think we could get that big of a loan. Owen said *yes*, he thought we could. I didn't sign the offer for the East Arlington place. I went home and talked to Caleb. He said *yes*, we could try for the Granite Falls farm again. Caleb said he wanted me to be happy, and so did his parents.

WOW!

Caleb I and I pulled the pictures of the Granite Falls farm back out and allowed ourselves a little thrill of hope. Yesterday in North Carolina my friend Sissy went to a Starbucks with my sister Jeanne, my sister-in-law Sunni, my niece Kelly, and my mom. When they looked at the pictures of the house and farm I had sent my friend Sissy they all said "Wow. This is *Bean*" (that's my family nickname).

God was having great fun with this, I could tell. I was a little anxious because I didn't want to deal with another disappointment if we didn't get it. I knew God would see us through and he would throw the ball again and we would chase it again. I had to take another deep breath and exhale. I was getting pretty good at those! *Practice makes better.* That's what I tell my students.

We found out through Owen the farm in east Arlington place wouldn't finance because of the mobile home that was on it without a permit. Good thing I didn't sign those papers.

We had the Granite Falls place inspected. There were dozens of little things to fix, some medium size things and even a largish thing or two, but nothing to make us turn away. It would probably take about five thousand dollars to make all those repairs. We knew Elaine wouldn't do that. She didn't have the money for repairs, and she didn't want to lower the price. Caleb went to Bank of America to talk to Owen's cousin, a loan officer, who told him, "You'll need 6 months of income in the bank to qualify for this loan."

Because of all the practice we'd had trusting God, we did not panic and give up as we would have in the past. I was so thankful for all the guidance and foretelling of this story that Abba had given me. I had spent a lot of time reading the Book of Exodus over the past months. Caleb had spent a lot of time reading Joshua. We reacquainted ourselves with the stories of the Israelites' escape from bondage, their journey and conquest of the Promised Land. We really identified with their story. All the obstacles in the way of getting a farm were like the giants the Israelites encountered on their epic journey. Ours was feeling pretty epic too.

Once again things came to a screeching halt because we did not have the large sum Bank of America said we needed to have in order to get the loan. Owen came by to drop off some papers and the lack of funds came up in our conversation. I told Owen, Well, *we* don't have that money, but I have a rich Heavenly Daddy who does!" Owen just smiled. I was just his *Crazy Head-Bonk Girl* client.

Caleb's step-dad stopped by our house to pick up the inspection papers. I could hear him talking on the phone to a man with a very deep voice. I thought it might be Caleb's cousin's husband. It turned out I was right. By the end of the day Caleb's cousin, who used to be a mortgage broker before the economy crashed, took matters into his hands and gave us all a plan of action that made what Bank of America said null and void.

There was a lot of real estate vocabulary that went over my head, but I was learning a ton. That was really cool, because I had always thought never buying a home was a big chunk to be missing from my personal development. Not any more! Rafe and Evie said they were willing to go down to Yuma and sell their motor home so we will have the money we need for the property. We asked Elaine for more time, and she said okay. I guess there *was* something to this Crazy Head-Bonk Girl's ramblings about her rich heavenly Daddy.

Day after day after day we pressed on. Caleb tried to get a true interpretation of the VA terms, as each of the banks we had contacted had their own understanding. Poor Elaine was unwillingly stuck dealing with the sale of her parents' estate. There were the estate's lawyers to deal with also. There were Caleb's folks who kept running around looking at different properties we weren't interested in. There was Caleb who kept having to work his terrible job. He had gotten skin cancer from the sun shining through the car windows on his delicate post bone marrow transplant skin. He had to keep going to the clinic to have it dealt with,

A lovely young horse trainer I knew had found out we were trying to buy the equestrian center in north Lake Stevens. Like me, she was tired of moving from barn to barn every few years. She was hoping to move her business to that barn if we got it, and I was excited about having her come, as I really liked her. She was an excellent vaulting teacher as well as rider and trainer. But we did not get that farm and the girl found a lovely place to lease. I was disappointed but it was just another thing in my little box to give to Abba. Thanksgiving was upon us and Christmas right around the corner. I knew I was not to become anxious or frazzled. If it weren't for curling up every morning with God, Hallie and the kitties on the couch wrapped up in the wonderful fleece "wubby" Sissy had given me, it would all have become too much.

At least I had a handle on getting my four "Punk Boys" boys worked; Jazz, Ticket, Gus and Memphis. They were such *nice* ponies. I had to trust Abba the money would be there to show them when they were ready. I had to trust Abba for *everything*.

Later I sent a text to my lovely young trainer friend that read, "The level of constipation concerning the property in Granite Falls has reached epic proportions. Please pray that the bankers, lawyers, and Elaine would receive a huge spiritual enema from God. In a *good* way, of course!" She laughed and said she would pray. I thought we should cover ourselves with heavenly tarps to keep from getting splattered by the aftermath!

In short order bowels started to move. Owen called Caleb requesting permission to chew on the banks a little for being so obtuse about the VA loan. "From what I've read they do joint loans all the time!" Owen said. That was in regard to Caleb and Rafe filing for the double VA loan because they both are Veterans. Caleb said, "Sure, go for it." If Owen didn't work just like Ex-Lax the banks had a *lot* of control. I texted my friend to keep praying and said we'd better duck under the tarps.

WOW-ZER!

God's *Ex-Lax* is very potent stuff. In two days the banks and a mortgage lender we first contacted a year ago called to say we were right about the joint VA loans. The mortgage guy even apologized, bless his heart. Key Bank gave us pre-approval for the loan. ***Thanks, Abba!*** Plop #1 went in the potty. A few days later Elaine agreed to the loan. Plop #2 down the toilet. There was one big plop left; a V.A. appraiser had to come out and approve the property for the loan. If it got approved, once the papers were signed plop # 3 would go down the hatch, and *Wah-la*, the farm would be ours. I was starting to get more excited than scared. If the appraiser said no, then we would have to wait for Abba to throw the ball again. I felt better trained on this ball-throwing thing, but I hoped Abba felt we had *enough* training.

One night Caleb and I drove to the farm in Granite Falls to get a well water sample for a bacterial test. We had a lovely chat with the woman staying at the place. We met her oldest son and her husband.

She was a good friend of Elaine's. It was very good to talk to her and get to know Elaine's story. We let them know we were not trying to push our way through this sale to Elaine's detriment and sorrow. Elaine had been through so much with the death of her parents, her difficult siblings and the handling of the estate.

We had a short breather as we waited on the VA to inspect the property. My birthday came and went. Our 32nd anniversary came and went along with the usual anniversary spat. Oh well, we were getting along beautifully before that! All I can say is, I believed God was doing some pretty heavy roto-rootering in Caleb. I did not feel I should back down this time. I felt neutral, like I needed to stand my ground, but let God do His "thing". Lord knows, I didn't have a "*thing*" I could possibly do. *Been there, tried that.*

Our anniversary spat centered on Enya's very rude behavior. I won't put up with it and Caleb shields her from me. He does the same thing for Ryan. No wonder the kids don't listen or regard the things I say or the instructions I give them. If Caleb sets the standard, why should *they* raise the bar? They blow me off when I say it isn't high enough. Well, if I am wrong, God will surely show me; He always does. He doesn't let me get away with much! Not that I would want to; I *want* to be right with Abba. I can understand people "missing the mark" because of ignorance, but to do it *deliberately?* I sure hope there are not too many people like that.

Chapter Seventy-seven

THE VA PROMPTLY INSPECTED THE house. Just after dark one evening I drove to Snohomish to pick up our dryer from the Appliance Recycling Center, where they had replaced the thermal fuse. Train tracks crossed the road just north of the place, which was almost across the street from Maeve's coffee stand. Just as I pulled out of the parking lot, down came the guard rails, red lights flashing. Normally I would fret impatiently at the delay, but I had come to love trains going by. It seemed to me Abba was on the train checking on me and chuckling to himself as he passed by. It was always timely encouragement. This time it was a swiftly moving Amtrak passenger train. All the cars had little green lights on each stairwell. Lately I saw a lot of green on every train that passed me by. It was Abba's endearing playfulness; green because, *well,* we're the Greens, green because that's the type of farming we will do, green because that color means GO! All systems *GO.*

But winter weather came rolling in which brought all movement on purchasing the property to a halt. At least it *felt* that way. I am sure that is why Abba sent the trains all decked in green so I would not lose hope. You could say, "*Duh,* Those trains roll through town on a daily basis whether you are there to see them or not! What makes you think Abba sent them just for you?" I don't think that he sent them just for me. Of course they roll through Snohomish like clock work. I just *choose* to believe Abba rides through town on the trains. I even imagine He is driving the train in His *Bad Outfit,* and I wave at Him. Crazy Head Bonk Lady? Sure. "Hey I'm Craaaa-zy Head Bonk Lady! *Now give me some candy"* (look up Adam Sandler's Halloween skits from Saturday Night Live on YouTube).

Things seemed slower than molasses concerning the Granite Falls farm, but I just kept on *gettin' it*. I kept riding and teaching. My riding and teaching got better and better. My students were riding beautifully. My horses were going beautifully. It was so cool. Abba was with me in everything. *All systems GO.*

Sissy came for a visit in early December. I met her at a car rental place near the airport. She gave me directions to the place on her cell phone. I found it and her, but was in an unfamiliar area and I had no idea how to get home. I asked Abba to help me. You would have thought I drove that way all the time. I didn't miss a single turn. *All systems GO.*

Sissy had come to visit me and ride Gandalf, but also to scout out potential houses to buy. She was thinking of moving out to the Pacific Northwest. She went with us to cut our Christmas tree at Promised Land Christmas Tree Farm. We had gone there the year before and met the owners, absolutely terrific folks who loved the Lord. They told us their own amazing story about getting a farm. The wife had written a book about it and gave us a copy. A beautiful story, it was a great encouragement to me. *Thanks for going before us, guys.*

We went to sign more bank papers. Our loan though Key Bank just got more and more miraculous. Every time we saw a roadblock (a giant), just before we hit it (or it hit us), it disappeared! Remember in *Star Wars* how Obi Wan would just wave his hand slightly in front of any creature blocking his way? As he did that, he would also speak forth what that creature would do, and that creature would do just as Obi Wan said. That is how it went with the whole process. We saw lots of scary, ugly giants standing in the roads and in the doorways. They were grunting and drooling and brandishing big sticks. Our eyes got big. We trembled and grabbed Abba's hand. He just waved his other hand a little bit and said a few words to the giants. *Poof!* They disappeared into thin air.

Star Wars was huge back when Caleb and I were young married believers. We used to talk about it a lot in The Church at Raleigh. The movie had so much to see, so much to hear. During my early morning hours on the couch with Abba, Hallie, and the kitties He started speaking to me about *Padiwan Learners*. In the movies, those are the young folks gifted with *The Force* who are chosen to go into rigorous training and become Jedi Knights. At first I thought my kids were the Padiwan Learners, learning to function as adults living with us, instead of acting like little children. The recession and my head injury had brought Maeve back home, and Ryan and Enya were still living at home. We were trying to pack for the coming move. I was trying to ride four horses and teach. Caleb was trying to keep his now twelve Arby's® stores afloat. We were trying to make ends meet. Ryan, Maeve, and Enya were trying to grow up and have their own lives. Caleb and I were trying to be patient. We were trying to love one another. It was hard. We had to "unlearn what we had learned."

The Padiwan Learner concept started small and then gradually expanded, like ripples on a pond when someone throws a pebble into it. It not only applied to our little family and what we were doing, it extended to our dealings with Caleb's parents, Owen, my family back East, Sissy, my friends out here, Caleb's employees, my students, and so on. We began to learn so much about communication and *mis*communication. About understanding and *mis*understanding. I began to see that the ball Abba had put up His sleeve was a magic ball! A *Oneness* ball.

Chapter Seventy-eight

ON A TUESDAY BOTH MY students were sick, which was just as well because my truck wouldn't start. My 2004 Chevy Silverado had been totally reliable since I bought it. For my truck not to turn over normally would have made me frantic, but this time I took it and my students' cancellations as a sign from Abba that I needed to rest. I had a whole day at home. I couldn't go anywhere and my ponies were in my "back yard," so no worries except for getting my daily 20 oz. extra hot dilettante mocha from Maeve's coffee stand. She *brought* me one. I was able to linger over my email. One from my 94 year old uncle caught my eye. He sent so many politically slanted emails I delete most of them. For some reason I opened this one. It was called *Change for a Dollar,* a short video on YouTube directed by Sharon Wright. https://www.youtube.com/watch?v=9DXL9vIUbWg

It blew me away.

Bubble and *Squeak* time. I watched it over and over, sobbing profusely. It was profound and beautiful.

> ... *a homeless man sat on a shop step in a city, panhandling for change with a cardboard sign. Most people ignored him as they hurried by, but one guy put some change in his small tin can. The homeless man got up and entered a grocery store, where he bought a cup of coffee and a book of matches. At another checkout, a mom was struggling to find enough change in her purse to buy a loaf of bread, while her young son patiently waited. The little*

boy's eyes and the homeless man's eyes met and lingered on each other a little while.

The homeless man took his matches and coffee and left. As he walked he spotted a sad looking homeless woman sitting on a bench holding a stuffed animal, surrounded by her bags and baggage. He gave her the coffee. She took it and a shy, wondering smile lit up her weary face.

The homeless man walked past a coffee shop with a Help Wanted sign in the window. He purposefully dropped a penny on the sidewalk in front of the store. Shortly afterward the little boy and his mom from the grocery store rounded the corner. The little boy spied the penny on the sidewalk as they walked past the Help Wanted sign. He stopped, picked up the coin, and handed it to his mom. She kissed it and gave it back. The boy put it in his shoe. The mom spotted the Help Wanted sign in the shop window. She kissed her son on the forehead and said, "Stay here. I'll be right back!' She went into the café. The boy looked up and saw the homeless man looking at him a few yards down the sidewalk. Their eyes met. A moment later the little boy's mom burst out the door, scooped up her son and twirled him around. She got the job!

The homeless man smiled a faint smile and walked on. He came to a little girl collecting change for a baby with cancer; a poster with the baby's picture hung behind her on a fence. He gave her a couple of coins. She thanked him and handed him a white carnation.

As the homeless man kept walking, day turned to night. The homeless man walked past a coin laundry where he saw a young couple fighting through the plate glass windows. As they were arguing the man dumped the basket of laundry on the floor. The woman threw some of the laundry back at him and then sat down to sob into her hands. The man stomped out the door and slouched against the windows of the laundry mat, angry and upset. The homeless man stopped and offered him the white carnation and gently patted his upper arm. The angry man was surprised, but he accepted the white carnation. Then he went into the laundry mat and presented it to the woman, who threw her arms around him. They embraced in reconciliation.

The homeless man came to a gathering of people on the dark, cold street. Two young men were standing near an unlit barrel of scrap wood, struggling to stay warm. The homeless man gave them his book of matches. He walked over to a young girl who sat huddled against the cold night air. He gently touched her shoulder and she lifted her beautiful tear-stained face. He placed 35 cents into her palm and looked over to a pay phone booth. She did, too. She walked over to the phone booth, dropped in the coins and placed a call. "Mom? I want to come home."

The homeless man saw, heard, and walked on. Behind him the other men had started a roaring, comforting fire in the old barrel.

The next morning he was sitting on the same steps in the same city, holding the same cardboard sign that said, "Change?" Along came the little boy and his newly employed mother with a bounce and a swing in their step. The little boy and his mom stopped in front of the homeless man. Their eyes reflected the wonder and goodness of what had taken place the day before. The little boy took the penny from his shoe. He placed it in the homeless man's tin can. Then he and his mom walked on.

The wonderful short video ended. It was about *The Beginning*.

Chapter Seventy-nine

My beloved little Amazon Princess Beagle Hallie had become my alarm clock. She made sure I got up early and spent time with Abba. That's her job. That, and looking after the family and farm. She *needs* to be an Amazon Princess Beagle.

She usually scratches on our bedroom door between three and four in the morning, but occasionally at one-thirty. That's how I have come to have incredible visits with Abba. That is how this book got written. She has helped me continue to be the morning person I have been asking God to help me be for so many years. I'm not exactly a jump out of bed and hit the door running at 5 a.m. kind of morning person, but that's okay.

One of those 1:30 a.m. mornings got the best of me and I went back to sleep on the couch with Hallie wedged in there somewhere. I had a million things to do, but I fell sound asleep till nine o'clock. Caleb missed the list I left for him in case that happened, but he did know to give the horses some hay. *Good man.*

When I woke up I had to cancel going to a clients' home to teach and train as my truck still wouldn't start. I called for a tow truck. I called the Chevy dealer for an appointment to get it fixed. I made arrangements for my scheduled school-horse riding student to come to our place for an unmounted lesson.

I did housework while waiting for the tow truck. It finally arrived driven by a nice, petite, somewhat Mediterranean-looking man. I filled out paperwork and he took my credit card information. When he started winching my truck up on the flatbed part of his tow truck, I went back inside the house to watch *Change for a Dollar* again. As I sobbed through it again, I felt like I should go tell the tow driver to come in and watch it, as he was just sitting quietly in the cab of his truck. When I asked him if he had ten minutes to watch it, he came in, sat down, and put Ryan's headphones on. *That* was very out of character for me to let a strange man into my house. I went about emptying trash cans around the house while he watched the video. I could hardly believe I let a total stranger, a *guy* stranger, into my home; a very cluttered and messy home at that. He finished watching it and said *wow*. I said, "Yeah. Merry Christmas!" He and his tow truck and my beloved, beat-up Silverado left for the truck hospital. I called Caleb to see if he was having a Magical Mystery Tour day like mine was turning out to be.

Yeah. He was.

Wow.

I found out my truck needed two new batteries and a new fuel pump. As soon as that was taken care of, *I kept right on gettin' it.* The Christmas "holiday season" was in full swing. Normally it kicked off a bout of anxiety and depression in me, but that year I was completely at peace. I had not enjoyed most Christmases past. We never seem to have any money to spend on gifts and we were so far away from my family. Since the *Great Head Bonk,* however, everything has changed. The first Christmas after it happened was amazing. We were all celebrating the fact that I was alive! We had a little money to spend on gifts. That year we invited our homeless buddy to spend Christmas Day with us. We picked him up in the late morning. He was deeply touched by our gifts and to be included in our little family gathering. That in turn ministered deeply to us. Later the kids and Caleb and I went to see *The Voyage of the Dawn Treader.* We asked our homeless friend to come along, but he declined our offer. The movie was magnificent.

I'd been in a different mode since my truck broke down. I had really slowed down. I texted my friend Sissy about it and told her she would be proud of me. She had given me a lecture when she was here about slowing down to smell the roses. I replied she did not understand my situation or most dedicated horse people. I told her to imagine having eight little kids; it was not much different. When I told her I *had* really slowed down, Sissy asked me how it felt. I said it felt weird, but kind of nice.

I was actually more on top of preparing for Christmas than I had been in years. I had not been riding much and December was always a slow time for teaching lessons. My Tuesday riders had been out sick for two weeks. The rest were hit or miss, except for two sisters who were as regular as Puget Sound rain in winter. Speaking of rain, this had been the driest December in 50 years! The weather had been so cold and foggy it made me want to hibernate. I guess I had a little bit. The wonderful thing about having the horses home is that I didn't have to go anywhere to take care of them. They were in my back yard. They may have been wondering why I was not riding them. Other than being a little bored they seemed fine.

We were a little bored too. We were still waiting. We were waiting for the VA final approval and then the underwriters to do their thing. We were waiting for the bank to finalize, then waiting for Elaine to say "Yes" and sign the papers. All which *really* translates into waiting on Abba. I was still pretty sure, 99.9% sure this farm was *'the one."* All the little "faith formulas" I had learned, every prayer breathed, every toe stubbed, every thorn in my heart big or small over the years had prepared me for this time. Now was not the time to give up or cave in. Even if I did Abba would still be with me unchanged and unmoved. Caleb said something about Him throwing the ball again. *Lord,* I hoped not. But if He threw it, He threw it, and you know how Golden Retrievers are about chasing balls. With all the rest I've had, for sure I'd go galumphing off! But I hoped he didn't throw it anywhere else. I wanted to go home to Sherrer Road. I wanted to drive through those majestic old trees, open the gate and see that ancient, majestic, mystical log cabin.

Chapter Eighty

A WEEK BEFORE CHRISTMAS I got broadsided by a horrible flu. Enya came down with it first. Caleb and I spent several hours helping her after projectile diarrhea struck along with violent heaving. I had been up since two-thirty a.m., so that was not exactly what I had in mind for the evening. I had noticed during the day that I felt really strong and healthy; perhaps Abba had given me extra vibes because He knew what lie ahead. We finally went to bed and I got about six hours sleep; pretty normal those days. I got up, worked on this book, fed the pones and turned them out. After checking on Enya's welfare I headed to work with a client and her horses at her farm, as I usually did on Fridays. I got done with that, stopped at a health food store, stopped at the coffee stand for a second time and stopped at my hairdresser's to buy Enya's gift certificates for Christmas. As I drove home I felt sleepy even being loaded with caffeine, and I had a little heartburn. I was feeling a bit odd and guessed I overdid it this time on the coffee. I had drunk an awful lot, even for me.

After I fed the horses lunch and changed the turn out, I laid down to rest for a few minutes before heading out to Trinity to teach and ride. My in-laws stopped by to pick up their mail. "Are you sick?" they asked worriedly. "No, just resting," I replied, and we chatted a little before they left. In the meantime I started to feel queasy. I texted my student to let her know I might not make it. She didn't answer, so I thought I'd better call. As I was talking to her I had to excuse myself to barf. She was *quite* understanding when I cancelled. Then I threw up again. And again. I finally made it to the bathroom where I sat on the pot with my head in a plastic trashcan. It was lovely ... *not*. I finally stopped barfing long enough to lie down for a few moments. The moments between heaving got a little longer. Somehow I got the pones to bed for the evening, though I did ask for Ryan's help. Walking down to the barn was exhausting. I finally got to bed for a good nap. Caleb came home from work bearing ginger ale. It tasted like Nectar of the Gods. He opted to sleep in an empty bedroom on Sissy's air mattress. About ten o'clock it hit him, poor guy. I was so out of it I couldn't get out of bed to tend to him. By the sounds of it, his flu progressed about the same as mine. I started feeling almost normal. Caleb crawled back to our bed and crashed. I typed on Caleb's laptop as he snoozed next to me.

During one of my wakeful periods as I lay melted into the covers, it came to me that I should host another New Year's Eve gathering. I had hosted one a year ago, but it didn't go exactly as I planned. I had envisioned one like we used to have at the old Church at Raleigh. We would gather after fasting for the day, to worship and wait before the Lord until his gifts would flow and he would speak through us, to us. At my house last year there was a lot of talking, a little eating, but no worship and no manifestation of *anything*. I guess I had wish-dreamed--a lot. This year I needed to be clearer about the purpose. I figure people would either come or I would totally scare them off. Here is the invitation I sent off when I was recovered enough to type an email without barfing:

Hey Y'all,

I am going to have a New year's Eve "thing" again. Not really a party, but kinda-sorta get together. Here is what I envision:

6:00p.m.--8:00p.m. Gather, eat and socialize. I think we will have breakfast for dinner ... at least quiches or something like that, hopefully fully cooked this year, ha-ha!

8:00p.m.---till: a time of sitting quietly together before God, to seek His face, to hear what He has to say about the coming year and let the Gifts of the Spirit operate.

All evening: there will be a few chairs set up in Kate's now empty room. These are so people can break off to talk, pray, take a break; whatever.

I am very excited about this coming year! I know that a lot of people are fearful or sad for various reasons or just maybe ferklumped, stumped, or stuck. This will be a time to put your heart and soul before the Father in the company of comfortable people. You don't have to share or bare *anything*. You don't even have to talk or pray out loud. Just come and *be*.

Everyone is welcome. All kinds of folks; all colors, all cultures, all faiths, or no faith! English riders, Western riders, Natural Horsemanship devotees, or not. You don't even have to like horses *(although I can't imagine why not)*.

No judging. Not allowed.

Come for 5 minutes or 5 hours.

Come stuff your face, wish everyone a Happy New Year, then split if you need to, at any time.

Bring a friend. Tell a friend. I don't have everyone's email addresses. Our living room is not huge, but we will try to make as much room as possible. Bring a snack to share if you want (not required).

Barn duds and muddy boots welcome ... just take off the boots inside the front door. Stinky feet okay ... Hallie will love them!

No place for kids to play if they get bored, and our house is neither clean nor kid-proof. Just so ya know.

No need to RSVP. Hope to see ya! If no one shows, more food for us. If we have a ton of folks, and we run out ... we'll order pizza!

May and Caleb

... the flu had come, kicked our bottoms, and left just as quickly. The morning after the flu hit, Hallie woke me up at 1:30a.m.. I let her out and gave her a little food, then went back to bed. I couldn't sleep, so I got up to write. I had to laugh; while scrolling down trying to find where I had left off, I read about the constipation and God's Ex-Lax getting the bowels moving. *Ha- ha,* Abba. Caleb, Enya, and I had been living examples of that, for sure! I had missed a ton of riding, missed teaching a lesson, and missed two Christmas parties with horse people that I was looking forward to, but I am sure it was all meant to be, even being so, *so* sick. There *is* something about being thoroughly roto-rootered. It is cleansing, it is healing, and I sort of prophesied it in theses pages.

WOW.

Now that Caleb and I had thoroughly been cleaned out, we could be refilled with Abba's wonderful Holy Spirit. Bring it on, Daddy!! That was actually a prayer that Caleb prayed over me Friday night when he brought me the heavenly ginger ale; now that I had been thoroughly cleaned out, to fill me with all of His good things. *AMEN* to that and ditto for Caleb, Abba! It was amazing to see the progression of things as I had written them down, and I was so glad that this book had become a daily journal.

Over the last few days as we dealt with Enya's illness together, then being ill together showed me the craftsmanship of Abba's magnificent skilled hands. Caleb and I were so much more ONE than we were a few weeks ago. Leave it to Enya to play a central part! Enya may have Down Syndrome, and she may be considered "incapacitated" by the courts, but she is NOT. Enya is a mystical being, a very spiritual being, a beautiful being. Yes, she can be difficult indeed. She is one of the most stubborn creatures I know. But what do *I* know? One lovely, lovely thing about Enya; after we butt heads about her stubborn refusal to do chores around the house there comes true repentance and she makes it right. If only *everyone* could be that way!

It got really cold; cold as a witch's bosom in a brass brassier. That's what my old high school sweetheart used to say. That's pretty typical for December in Puget Sound. In winter in the Pacific Northwest you either get wet and warm-ish, or dry and cold … as a witch's bosom in a brass brassier! If you can handle freezing your bottom off at the beginning and end of the day, the dryness and sunshine is really nice, in the middle of the day for a couple of hours. When the clouds and rain move back in it feels so balmy everyone walks around in shorts under their umbrellas. People here complain about the weather constantly; it seems they are never happy with it. The weather here constantly changes, that's for sure. I think that is one of the reasons why I love it here. It's never boring.

Chapter Eighty-One

CHRISTMAS CAME AND WENT. USUALLY I was exhausted and happy to be done with it, but this year I was at rest; a *heavenly* rest. Yes, there was a flurry of activity to get it all done, but there was no stress or anxiety. It all got done, and it was fun. My in-laws came over mid-morning; we had a nice time with them. We ate well, but we didn't eat too much. We didn't make a big deal out of the meal, but the teamwork in cooking and cleaning was downright amazing. I even got Finny and Sump brushed and Jazz's bridle cleaned, which had been on my "do" list for over a week. While I was doing that, Caleb, Maeve and Rafe cooked dinner. I was happy to clean up afterward. No fuss, no muss. We even made it to our annual Christmas movie on time. This year we saw *Sherlock Holmes II,* which was brilliant and amazing. If that day was a peek at how life together on our farm will be, all I can say is *WOW!* I chose a name for it: *Hissy Fit Farm.* It's such a *southern* saying, and it goes with where I grew up, in North Carolina. That's where I found Jesus, that's where I met and married Caleb...*down those red dirt roads.* Lord knows there has been enough hissy fits to fill *all* the states we've lived in. It's not just us having them; all our critters have had plenty of hissy fits both great and small. This whole deal, every bit of my life's journey has been guided and directed by Abba. It has been as *He Sees Fit.*

What Hissy Fit Farm Will Be

    A.   **It will be a place where Faith, Hope and Love abide. Faith in God to look after us and make it all (including us) work.**

Hope that what we believe is the truth and that what we believe will come to pass. Love because of everything and in spite of everything.

B. It will be a place of rest and refuge for the dusty, road-weary traveler. A place of refreshing springs from the River of Gladness. People will come because it causes them to find rest. To find peace. To feel joy. To feel right. To get right with God.

C. It will be a place to hide and heal from the slings and arrows of misfortune. A place to walk with God in the woods.

D. It will be a place like Dr. Doolittle's … a place to talk to the animals. To find out who *they* really are. To be amazed and humbled by their sacrifice and service to us.

E. It will be a place of learning. Of growing. One can learn how to ride. One can learn how to farm. Learn how to cook. Learn how to eat. Learn how to care for all of God's critters (us included). Learn one's place in the choir.

F. It will be *all* of the above. A place of oneness. With the land. With the elements. With the critters. With each other. With God, who is and was, and is to come. Who is all things.

I was reading about The Last Supper, and why Jesus chose a dinner setting to let his disciples know that His time on earth as a flesh and blood human being was drawing to a close. It was in the book *Love, God, and the Art of French Cooking* by James Twyman. "Every meal is The Last Supper", Alain Toussard, a fabulous and experienced older chef, asserted. "If every meal is considered as sacred as this (he and James were looking at a painting of The Last Supper), then it touches the soul and sparks our love. This is why it is so spiritual. Jesus knew what he was doing when he decided to teach this lesson around a table. Food isn't just something for our bodies. If it comes from our desire to love one another, then it's like communion. It gives us spiritual life. If I can remember that when I'm in this kitchen cooking for whomever walks in that door, then I will have accomplished what I am here on Earth to do. That is the only thing that is important to me."

Hissy Fit Farm will be a place of many, many Last Suppers for each and every person who comes through those gates. It won't matter if I am helping someone to be One with a horse, or if Caleb and his folks are helping someone be One with their food, or Ryan is helping someone be One with the river or trees. If each thing we do is an act of love, then we will have accomplished what we are here on Earth to do.

All God's Critters Got a Place in the Choir
by Bill Staines

All God's critters got a place in the choir,
Some sing low, some sing higher
Some sing out loud on the telephone wire
Some just clap their hands or paws or anything they got, now

Listen to the top where the little birds sing
With the harmonies and the high notes ringing
The hoot owl hollers over everything
The jaybird disagrees

The dogs and the cats they take up the middle
The honeybee hums and the cricket fiddles
The donkey brays and the pony neighs,
And the old coyote howls

Listen to the bass, it's the one on the bottom
Where the bullfrog croaks and the hippopotamus
Moans and groans with a big To Do
The old cow just says moo

Singing in the nighttime, singing in the day
The little duck quacks and he's on his way

The possum ain't got much to say
And the porcupine talks to himself.

It's a simple song of living sung everywhere
By the ox and the fox and the grizzly bear
The grumpy alligator and the hawk above
The shy raccoon and the turtledove

All God's critters got a place in the choir
Some sing low, some sing higher
Some sing out loud on the telephone wire
Some just clap their hands or paws
Or anything they got, now.

Chapter Eighty-two

THE ARRIVAL OF NEW YEAR'S Eve felt like the eve of something HUGE. I felt it in my bones. I had sent out email invitations to quite a few people but I didn't have a clue if anyone would come. A family that Maeve just met through her coffee stand *was* coming. I hadn't met them yet, but I was excited at the prospect. I invited our homeless friend. I hadn't run into him lately, but I found him on FaceBook, for crying out loud. Or *L.O.L.*.

The day before New Years had been a full one. I was up at three to sit with Abba and work on this book, check email and do the banking. Then I fed and turned out the horses, took Enya to work, and went to my client's farm to work her 3 horses. Afterwards I came home, loaded up Gandalf, Shadow and Jazz and headed up to Trinity. All 3 horses were really muddy, and we were in a time crunch because Stacy, my Trinity Farrier School graduate farrier, was coming to work a client's mare on the mechanical cow. I was hoping to ride Jazz with my students, but they were slow getting ready to ride. I had to leave Jazz for later.

Those girls had a really good lesson and we set long and short term goals for the coming year. The temperature had dropped over 10 degrees by the time the lesson was done, and the kids made a dash for their warm car. I was starting to feel chilly even with *Patagonia* long johns and a big down parka on. Stacy came to work the cow with Lisa and John. I tacked up Jazz and asked if I could ride. They said, "Sure!" When they started to work the cow I opted to stay on Jazz and take my chances. Jazz was startled when the funny looking and smelling creature that usually hung motionless in the corner started running and bucking up and down the north end of the arena. He grew two inches, his heart started thumping, his neck got beautifully arched and his fuzzy little Appy ears shot forward. He spooked … in place. *Good boy!* Lisa, John and Stacy let me join in, and Jazz had his first lesson on "cow." He didn't dump me! Afterward Jazz had a *most* beautiful, expressive trot; good cross-training. I bet Jazz would make an excellent cutting horse if I ever wanted to go that route.

By the time I got the horses loaded and the barn cleaned up I was so cold I hurt. It was good I turned the heater up full blast to warm up the truck before I got in. I stopped up at the house to get hot water for the pones and some hot tea I had called Ryan to make (it was *soooo* good). Next I unloaded the horses, threw hay, sorted everyone out for the night, and went to get the hot water buckets out of the back of my pick-up. They weren't there. *Rats.* I had left them in the house. I was too frozen and exhausted to go back to the house for them, so I sheepishly brought cold water from the trough instead. I consoled my guilt by the fact that it had warmed up a bit and started to rain. The horses didn't seem to mind.

I put more bedding down to make things really cozy, fed carrots, and unhitched the truck. I drove it to the house and got out with an armload of stuff as usual. I was so tired I dropped half of it on the floor. After I cleaned it up I crashed on the couch with the wubby Sissy had given me. Caleb hardly took notice. He was cooking and doing research on the computer. After a few moments I said "I'm going to bed." Caleb insisted that I ate what he just cooked.

I was too tired to eat but I grabbed a few bites. I ate them too fast. I got hiccups but washed them down the hatch with rice milk. I brushed my teeth and fell into the nice warm sack that Caleb had pre-heated by turning on the electric blanket and mattress pad full blast. Caleb joined me shortly. Pretty soon Hallie started barking. "She outside?" I mumbled. *"Yep,"* he replied as he hunkered down under the blankets. *Bark. Bark. Bark.* Ryan and Enya were on their X-Box and computer with headphones on. They were oblivious to Hallie's cries. *BARK. BARK. BARK.* Hallie was cold. "Could you please let her in? The kids can't hear her," I asked Caleb. I was thinking about how I had gotten up at three but Caleb at seven that morning. It seemed fair enough; he hadn't been out in the freezing cold for hours, either. "No. I'm comfortable," Caleb replied. He wouldn't budge, so I leapt out of bed, furious. I screamed at the kids as I let Hallie in. I stomped back to bed. Caleb was laughing at me, but I did not think it one bit funny! *"You're such a stinking **GUY**,"* I snarled as I got under the covers. *"And you must have volunteered to be a total jerk!"* That was in reference to the *Conversations with God* books by Neal Donald Walsh we were reading. Caleb kept laughing and said I was vastly entertaining. How nice. All I wanted to do after I beat him senseless was to fall asleep. It's hard to do when your chest is heaving, your breathing is rapid and shallow, and you have **DESTROY** level adrenalin running through your veins. I concentrated on breathing and allowed myself 20 ten-second-in-and-out breaths before I went back out to the couch to be rid of that moron. I don't even think I made it to ten before I was out.

The next morning Hallie woke me up at three. I got up, went to the bathroom, let her out, and fed her a little bit. I went back to bed, but I couldn't sleep. I got up a half-hour later, made coffee and sat down to write. Caleb got up at 7:28. I wondered how the day would day go. I went down to the barn to feed the pones. This time I remembered to take hot water.

I wrote a poem about the time years ago when Caleb and I took our kids to Jetty Island for a fun-filled day in the sun. Jetty Island is a mile long man-made strip of sand in Puget Sound just off the coast of Everett. It was built to protect the waterfront city from storms or earthquake-induced surges from the sound, and the city had taken pains to turn it into a lovely park and wildlife center. We loved going there in the summer. It had clean, sandy beaches and warm, shallow water stretching out into Puget Sound. It was the closest thing I could find to the beaches I missed back in North Carolina.

This time we took along some kites that Caleb's parents had given us. The kids were a little on the young side for flying kites. They were more interested in playing in the sand and water. Caleb and I flew our kites a long time while we kept an eye on the kids. This is what we discovered that day:

Sailing Kites on Jetty Island

My kite shot straight up to the heavens
Then crashed straight down.
It went up, it went down,
It shimmied circles all around.
Len's kite sailed serenely up
In an almost lazy way,
And there it stayed;
Calm, quiet, confident, not swayed.

Which kite was right?
Both.
Here's some insight;
It's not a matter of
Right or of wrong,
Because we are *One*.
Because we belong.

We belong to our Father,
We belong to each other,
To all of humanity,
To all living things.

We're the same,
We are different.
But I'll tell you this,
The emotional tangles,
The anguish, the bliss,

For sure we all feel it,

That part is the same,
But it's how we *deal* with it,
It's our crown, or our shame.

But who says which is which?
Which one-- me or you?
Who says---does it matter?
Oh judgment---*go!* **SHOO!** *By May Dilles winter 2011*

Caleb and I are a study of opposites. We are *so* completely different from one another. Watching those kites act out our personalities in the sky made us laugh and laugh. Amazingly, my kite slammed to the ground a couple of times and then jumped right back up into the sky! I wonder if it bonked its' little kite noggin?

Chapter Eighty-three

NEW YEAR'S EVE WAS A BIG day. I stayed up 21 hours straight, and it was gloriously easy. The day before I had been completely exhausted! On New Years Eve I felt absolutely *bionic*. I took care of the horses, worked a little on this book, gassed up the truck, went to the grocery store, the feed store and the coffee stand. I came home, unloaded hay and bedding pellets, then proceeded to get ready for my New Year's Eve "thing." I rarely cleaned house, so that meant *LOTS* of cleaning. I also prepared biscuit flour and filling for 4 quiches. I did about 5 loads of laundry. I brought up two old, filthy directors chairs that Caleb got from the movie set of *Gardens of Stone* years ago. I washed the cloth parts in the washing machine and Ryan cleaned the wood frames. I hustled Caleb's beautiful white leather chair that we got him one Father's day over tons of his stuff that was laying on the floor on his side of our bedroom and out our bedroom door. I moved more detritus from the hallway so I could slide the chair to Maeve's old bedroom door (she had moved into an apartment in Snohomish with some friends). I put a couple of chairs in there in case anybody needed a place to pray, cry or just talk. I wanted to be ready for *anything* the Lord had in mind.

I left the evening as open as possible. A few of my friends had let me know they had other plans already, and our sweet homeless friend said he was sick and probably shouldn't come. I didn't hear a peep from anyone else. I didn't require an RSVP and half the time even if you do, people still don't respond, guilty me included. I got ready for a crowd and I got ready for no one except us and God. My heart really warmed up when Maeve told me she was coming with some of the Sterling family that she had met through her coffee stand. Maeve thought we were a little bit out in left field with all the Neale Donald Walsh books we were into. I wasn't sure she would want to participate. Now she was coming too, and bringing friends to boot!

The Sterlings have 11 children. They are Christians. There is a "flavor" of Christianity where the families don't practice any birth control and have lots of kids. I think sometimes maybe they shouldn't have. I called them "Zombie Mothers for Jesus". But that's judging, isn't it? I didn't know what flavor the Sterlings were, and I didn't really care. I just hoped they wouldn't care too much about what flavor *we* were.

Our gathering ended up being Caleb, Enya, Ryan, Maeve, Marta Sterling, Bristol Sterling, and their son Dyson. We ate the quiches and some absolutely wonderful stuff Marta made, and we got to know each other a little bit. Dyson had been to Botswana, Africa several times on mission trips. He had contracted both malaria and typhoid. Recently he had come back to the states ill with cerebral malaria and passed into a coma while his family was visiting relatives in Oregon. His doctor gave him a 50-50 chance of survival. Marta was like, "hmmm … I guess that's pretty good! Fifty percent chance he returns to us, fifty percent chance he goes home to the Lord. I'm okay with that." The doctors thought she was one nutty babe. Dyson recovered.

It seemed like the Lord had been busy bonking heads lately. One head belonged to the director of *Bruce Almighty, Ace Ventura,* and many other movies. He recovered from his head bonk off a mountain bike a changed man and made the incredible film *I Am.* I ordered a copy and sent one to my family in North Carolina.

We had such a lovely evening. The Sterling's and the Green's life/ Lord stories were amazingly similar. Our hearts knit. We had a very good time of prayer. It was not a big forthcoming of the Gifts of the Spirit, but that's okay. It was as it should be … perfect.

Chapter Eighty-four

WE WERE WAITING, STILL WAITING on the Granite Falls place. It turned into a very long labor of love and forbearing. Caleb's folks were having constant hissy fits. They didn't like Pacific Northwest winters. They were tired of packing up and moving from R.V. campground to R.V. campground every two weeks. Caleb's mom said she was way too old for this; she's in her eighties and has had a couple of mild strokes. Owen was having a hissy fit too. He was worrying about Elaine having hissy fits about selling the place. He was worried about Elaine having hissy fits about the latest developments with the Veteran's administration. They would not require any repairs to the house but would only loan $450,000.00. Elaine didn't know about that yet. Key Bank had our finances under a microscope. That gave me the heebie-jeebies, but I avoided a full-fledged hissy fit.

Caleb kept me up on all the stuff to do with Granite Falls. He seemed resigned that the whole thing would fall through. I was thinking "NO!" I got angry and frustrated with him because he didn't seem to be "in the Lord" at all. He slept late, then got up and went straight to the computer and started his work day. Then he put in a long day visiting his stores, came home, poured a drink or two, and immersed himself in farming books, magazines or stuff on the computer. I would have loved it if Caleb got up early and spent time with Abba and me. When Hallie came and scratched on my door in the mornings, I didn't think it was just so I will let her out to pee or feed her. She works for *Abba*. Caleb heard her too. Why wouldn't he get up? Spending time with Abba every morning got me spiritually roto-rootered. It got the garbage cleaned out. It wasn't a chore; it was *wonderful.* It was me, Abba, Hallie, and the kitties curled up in that wonderful, soft wubby on the comfy old couch. There was a space on the couch where Caleb should have been, I thought.

After Hallie got me up one morning, I fed her some little biscuits and let her out. I figured "second breakfast" later, as it was only 4:00 a.m.. That usually suited Hallie the little Beagle hobbit, but not that morning. Within a hour she was back in the kitchen very noisily going through the recycling bins looking for snacks. She even turned them over, sending bottles and cans clinking and clanging over the kitchen floor.

I called her several times and she ignored me. I am sure all the noise woke Caleb up. I knew I would have to go in there and put a stop to her rummaging. As I was gearing up to peel my fanny off the couch, Abba poked me and said, "She's like Caleb. Too busy rummaging through recycling to hear my voice." WOW. Did I tell Caleb this? Did I have him read this? Yah, sure, you *betcha.*

That morning as I sat before Abba, my mind was busy and full. Full of my friends' needs hopes, worries and frustrations. I felt the same worry for my family, and the same for the world … it was like ripples on a pond. I felt a little overwhelmed. "I hope you can hear me, Lord," I whispered to Abba. I caught myself. Yeah, right. "Of *course* you can hear me."

Then God the Funny Man says to me, "I hope you can hear *Me,* May Dilles".

Yeah, right, *ABBA!* "Of *course* I can hear you."

Chapter Eighty-five

A week into January, I got another "download" from Abba. He was doing that more and more often. Usually the messages were clear as a bell. That morning when I woke up it was 2:30 a.m., and I had stayed up till 10:00p.m. watching *I AM*. I usually got right up to write down what I had received, because I didn't trust my brain like I used to. Sometimes I didn't because I just wanted to go back to sleep. My brain seemed to be functioning pretty well those days, so I took a chance on falling back asleep in the hopes it would still be there when I woke back up. *Yep!* It was. So here it is.

Maeve had given Ryan an absolutely humongous *Jaw Breaker* in his stocking for Christmas. Ryan loved those when he was a lot younger. He always had one he was working on close at hand. A Jaw Breaker changes color several times as you wear away the layers with your tongue. Ryan's Christmas Jaw Breaker came in a funny box with *Gobstopper Trivia* all over it, including a blurb about licking your way down to the core. They made it sound like going on a quest or a mission.

That January morning as I lay in a "mental mist" before I fully awoke, I was thinking about the different layers of knowing Abba. You can know him a little bit, like on the outside of a new Jaw Breaker, or you can lick all the way down to the core. Remember the quote, "life is like an onion; you peel off layer upon layer, and sometimes you weep"? I have really identified with that one. It's like working with horses. About the time you think you know a thing or two, along comes an article, a book, or a horse to let you know *you don't know Jack.*

With Abba the Eternally Big Jaw Breaker, you can lick a little or lick a lot. He's so huge it will take a lifetime; maybe several, maybe hundreds or thousands of lifetimes to get to His core. As you lick the sweet surface you absorb the sweetness of God. Abba started out as a Jaw Breaker on the shelf of whatever store you bought Him from, but when you take Him out of the package and start truly enjoying Him, you both change. He becomes a part of you and you become a part of Him. He shrinks and changes colors. Maybe *you* enlarge, but you are becoming one entity; no longer separate.

The goal of hardcore *Jaw Breaker* devotees is to lick down to the center, the core. I didn't know what color the core of Ryan's current *Jaw Breaker* was, but the core of the *Eternal* Gobstopper is pure gold. It's glorious, radiant energy. As we get closer and closer to the core, we feel it. We absorb it and we are energized. There aren't many of us who can lick non-stop to the core ... our tongues might fall off. Who knows if our teeth or tummies could handle such a steady inflow of sugar? *Only God.* At least it's metered out slowly.

As adults we are taught to put away such foolish behavior. Who has time to lick a *Jaw Breaker* anyway? There are bills to pay, mouths to feed, work to do, countries to run, wars to wage. I finally understood the Bible story of Martha and Mary. I used to think the Lord was being very unreasonable with Martha when he should have applauded her for being such a hard worker. Wasn't Mary being lazy and irresponsible, leaving Martha to do all the chores? If I were Martha, I'd be angry too!

But Mary chose *the best part.* She chose to savor the Eternal Jaw Breaker before she did anything else. Perhaps Martha could have used some of that sweetness! Finally, I get it.

Abba, I want to lick right down to the core of You! Right down to Your molten center of golden sweetness. Amen.

Not long ago my soul sister Sissy texted me in a funk. The house she picked out in Snohomish was in danger of foreclosure, and the bank that held the mortgage wanted her to hurry up and buy it. Sissy had to sell her house in North Carolina first. No one had shown much interest, and she was falling into despair. Could I please talk to God for her?

I told her if God wasn't talking to *her* about the house, I doubted He would talk to me about it, but I would ask Him. I sat with Abba on the couch with my coffee and Hallie. I said, "So what about Sissy and that house?" He said, "I don't have anything to say about the house, but I have *lots* to say about Sissy!"

Abba had much to say about how much He loved her. How she was an *Endtime Handmaiden*, just like my beautiful mare Velvet. (That was the show name I gave her.) Just like me. He had a lot to say about how she had been chosen for this time before the foundation of the world. How everything in her life both good and tragic had been training her for this moment in history. He told me to tell her about the wooden plaques that Caleb had carved me before we married. He told me to ask her if she'd read *The Harness of the Lord* yet. I had emailed it to her after the Caleb had found it on the internet one morning as we were side by side at the computer table. It was originally written in 1968. Caleb had first seen *The Harness of the Lord* as a pamphlet at a retreat he had been to in the 1970's. After he got to know horse-crazy me, he showed it to me thinking I might enjoy it. *I'll* say! It hit me like a ton of bricks back then. It still does.

THE HARNESS OF THE LORD
By
Bill Britton

There is a terrific operation of the Spirit going on today to bring the Sons of God into an absolute confinement to the perfect will of God. This is the Day of His Preparation, the day in which He is preparing the channel through which He shall pour forth His Glory for all the world to see. This channel is His Body in the earth, that glorious company of people who are being conformed through much tribulation and fiery tests to the Image of the Son of God. This is His "battle axe and weapons of war" with which He shall subdue kingdoms and overcome all His enemies. This is His "mighty and strong One" to whom He shall commit the work of judging this world. This is His Overcomer, His "great army" with which He shall bring the nations into submission. The weapons of their warfare are not carnal, natural weapons but they are mighty weapons, mighty through God to the pulling down of strongholds. These are those who shall "be strong and do exploits."

But before God can commit this great and tremendous ministry into their hands they must submit themselves to the discipline of the Lord, letting Him truly be the Lord of their entire lives. We have long since dealt with the question of open sin but now God is dealing with the inward rebellion of our own wills. Some good Christians are not now being so dealt with for they are not in this First-fruits Company, but nevertheless there is a real dealing of God going on within those who are called into the High Calling of God. This is a very real thing and is the work of the Refiner's Fire. To those who are going through it, some of its aspects are horrible but very necessary and the end result thereof is glorious, as we are brought into absolute and complete submission to the will of our Lord.

It was in a minister's conference and convention in Tulsa, Oklahoma that God gave me a vision which I want to share with you concerning this harnessing of our own wills. There were more than 30 ministers present in this particular Thursday morning service and God, the Father of spirits, was present to deal with His sons; to correct them and discipline them to absolute obedience to His will. There was such a stern dealing in the Spirit that no one could go to the pulpit and minister. There was a reluctance among the ministers to say anything except that which was directly ordered by the Spirit. And as those men of God sat there in the awesome presence of Almighty God, some of them having many years of ministry; some missionaries, all of them capable of getting up and preaching a powerful sermon, I was impressed by the way they responded to the discipline of the Spirit. And in the midst of this terrific dealing of God with our spirits, the Holy Ghost gave me a vision ...

I SAW THE KING'S CARRIAGE

On a dirt road in the middle of a wide field stood a beautiful carriage, something on the order of a stagecoach but all edged in gold and with beautiful carvings. It was pulled by six large chestnut horses: two in the lead, two in the middle and two in the rear. But they were not moving; they were not pulling the carriage, and I wondered why. Then I saw the driver underneath the carriage on the ground on his back just behind the last two horses' heels working on something between the front wheels on the carriage. I thought, "My, he is in a dangerous place; for if one of those horses kicked or stepped back, they could kill him, or if they decided to go forward, or got frightened somehow, they would pull the carriage right over him." But he didn't seem afraid, for he knew that those horses were disciplined and would not move till he told them to move.

The horses were not stamping their feet nor acting restless, and though there were bells on their feet, the bells were not tinkling. There were pom-poms on their harness over their heads, but the pom-poms were not moving. They were simply standing still and quiet, waiting for the voice of the Master.

THERE WERE TWO YOUNG COLTS IN THE FIELD

As I watched the harnessed horses I noticed two young colts coming out of the open field and they approached the carriage and seemed to say to the horses: "Come and play with us, we have many fine games. We will race with you, come catch us!" And with that the colts kicked up their heels, flicked their tails and raced across the open field. But when they looked back and saw the horses were not following, they were puzzled. They knew nothing of the harnesses and could not understand why the horses did not want to play. So they called to them; "Why do you not race with us? Are you tired? Are you too weak? Do you not have strength to run? You are much too solemn, you need more joy in life!" But the horses answered not a word, nor did they stamp their feet or toss their heads. They stood quiet and still, waiting for the voice of the Master.

Again the colts called to them: "Why do you stand so in the hot sun? Come over here in the shade of this nice tree. See how green the grass is? You must be hungry, come and feed with us, it is so green and so good. You look thirsty; come drink of one of our many streams of cool clear water." But the horses answered them not so much as a glance, but stood still waiting for the command to go forward with the King.

COLTS IN THE MASTER'S CORRAL

And then the scene changed and I saw lariat nooses fall around the necks of the two colts and they were led off to the Master's corral for training and discipline. How sad they were as the lovely green fields disappeared and they were put into the confinement of the corral with its brown dirt and high fence. The colts ran from fence to fence seeking freedom but found that they were confined to this place of training. And then the Trainer began to work on them with His whip and His bridle. What a death for those who had been all their lives accustomed to such a freedom! They could not understand the reason for this torture, this terrible discipline. What crime had they done to deserve this?

Little did they know of the responsibility that was to be theirs when they had submitted to the discipline, learned to perfectly obey the Master, and finished their training. All they knew was that this processing was the most horrible thing they had ever known.

SUBMISSION AND REBELLION

One of the colts rebelled under the training and said, "This is not for me. I like my freedom, my green hills, my flowing streams of fresh water. I will not take any more of this confinement; this terrible training." So he found a way out, jumped the fence and ran happily back to the meadows of grass. I was astonished that the Master let him go and went not after him. But He devoted His attention to the remaining colt. This colt, though he had the same opportunity to escape, decided to submit his own will and learn the ways of the Master. The training got harder than ever, but he was rapidly learning more and more how to obey the slightest wish of the Master and to respond to even the quietness of His voice. And I saw that had there been no training, no testing, there would have been neither submission nor rebellion from either of the colts. For in the field they did not have the choice to rebel or submit, they were sinless in their innocence. But when brought to the place of testing and training and discipline, then was made manifest the obedience of one and the rebellion of the other. And though it seemed safer not to come to the place of discipline because of the risk of being found rebellious, I saw that without this there could be no sharing of His glory; no Sonship.

INTO THE HARNESS

Finally this period of training was over. Was he now rewarded with his freedom and sent back to the fields? Oh no. A greater confinement than ever now took place as a harness dropped about his shoulders. Now he found there was not even the freedom to run about the small corral for in the harness he could only move where and when his Master spoke. And unless the Master spoke, he stood still.

The scene changed and I saw the other colt standing on the side of a hill nibbling at some grass. Then across the fields and down the road came the King's carriage drawn by six horses. With amazement he saw that in the lead, on the right side, was his brother colt now made strong and mature on the good corn in the Master's stable.

He saw the lovely pom-poms shaking in the wind, noticed the glittering gold bordered harness about his brother, heard the beautiful tinkling of the bells on his feet -- and envy came into his heart. Thus he complained to himself: "Why has my brother been so honored, and I am neglected? They have not put bells on MY feet nor pom-poms on MY head. The Master has not given ME the wonderful responsibility of pulling His carriage, has not put about ME the gold harness. Why have they chosen my brother instead of me?" And by the Spirit the answer came back to me as I watched: "Because one submitted to the will and discipline of the Master and one rebelled, thus has one been chosen and the other set aside."

A FAMINE IN THE LAND

Then I saw a great drought sweep across the countryside and the green grass became dead, dry, brown and brittle. The little streams of water dried up, stopped flowing, and there was only a small muddy puddle here and there. I saw the little colt (I was amazed that it never seemed to grow or mature) as he ran here and there across the fields looking for fresh streams and green pastures, finding none. Still he ran, seemingly in circles, always looking for something to feed his famished spirit. But there was a famine in the land and the rich green pastures and flowing streams of yesterday were not to be had. And one day the colt stood on the hillside on weak and wobbly legs wondering where to go next to find food and how to get the strength to go. It seemed like there was no use, for good food and flowing streams were a thing of the past and all the efforts to find more only taxed his waning strength. Suddenly he saw the King's carriage coming down the road pulled by six great horses. And he saw his brother, fat and strong, muscles rippling, sleek and beautiful with much grooming. His heart was amazed and perplexed, and he cried out: "My brother, where do you find the food to keep you strong and fat in these days of famine? I have run everywhere in my freedom searching for food, and I find none. Where do you, in your awful confinement, find food in this time of drought? Tell me please, for I must know!" And then the answer came back from a voice filled with victory and praise: "In my Master's House there is a secret place in the confining limitations of His stables, where He feeds me by His own hand. His granaries never run empty and His well never runs dry."

And with this the Lord made me to know that in the day when people are weak and famished in their spirits in the time of spiritual famine, that those who have lost their own wills and have come into the secret place of the most High, into the utter confinement of His perfect will, shall have plenty of the corn of Heaven and a never ending flow of fresh streams of revelation by His Spirit. Thus the vision ended.

INTERPRETATION OF THE VISION

"Write the vision, and make it plain upon tables, that he may run that readeth it," (Habakkuk 2:2). "Harness the horses; and get up, ye horseman," (Jeremiah 46:4). I am sure that many of you who can hear what the Spirit sayeth to the Church have already seen what God was showing in the vision. But let me make it plain. Being born into the Family of God, feeding in the green pastures and drinking of the many streams of the unfolding revelation of His purposes is fine and wonderful. But it is not enough. While we were children, young and undisciplined, limited only by the outer fence of the Law that ran around the limits of the pastures (that kept us from getting into the dark pastures of poison weeds) He was content to watch us develop and grow into young manhood, spiritually speaking. But the time came to those who fed in His pastures and drank at His streams when they were to be brought into discipline or "child-training" for the purpose of making them mature Sons.

Many of the children today cannot understand why some of those who have put on the harness of God cannot get excited by the many religious games and the playful antics of the immature. They wonder why the disciplined ones run not after every new revelation or feed on every opportunity to engage in seemingly "good and profitable" religious activities. They wonder why some will not race with them in their frantic efforts to build great works and great and notable ministries. They cannot understand the simple fact that this Company of saints is waiting for the voice of the Master and they do not hear God in all this outward activity. They will move in their time when the Master speaks. But not before, though many temptations come from the playful colts. And the colts cannot understand why those who seemingly appear to have great abilities and strength are not putting it to good use. "Get the carriage on the road," they say, but the disciplined ones, those in God's harness, know better than to move before they hear the voice of the Master. They will move in their time with purpose and great responsibility.

And the Lord made me to know that there were many whom He had brought into training who had rebelled against the discipline; the chastising of the Father. They could not be trusted with the great responsibility of mature Sonship, so He let them go back to their freedom, back to their religious activities and revelations and gifts. They are still His people, still feeding in His pastures, but He has set them aside from the great purposes for this end of the age. So they revel in their freedom, feeling that they were the Chosen Ones with the many streams of living water, not knowing that they have been set aside as unfit for His great work in this end of the age.

He showed me that though the chastising seemeth grievous for the time and the discipline hard to endure, yet the result with all the glory of Sonship is worth it all, and the glory to follow far exceeds the suffering we endure. And though some lose even their lives in this training yet they will share alike in the glory of His eternal purposes. So faint not, saints of God, for it is the Lord that doth bring thee into confinement and not thine enemy. It is for thy good and for His glory, so endure all things with praises and thanksgiving that He hath counted thee worthy to share His glory! Fear thou not the whip in His hand for it is not to punish thee but to correct and train thee that thou mightest come into submission to His will and be found in His likeness in that hour. Rejoice thou in thy trials; in all thy tribulations, and glory thou in His cross and in the confining limitations of His harness, for He hath chosen thee and He hath taken upon Himself the responsibility of keeping thee strong and well fed. So lean thou upon Him and trust not in thine own ability and thine own understanding. So shalt thou be fed and His hand shall be upon thee and His glory shall overshadow thee and shall flow through thee as it goes forth to cover the earth. Glory to God! Bless the Lord! He's wonderful! Let Him be Lord of your life, friends, and complain not at that which He bringeth to pass in your life.

PLENTY IN THE TIME OF FAMINE

For in the hour when famine sweeps the land He shall feed by His own hand those who are submitted to His perfect will and who dwell in the secret place of the Most High. When terror stalks the land those in His harness shall not be afraid for they shall feel His bit and bridle and know the guidance of His Spirit.

When others are weak and frail and fearful there shall be those who shall be strong in the power of His might and shall lack for no good thing. In the hour when the traditions of the religious systems have proven false and their streams have dried up, then His Chosen Ones shall speak forth with the true Word of the Lord. So rejoice, Sons of God, that you have been chosen by His grace for this great work in this last hour.

The fence which kept the colts in their own meadows and their own pastures mean nothing to the team in the harness, for the gates open to them and they go forth pulling the King's carriage into many strange and wonderful places. They do not stop to eat the poison weeds of sin, for they feed only in the Master's stable. These fields they trample under their feet as they go forth on the King's business. And so to those who are brought into absolute subjection to His will, there is no Law. For they move in the Grace of God, led only by His Spirit where all things are lawful, but not all things are expedient. This is a dangerous realm for the undisciplined, and many have perished in sin as they leaped over the fence without His harness and His bridle. Some have thought of themselves as being completely harnessed and submissive to Him, only to find that in some avenue of their life there dwelled rebellion and self-will. Let us wait before Him until He puts His noose around us and draws us to His place of training. And let us learn of the dealings of God and the moving of His Spirit, until at last we feel His harness drop about us and hear His voice guiding us. Then there is safety from the traps and pitfalls of sin and then shall we abide in His House forever!

Bill Britton served as Vice President of Pinecrest Bible Training Center for the first three years of its existence and was a great blessing in helping to establish the work at Pinecrest.

As I talked with Sissy about *The Harness of the Lord,* I had a vision of the airplanes flying into the twin towers of the World Trade Center. I saw terrified, injured people trapped in the inferno, not knowing the way out. Then I saw the fire fighters go in and bring out as many as they could. I saw them bringing the frightened and wounded out to safety. At that moment I knew Sissy and I were spiritual firefighters. We know the way out. Our life's training has been hard; It's been painful. But trained we are. We will get the people out. That made worrying about her little Snohomish house and my big Granite Falls farm kind of insignificant for the moment.

Chapter Eighty-six

Talking with Sissy brought back the horror of September 11, 2001, the bombing of the World Trade Center. Or rather, when the airplanes were flown into the buildings by terrorists and *became* bombs. How well I remember! It was a Westshore Home School Networks day for my kids, and I went in to wake up seventeen year old Enya. Her radio was playing because she left it on day and night. It was time for the news and as I entered her room to wake her, I heard the radio announcer talking about a plane flying into one of the Trade Center towers. It sounded like a pilot had made a horrible mistake.

I went into the living room and turned on the television to watch the news. One of the towers was billowing smoke and fire. I hurried off to get Caleb, Ryan, and Maeve. We watched in horror and shock as the tower burned and people starting jumping from the buildings, certain of their death either way. Then a second passenger plane flew into the side of the other tower. It was unbelievably terrifying. Maeve broke down and collapsed sobbing in my arms. The rest of us had tears streaming down our cheeks. We watched as people screamed and ran down the streets of New York City. As we sat there glued to the T.V. screen and stunned to the core of our souls, more news came in. A third plane had flown into the Pentagon, and a fourth had crashed into a field in Pennsylvania. That plane had been bound for the U.S. Capital building, but the passengers on board had heroically overtaken the terrorists who had hijacked the plane and killed the pilots. The plane had crashed during the melee on board.

The entire country was paralyzed in fear. No one knew if there were more planes or where they would strike next. I called Home School

Networks to see if they were even holding classes that day. My call was the first they had heard of it, as they were already hard at work. We decided to go on in. We somehow got in the car and got on the road. As we made our way down highway 522 we searched the skies for errant passenger jets. Everyone was driving very slowly that day. We made it to campus, but our time there was mostly spent huddling with the staff and parents for security and comfort.

The next several days were spent glued to the news and trying to get on with life. People stopped hurrying to work, and most cars were adorned with a half-mast flag on their antenna. Both trade towers had collapsed, killing thousands of people. It seemed every road and street was a mass funeral procession even though Washington State is 3,000 miles away from where the tragic events took place.

Of course the rest is very well known history. The United States' retaliation in Iraq. The Dixie Chicks protest at a concert in England. The war in Afghanistan, the capture and execution of Saddam Hussein. The eventual murder of Osama Bin Laden. George W. Bush rallying the troops. Shock and Awe. Watching Bagdad get pummeled. The terrible aftermath. The toll on American soldiers and their families. PTSD.

This was all on my mind before my Father early that morning. Even though the vast majority of Americans were outraged at the Muslim terrorists, somehow I understood why they did it. Yes, it was base and terribly brutal but in reality they were just like little kids acting out when their parents don't pay enough attention to them. But the terrorists were BIG kids with big, bad toys, funded by other big kids with big, bad money. They wanted what they wanted, be it recognition, respect, time, or toys. They weren't getting it, and they were having hissy fits. They had all kind of lofty sounding ideals and ideas for what they did, and are still doing. The United States government did not play the way the Muslim extremists wanted them to, so they acted out, big time.

Did that get our attention? You bet it did. Just like parents would yell at their kids or spank them or at least talk to them and put them in time-out, the United States did all of it. More lives lost, more hate, more destruction.

People like the Dixie Chicks who spoke out against greed and the war machine that America had become were censured. Most Americans were pounding their chest like gorillas and pounding the drums of war and retaliation. Not me, not Caleb. We wanted to stick socks in W's mouth and censor him---*and* his cronies.

But we kept it to ourselves. I inwardly cringed the few times I flew out to North Carolina to visit my family and I saw an autographed photo of George W. and Laura Bush proudly displayed on my sister-in-law's refrigerator door.

As I was mulling all this over before Abba, I started thinking about Sarah and Abraham from the book of Genesis. Sarah had been unable to conceive, and now she and Abraham were quite old. God had promised them a son who would be the father of many nations. This had made Sarah laugh, a "Yeeeaahhh, *right*" sort of laugh. Then she took matters into her own hands and asked Abraham to sleep with her servant girl, Hagar. Sure enough, Hagar became pregnant and Sarah, jealous, accused Hagar of putting on airs. Sarah harassed Hagar so much that Hagar ran away. God met Hagar in the desert. He comforted her and told her to return to Abraham and Sarah. When she gave birth she named her son Ishmael, as God directed, and spoke this to her about him:

"He'll be a bucking bronco of a man; a fighter and being fought,

Always stirring up trouble, always at odds with his family." *Genesis 16:12, The Message*

Ishmael is the founding father of the people of the Muslim religion and culture. They are who they are, just as God spoke it. Even though Hagar was Sarah's maidservant, she still belonged to God, and He looked after her when she fled Sarah and Abraham's campsite. Even though her son founded a new religion, they still belonged to the God of Abraham. Doesn't that make us brothers and sisters? Family? Family feuds are the most painful of all.

So how *ridiculous* it is to fight religious wars! It is not much different than a family arguing about where the furniture will go, or whose turn it is to wash the dishes, or who gets what portion of the dessert, or the inheritance! We really *are* all the same, yet we are all a little bit different.

What do we desire? To be loved. To be understood. To be appreciated. To be fed and clothed and sheltered. To have purposeful work. To rest. To play. **To matter.** We all want these things, but how we perceive them, *that* is how we differ. We have different ideas. Different opinions. Different tastes. Different viewpoints. Just because it is different does not make it better or worse than the other.

Any kind of war, no matter what the fight is about, is utterly insane. We are all one family. God is our *Dad*. Why do we fight? Because one of us wants what the other has? Because one of us feels slighted? Because one of us slacks off on chores, which makes it harder for the rest of us? Because one of us looked at one of us funny or said something that we didn't like? Why do little kids fight? Over toys, or food; or attention from our caregiver. Why do **big** kids fight? For the very same reasons.

Now abide these three things: *faith, hope, love.* Apply these things to the universal desires of man. We should have **Faith** in God to provide these things *through* our brothers and sisters as we do the same for them. **Hope** that all will be well and peaceful in the doing of it. **Love** for our Mother and Father and our brothers and sisters in the midst of working it all out. The greatest of these three is **Love**. Love covers a multitude of sins (goof-ups, failures, misunderstandings … *missing the mark*). **Love** never fails. *God is love.* We are his kids. Therefore we are love too. My brothers and sisters, *let us love one another.*

… as Sissy and I wound up our phone conversation that day we started talking about training horses. We talked about how some horses are trained just a little bit and some extensively. It depends on what a person wants to use them for. If it's just to go on pleasure rides occasionally, a little basic training is more or less sufficient. If a horse is destined for the Olympics, that's another story. That training takes years and years. The concept of Three-Day-Eventing in the Equestrian Olympics was originally based on war horses that were trained to bravely carry their masters anywhere they wished in rugged terrain, even into the mouths of cannons.

Sissy grasped the fact that horses that pull the King's carriage are even beyond Olympic level horses. After we finished our conversation and we hung up I thought to myself, "Oh! No *wonder* I have had such a single mindedness to ride in the Olympic Games since I was a little girl! I still would if given half a chance, even though I am probably a little too old now. But to serve God in *His* Olympic Games, now that would truly be an honor. How I want to shine for Abba! How I want to win. I want to win *souls* for him, not just a gold medal. I want to *get them out* of the world mindset that will eventually collapse on itself. All my years of hard training now make perfect sense.

Chapter Eighty-seven

ANOTHER "MORNING MIST" MESSAGE I received made me feel that Caleb and I are not done raising children. Thirty five years ago on our wedding day, Makeda Ennishad prophesied over me as she was helping me put on my dress: "Thus sayeth the Lord, I have made this union to reproduce. Thou shalt have many children, and they shall rise up and bless you." When I heard that I quaked a bit. Was I destined to be barefoot and continually pregnant? As it turned out I just had three babies, not twenty-three. *Whew.* Thank you, Abba. We are done making babies, but not raising children. The Lord will send them to us. One of them might be a Native American boy. Our task will be to restore unto him the knowledge and experience of his beautiful heritage. The farm in Granite Falls felt like it was sacred ground. The huge old trees felt holy and so did the wood in the house, especially the ancient cabin.

When our kids were young and we were home schooling, we attended *Wilderness Awareness* classes held at Lord's Hill Park, and Ryan took one of their summer camps. It was really, *really* good. We learned how to survive in the woods and how to be one with the trees and the dirt and the wildlife. I was hoping Ryan would pursue it as a life path and eventually become a teacher/mentor with Wilderness Awareness, but we never could afford to send him to the required classes. Oh well. He still learned a lot of great stuff.

One thing that we all learned in those classes is to have a "secret place" of your own in the woods. There is nothing to make or build, just a place where you can go sit and just "be." I was looking forward to finding my secret place in our farm forest. God has a secret place in

His enormity for every one us; a place to hide, sit, and just *be*. A place to rest. A place to be restored. Having a secret place in the woods on a farm is just a physical manifestation of that spiritual place in God's bosom. As Makeda Ennishad always said, "first the natural, then the spiritual." Your secret place in the woods will show you the path to your secret place in God's arms.

Chapter Eighty-eight

I WOKE UP TO A beautiful snowfall one January morning. I went down to feed the horses and enjoyed the exquisite beauty of near-dawn. What a precious time that is. It is wonderful to be up at that time and to be so incredibly *aware*. No wonder the Lord encourages us to be with Him in the early morning hours.

Some funny and interesting things had been happening. It had been pretty cold outside so one morning I decided to make a fire in the fireplace and finish burning all the dried-up Christmas tree branches that Len had chopped up to burn. Soon I had a roaring fire going, and *oops* ... smoke was pouring into the living room and flames were licking the edges of the fireplace, torching the old wooden clock hung above the fireplace my Mom had given us years ago. Caleb had shut the damper to the chimney and didn't tell me. The fire was too big and too hot to try to open the damper, so I just had to wait and hope the fire didn't get out of control. I did manage to remove the clock and take it smoking to the kitchen sink. As I was opening doors and windows to let the smoke exit, the fire alarm went off. That caused Enya to go off. She sure hates the sound of it. I tried to shut off the alarm but couldn't figure it out. Caleb got up, shut it off and went back to bed.

Later I told Caleb I thought God was pulling out all the stops just to try to get him up in the morning. I said I hoped it didn't get any more drastic than me accidentally trying to burn the house down.

When the vet came to look at where Finny kicked Gus in the hock, she very gently warned me about the dangers of keeping horses in a herd, especially mares with geldings. I got the same kind of lecture in an email from my friend and jumping instructor from the Potomac Horse Center era, Lana Wagner.

I knew about the risks. I followed the rules most of the time, but now seemed to be a little different. Abba was teaching me so much through the horses' herd life. My little horse family is very, very good at settling disputes and keeping harmony and order *most* of the time, but just like people, they make mistakes. Some of the horses are very greedy and pushy about food. Some are trying to improve their position in the pecking order. Others are just trying to keep their place. A couple of them just keep to themselves. Doesn't this sound like an office where people are gathered together? One solution is to make little cubicles where everyone is separated, just as when each horse has its' own stall. That gives everyone their own space so they can concentrate and get their work done, but it also isolates them. Then there are the co-workers who want to visit or give directions over the cubicle walls. Maybe they unintentionally invade your personal space and block the exit that you want to take. Often they don't have a clue they are in the way.

After Gus's injury I could have gotten all concerned and gone about separating everyone, especially Finny and Shadow from the boys. Shadow was a bit resentful of Finny showing up and getting Jazz's attentions, so I wasn't sure if they would get along. If I separated everyone and maybe bubble wrapped them, I would cut back on injuries, but I think it would take away from their lives. I have never seen my horses so … *whole.* They are fabulously happy. Watching them as a family has been incredible. They have arguments, yes, but they work them out. They get boo-boos, yes, but it is mostly because of their environment. If I had shelter and fencing to accommodate herd behavior, the injuries would lesson or disappear. If you look at the very finest breeding farms, you will see fences with rounded corners so no horse can get trapped in one. You see groups of horses living in pastures with loafing sheds that are very open, yet very protective. Most professional horse people would not group mares and geldings together because of the heightened risk of injury, even among geldings. People don't want their horses to get hurt; barn owners don't want to get blamed and possibly sued.

But what do wild horses do? They work it out. I'm not saying all is calm and bright all of the time. Stallions compete for mares. Mares compete for place. Youngsters are disciplined along with wayward adults. Sometimes injuries, even deaths, occur. I am sure there are anger, jealousy, grief, and fear. But there is also *life*. There is joy, friendship, fellowship, peace. The young mature with ease or with difficulty. It's the circle of life. **LIFE.** To try to interfere with herd life for the sake of our pocket books and our dreams creates a different kind of death. Perhaps that is why Jesus died a physical death so that the rest of us would be freed from dying a *soul* death. Jesus' soul was alive and radiantly whole. He came to show us what that looked like and how to have a healthy soul too. He was crucified by people whose lives were so corrupt and diseased they couldn't stand seeing their sorry selves revealed by Jesus' teachings.

Chapter Eighty-nine

I WENT TO SEE THE movie *War Horse* twice; once with Caleb and once with Maeve and Dyson Sterling, who were now "courting." It was really something. I found it very interesting that two major movies focused on a horse should come out in the last two years. The other one was *Secretariat.* Caleb took me to see that shortly after I was released from the hospital. I bubbled and squeaked through both movies. There was God in two different BAD horse outfits on the big screen. He was also in his BAD outfits as the humans who loved the horses, but I won't get started talking on that subject. I could go on and on, like ripples in a pond.

Having seen both movies twice and pondered over them, I could see that they were also movies of my life and my horses. *War Horse* especially sticks in my soul. Horses and I have been through the wars of life together. We have been together, separated, reunited over and over again, literally and figuratively. We have grown up together, literally and figuratively. We have experienced everything that boy and that horse have in that movie, figuratively. We have been blinded and stuck in tangles of barb wire physically and figuratively. But *we made it out.* We have gone the distance. Soon we will get to go home. Home to our beautiful farm in Granite Falls. We are already home with God. We have and will always be home with God.

I had the Christian radio station blasting as I drove the truck to the feed store and back. In the recent past I could not stand to listen to it. The songs seemed so shallow then, but they are different now. They are deep and real. Young people are singing from their hearts, from their guts and from their souls. Their songs are anointed.

In between songs they had a guest on that was talking about her new book. It was about taking in orphans. She talked about giving help to people who were taking in orphans. An electric spark leaped in my heart. I heard the woman speak twice this morning as I drove through town running errands in the snow. I knew it was significant. I wrote down her name, her website and the name of her new book. I thought about the morning the Lord spoke to me about taking in a Native American child. Soon I was bubbling and squeaking wholeheartedly as I unloaded hay bales and grain sacks from the back of my truck.

Chapter Ninety

MID-JANUARY BROUGHT A FOOT OF snow. Everything came to a screeching halt. The snow was breathtakingly beautiful. It was dry snow, so not so slippery and treacherous. Len and I drove up to Granite Falls to see "our house" in the snow. The long drive down Scherrer Road looked absolutely majestic; so did everything else. I could not ride or teach lessons for days, so I worked on this book.

During this period Key Bank approved an adjustment to our loan, and Elaine approved it too! Now it was heading for the Veteran's Administration. One more giant head to lop off in the 3-headed "monster" I nicknamed ELAKEVA. (Elaine, Key Bank, V.A.). Caleb and I felt like the Joshua and Caleb in the Old Testament conquering the giants in the Promised Land. We were counting on Abba to help us be brave and make the hands holding the pens at the V.A. write swiftly and easily!

While we were waiting on the V.A. I would more and more often get what I called "Daddy Downloads" as I sat with Him in the mornings, or as I was waking up. Here's one:

It seems like most people spend all their time and energy working to make life better for themselves from the outside *in*. Their minds are fixed on tweaking their environment to make it better so *they* feel better. That environment can be their world, their country, their state, their county, their city, their home, their family, their own personal exterior, i. e. *skin*. When the exteriors of these things manifest themselves with sores or other types of visible ailments, people usually try to put band-aids or lotion or ointment on the boo-boos they see on the outside. But these manifestations are symptoms of something unhealthy brewing on the *inside*.

God, on the other hand, is interested in working on *interiors*. He wants to get to the deepest, tiniest part of us, the most microscopic particles. If those tiny elements experience his healing love, the rest will follow, in bigger and bigger chunks, until the whole universe is, *well*, whole.

It's the **macroscopic** versus microscopic viewpoints, just like Len and I learned almost 30 years ago in Biology 101. We learned that you can look at the study of life in basically two ways, from microscopically out or **macroscopically** in. You can start at the atomic level and build from there until you have a body built by those atomic structures, or you can take the body as a whole and break it down until you get to the atomic or even sub-atomic level.

Spiritually speaking, at the sub-atomic level, God *is*. He *is* love. My brothers and sisters, let us love one another. Love makes the world go 'round. Love makes the universe exist.

Chapter Ninety-One

WITH THE PREVIOUS CHAPTER I felt I had "finished" the rough draft of this book. It wasn't *really* finished any more than my life was finished. Even when my physical body dies, it's *still* won't be finished. As I was pondering this a Daddy download came in. Caleb had asked me to read a few pages from the book, *Gardening for Health and Nutrition: an Introduction To the Method of Biodynamic Gardening,* by John and Helen Philbrick. He said that reading the introduction helped him understand why I was writing *this* book.

John and Helen's book is about *life*. The Circle of Life. It's a book about connectedness and oneness; how we are all joined with God, who is the Center. Because we (meaning absolutely every thing) are joined to God, we are all joined to each other, too. I mean *every* thing, down to the tiniest microbe in the soil. It's amaaaaa-zing (as my southern born-and-bred sister-in-law likes to say) it's cosmic (that's Caleb's line), and it's beautiful (that's mine*)*. You fill in here with your own exclamation.

I woke up thinking about that book. Actually, Hallie woke me up at 3:30, same time as yesterday. Oops. I forgot to tell her I was done writing my book. I let her out, gave her First Breakfast and went to back to bed. As I lay there I turned to Abba. It's so easy now ... *now everything is easy 'cause of you ...*

I was thinking about John and Helen's book; about the connectedness of everything. We really are, *all* of us, made up of the same stuff. It lives long or briefly, it dies, it changes form, it comes back. That stuff is Abba. That stuff is us! We are all the same stuff!

I thought of God in His *Bad Out-Fit* on the train. Really, we are all in our Bad Out-Fits. Some of our outfits look human, some look horse, dog, cat, plant, etc. etc.. If you take off the outfit, we all look the same. That is because we *are* all the same! Caleb said one time when he was a young hippie dude building a cabin in the wilds of Idaho, he dropped acid and went for a walk. As the drug swirled through his veins, everything started to break down into its' molecular structure. Familiar forms fell away. Everything was whirling and swirling atomically, just like the acid in his bloodstream. It was both amazing and terrifying. Caleb became disoriented and began to panic. Then he heard the **Voice**. It told him step-by-step what to do, how to think, where to go. The Voice led him to safety. What an amazing trip *that* was. You wouldn't think it was at all, at all, but it was a taste of reality.

When we die, we don't *really* die. We just change life forms! We just change Bad Out-Fits. When I look at Gus, I see life in a silly young *Punk Boy* horse suit. When I see Caleb I see life in a middle aged hippie suit, or a *Big Jerk* suit, tee-hee, depending on what's going on at the time. I see Hallie in her *Amazon Princess Beagle* suit and Pippin in his *Kamikaze Orange Kitty* suit. I see Abba in his pleated muslin gown and *Captain Kangaroo* bangs.

I see myself in each of them.

Biodynamics. Biodiversity. Bio=life. Dynamics=energy; *doing*. Diversity=all of the varieties of us. Life energy in all of us. *All* of us. And ... We All Come Out in the Wash.

Whew.

Chapter Ninety-two

SHADOW WAS SURE WORRIED ONE morning. I had turned her out with Sump so Gandalf could have a break from Sump-sitting. Perhaps she was anxious without Jazz, or it may have been our landlord's terrifying cows, or both. Shadow did not want to be without her leader and buddy Jazz, especially with zombie cows nearby. Finally Shadow got up the courage to go out to the pasture without him.

I saw myself in Shadow. Do you? We often don't feel that we are ready or capable for the work God sets before us. We cling fearfully to our leadership figures and our comfort zones. But if God (God alone; not one of His avatars) tells you to do it, rest assured you will be fit for the task. Shadow's task was to go baby-sit Sump without her leader, Jazz.

It was hard, but she finally put her big filly pants on and *did it*.

I saw parallels both in my family life and my circle of horse people friends, peers and acquaintances. In my family life, I have always looked to Caleb for leadership, advice and protection. I wanted him to be my Prince Charming who carried me away on his white horse. If he had indeed been the Prince Charming I fantasized about, I never would have grown into the strong, capable, independent woman I am today. I would have remained a spoiled little brat, as I *am* the baby in my family of five siblings. Bravo, *bravissimo* to Caleb who put up with a million hissy fits (a.k.a. temper tantrums) when he refused, and sometimes still refuses, to put on those silly P.C. tights and knickers. Abba knew the man I needed was not necessarily the one I wanted.

As far as my horse family is concerned, when I started teaching and riding again ten years after Enya was born, I knew I needed some lessons. One never, *ever* outgrows the need for a riding and training coach anymore than we outgrow the need for our heavenly Father. As we mature both as a human being, and in whatever our profession or calling is, our relationships change. Abba becomes our friend, advisor and co-worker. Our mentors hopefully become the same. I began riding with a wonderful dressage instructor at Pebble Creek, but then we moved away, and for a long while I was too broke to pay for any lessons. When I taught at Woodland Farm I was able to ride a little bit with Sarah Jane and take an occasional clinic. Then I moved to Wooden Nickel Stables. I was very close to Ellie Simpson's barn, so Ryan and I took our horses over there for lessons. It was pretty good, but there were things I didn't quite understand. That's when I began to see that there is not much time for discussion in a lesson. There isn't much time outside a lesson either. Horse trainers are very busy people.

Then I moved to Northern Lights Farm and bought Valentine. I got lessons on him with Mimi. Lessons with Mimi were okay for awhile, and I ended up going, at her suggestion, to *her* trainer. That coach's lessons were good, but again there was no time for discussion. I sold Valentine and bought Jazz, and I went from trainer to trainer until I ran out of trainers to ride with. Then I had an epiphany after *The Great Head Bonk* in a lesson with my friend Sonja. Good grief, I must be extremely thick-headed. I guess that's a good thing considering how many times I've fallen off a horse.

That pivotal lesson was at a barn I where I had hauled Jazz to have a lesson with Sonja Masterton when Trinity Farrier School was hosting a clinic. Sonya was trying to help me get Jazz relaxed and working through his whole body, but it wasn't happening. Every suggestion she gave me was contradicted by a voice in my head. There were a lot of them and they each had something a bit different to say. They were the voices of all the other trainers with whom I had ridden Jazz. They were all talking over each other and it was driving me crazy. That in turn was driving Jazz crazy. Jazz was frustrated because I was frustrated and Sonya was frustrated with both of us. Finally I pulled Jazz up. Sonja was ready to end the lesson and get out of there, but I needed to vent. I told her about the voices of past trainers in my head. I told her I couldn't hear her because of them.

She said, "May, *you* know what to do. Stop listening to all those other voices."

The storm clouds of confusion and anger parted and the sun shone through. That lesson was probably the very best lesson I have ever had. I told all those voices to shut up! They hi-tailed it right out of my mind, and I was free.

It wasn't because the instructors were teaching me incorrectly. It was just that I didn't quite understand what they were telling me to do. I always wanted clarification and had a lot of questions, but I never got to ask them. At least I never thought I could. They always seemed to be in a huge hurry to get to the next lesson or next horse to ride, or just be done for the day. I understood. I knew what it was like. So I never pressed to get answers to my questions. I just moved from trainer to trainer to trainer, hoping for enlightenment. I did finally see the light, but it wasn't from an instructor. It was God in His bad outfit tenderly looking into my eyes and taking my elbow to steady me as I departed that train. It was all the love from family and friends that poured in while I was in the hospital. It was love in the form of the Caring Bridge Website where people wrote the most wonderful things. It was in the form of daily visitors to my bedside. It was in the form of dozens of cards, letters, emails and gifts that poured in. It was in the form of Sonja choosing to stay with me in that arena while I vented, and then talking things out. I finally saw the light. The light of *love*.

… so just like Shadow, I didn't think I could go it alone. Actually, I *was* going it alone, but I still wanted help. I just couldn't find the help I needed until that fateful dressage lesson. I needed someone to listen! I needed to know that what I had to say *mattered*. Sonja made me feel like I mattered. I still want support; I still want coaching. But I didn't need someone to hold my hand like I thought I did. I can do it. I'd *been* doing it. I just needed the self-confidence to enjoy it instead of doubting and worrying all the time.

Thank you Abba. Thank you everyone who was so kind to me during *The Great Head Bonk*. Thank you, Sonya.

Chapter Ninety-three

As I FINISHED FEEDING THE horses one morning, I talked affectionately to each one and gave them a carrot. Each horse responded differently. Ticket looked guarded and worried. He was never sure of his place, if I loved him, or if he measured up. Gus was a pretty good boy but I knew not to linger or he would inevitably try to nip me. Memphis was the sweet kind soul he always was. Shadow gave me her modified Dragon Lady scowl, but I know she didn't *really* mean it. Jazz said, "Hrb ba bub ba bubuh!" When you translate that into English that means, "*Yes,* I love you too, but I am BUSY eating here and also I am the guy in charge so I mustn't appear too mushy in front of the others or let my guard down in case there is danger right around the corner!" Gandalf was his beautiful, clear-eyed loving and stately self. Sump was busy licking every last morsel out of his bucket. He did stop for a second to take the offered carrot with a muffled, "Thanks, Mom!"

How much we humans are all the same! Do you see yourself in any of these horses? In all of them? Perhaps you see your husband, your wife, your kids, your boss, your best friend, and on and on ... (like ripples in a pond).

How I loved my horses. Yes, it was a little easier (and *safer)* to love the saintly ones and the ones that returned the affection in obvious ways, but I knew they all loved me back, each and every one. Because I spent so much time with them I knew them intimately. I had come to understand them so much better.

How easy it is to judge when we *mis*understand. How easy it is to take offense. To feel hurt. To become angry. To retaliate somehow.

Time, observance, and communication. Patience. Faith. Hope. Love. This was what saw me through with the horses, with my husband, my kids, and so on and so on. Like throwing a pebble in a pond. In the center of the expanse is The **Rock**.

Everything else flows out from *Him*, w--i--d--e--r and

D
E
E
P
E
R.

Chapter Ninety-four

I'D GOTTEN QUITE AN EDUCATION watching the horses interact ever since I'd brought them back to join the ones already at home. At the farm we rented, they lived about as natural and comfortable as I could make it for them. They had shelter from wind and rain when they needed it, and a covered place to hang out away from the sun and bugs. We rarely shut them in the stalls. If Gus would have left Sump alone, we wouldn't have locked them in at all. We ended up shutting Sump in at night so he would be safe. Gandalf preferred a stall to himself with the door shut as well. It ended up that all the horses except Memphis enjoyed a turn in *The Hilton*; that is what I ended up naming the two cozy stalls Len built in the aisle when we brought everyone home. Ticket and Finny especially liked the Hilton and would have been happy to spend every night in there. Shadow liked it on occasion, but she really preferred being *in* the stall with Jazz. Jazz put up with being in the Hilton every now and then. Gus thought it a curiosity. Memphis did too, at first, but in the end he thought it too confining.

The pecking order in our herd at the time was: Jazz, Finny, Shadow, Memphis, Ticket, Gus, Gandalf and Sump. Jazz was our little horse family's *Man in Charge* and he was pretty good at it. He didn't hurt anybody but his fierce body language and facial expression sent the others packing when he wanted to come in a stall to see if there was anything in there to eat. The other horses respected him and did what he said. He led them out to the pasture and when he thought it was time to go back, he led them all back in, usually at full throttle. The only horses he allowed in the same stall with him were Shadow and Finny, for they were his *women*. The three of them do *not* share a stall. For a while each mare got booted out when he wanted their food, but Finny finally let him have it with her heels. Shadowed followed suit when she was in there with Jazz. He became much more of a gentleman. Usually Finny was in a stall with Jazz and Shadow was by herself, and I saw both mares take a turn with Gus or Memphis at times. But not Ticket. He is probably just a little too effeminate for those mares.

Gandalf *should* have been the herd leader, one would think. He was the tallest and his white coat shined bright in the sun. He had lived a long, accomplished life and was very wise. He was incredibly kind and caring to both people and animals. Yet he chose *not* to be in charge, and would not challenge any of them for a higher place in the pecking order. He slipped beautifully and easily into his role as Sump's caregiver. Jazz respected him, as did Finny and Shadow. Finny adored and looked up to him. The Punk boys liked to intimidate Gandalf, which made me pretty angry; how *dare* they. One of them grabbed him by the withers one day and took off some hair and skin, making him pretty sore. I'm pretty sure one of them was a little too zealous about getting him out of a stall so they could check out the grain buckets.

Sometimes I wished he would stick up for himself a little bit. His personality, age, wear and tear on his joints from all his varied careers had left him pretty fragile. He needed protection from the all the "rowdies" which was pretty much *all* of them, in his opinion, except for Sump. Shadow gave him a small nod of approval, which for her was big! *The Punk Boys* and Ticket let him slip fairly easily into the herd. Jazz did too. If he wasn't so fragile, perhaps he *would* have tried to be the leader. Gandalf was content to let Jazz run the show. He didn't seem to need the status, and maybe he preferred to pass the torch to a younger, more sound individual. They all seemed to recognize that. Sometimes, however, *The Punk Boys* forgot their manners.

Chapter Ninety-five

As I dropped Enya off at work and drove to one of my favorite espresso stands I was thinking about what God is up to these days. Some people think we're in the End Times. Others call it The Shift. Still others call it the Quantum Leap. Lots of folks don't know WHAT is going on, just that it reeks! But something *is* going on, no doubt about it.

Jesus said not to put new wine into old wineskins. If you do that, the new wine causes the old wineskin to burst. Then you lose both the wine *and* the wineskin. When I was a new believer in The Church at Raleigh a long time ago the wineskin parable was discussed. At that time lots of new wine was pouring. Our church was considered radical; some were even worried it was a cult. Many old wineskins burst as the new wine poured in, or puckered up so tightly that none could get in. I thank God I was a fresh new wineskin, as were my brothers and sisters in The Church at Raleigh. Now, *we* are the old wineskins, and the new wine that we received forty or more years ago is now vintage vino. In some vessels it unfortunately soured. In others it aged to perfection.

Now more new wine is coming down the pike and I refuse to be an old wineskin! This new outpouring of the spirit is, well, *newer* than the last one. This one has a whole lot to do with *oneness*. So did the last outpouring, but this one is even bigger. This one is huge. In the sixties in America we were concerned with *our* war, *our* civil rights and the liberation of *our* women. There was the Charismatic movement, and I'm sure it was bigger than America, but we didn't seem to see much past our shorelines. This time we need to look beyond our borders to a much broader vista. There are the same old issues and some new ones taking front and center stage, but the boundaries have expanded to include the whole world. Old wineskins may fuss and sputter about all the new wine, claiming to have a corner on Biblical interpretation. Remember, it's *people* doing the interpreting. H-u-m-a-n-s. I think that is why Jesus said, "Are you listening to me? *Really* listening?" *Matthew 11;15. The Message*

This time, *Oneness* will expand to include many races, many cultures and many religions. It will be a message of Oneness beyond the borders of religion and will expand into many, many areas. People will celebrate and make room in their hearts for our diversity and uniqueness. In the horse world, the world I know best, I think it will be a shift away from English vs., Western styles, show-ring riding vs. field trial type competition, natural vs. traditional horsemanship. It will go on and on through everything, you name it, just like ripples in a pond. At least, I sure hope so. We will have the choice to be old or new wineskins. Those of us who have eyes to see and ears to hear, let's get our lips moving to the Lord, asking for a great harvest of enlightenment. ***Shine a light, Oh Lord!***

On 1/11/11, there were tons of presentations all over the internet about the significance of the day. I was going to plug into a computer telecast to watch a prophetic message given by a man I used to call one of the *"Woo Woos."* That was the name we gave to people who were in to New Age stuff. That was basically anybody who was tuned in to other wavelengths *besides* Christianity. As though Caleb and I and fellow Christians had the corner on the spirituality market! We no longer think that way. Now *that's* new wine for you.

A few days ago I was up very early making a cheesecake for Maeve's 24th birthday. She was coming over in the evening and we were gonna eat pizza and wash it down with Kahlua Chocolate Cheesecake; basically we aimed to pig-out. I opened the refrigerator to grab two eggs, to find there was only one left. I aborted the cake mission until it was time to feed the horses. Maybe one of landlord's hens would telepathically discern (in a very *woo-woo* way) that I needed an egg and lay one for me in my barn hallway. They'd left me eggs before as a thank you for throwing them some of the horses' grain in the mornings. If not, at least little Roosevelt Store would be open by then.

I spent some time on the computer writing and checking email. I sent Caleb a link to a YouTube song I wanted him to hear. It suddenly dawned on my 55-year-old-headbonked brain that I could probably listen to another song I really liked on YouTube! *Duh.* I Googled to see if I could find Chris Sligh's beautiful song *Make Us One.* Wah-la. There it was. The power of that song soon had me burnt to ashes; they mixed with my tears. *Make us one! Make us one! Lord, make us one!* That was the cry of Chris Sligh's heart. That is the cry of my heart, too. It is the cry of Jesus' heart. It is Abba's heart's desire for *all* of us to be one. Starting with the microbes in the soil and expanding ever outward until we are all united as One.

I was overwhelmed in the Spirit. I called my dear friend Makeda Ennishad in North Carolina and left her a message. I probably sounded like a crazy head-bonked lady. Good thing there's a three hour time difference between the East and West Coasts! I went down to the barn and fed the horses, looked for an egg (no egg because my chicken pals were penned up in their coop). I got eggs at Roosevelt Store. I was so joyful I almost hugged the store owner. I came home and anxiously waited for Caleb to have his first sip of coffee as a courtesy before I launched into sharing my experience of the morning with him. I managed to let him swallow *half* a sip.

I never did get to see or hear the *Woo-Woo* guy; I got busy with my day as usual. I'm sure the *woo-woo* guy was interesting. There is so much happening right now that almost daily I get an e-mail invitation to an event of some sort being telecast. Other than that, the rest of the world seems to be oblivious. It seems like business as usual with everyone slogging it out. But what do I know? I'm just a farm girl.

Chapter Ninety-six

WE REGULARLY RECEIVE *FRIENDS OF Fred Hutchinson* bulletins in the mail. Fred Hutchinson Cancer Research Center, where Caleb had his bone marrow transplant 21 years ago. Wow, that seems like eons ago. My head-bonk seems like a long time ago too. Aren't we a pair? Here is a poem that really rang my chimes on one of the pages of the most recent bulletin.

Hope

Begins in the dark,
The stubborn hope that if you just show up
And try to do the right thing,
The dawn will come.
You wait and watch and work:
You don't give up.
                    Anne Lamont

This was my commentary after reading it:

That is it!
That is what we have done.
Sometimes we had great hope;
Sometimes none.

Buying the farm in Granite Falls had become a vast exercise in faith and hope. Years and years ago as new believers, Caleb and I heard lots of lessons on faith. What we didn't realize was that you cannot just acquire faith by hearing a message about it. Even before Caleb and I married, we would hear a great teaching and then set about to manifest faith as we thought we understood it from the message we heard. We didn't understand that the message was one person's experience and we couldn't just copycat it in our own power. We didn't think to sit quietly before him in the morning to see what He had to say about that message for *us*. We just received the information and with all the fervor and energy of truly *young dumb single people* (as our pastor in Maine liked to call them), we set about to act on faith and have it manifested immediately. We were like all the heavy equipment our landlords were so fond of driving and roaring around on the farm! Now after many years of crashes, fender-benders, flat tires and seized-up engines, we have finally learned that it is wise to wait on God, even if you must wait a very, very long time. It is wise to have your *own* intimate relationship with Abba. It is good to "be still and know that He is God." *Psalm 46:10.* It makes no sense at all to "plan your work and work your plan" if they are *your* plans, not His.

This time I HOPE is different. This time I HOPE that all the things I've been hearing are from Abba. This time I have spent lots and lots of time sitting quietly with Him. The idea of getting our own farm came out of those quiet times; so has everything else I've been hearing. No more jumping on a huge tractor or bulldozer that rattles the windows and tears up the ground.

As it turns out we were in for even *bigger* lessons on waiting. We didn't close on February 29th, 2012, as *we* planned. We were currently waiting for the final V.A. approval, so Owen asked Elaine for an extension on the closing date. The loan manager at Key Bank thought the V.A. approval might come in a couple days past the closing date. When Elaine contacted the estate lawyers, they counseled her that since the estate was hugely in debt our offer was not big enough. They advised her to take it off the market in hopes that the housing market would improve, and she agreed. All this happened the evening of the day before we thought we would get the farm. Owen was quite angry and called his lawyer. He advised us to do the same. *Um* ... we didn't know any lawyers and we certainly couldn't afford to pay one. Caleb and I felt like little kids whose wonderfully sweet and huge all-day suckers had been snatched from them by big bullies. Even Caleb's kite faltered in the air a moment; my kite took a nose dive.

That very same week two of my longtime students' wonderful mom passed away. That very same week Hallie became afflicted with glaucoma. My wonderful house call vet that I'd had since we brought Jim home from Equifriends taught me to look for the symptoms, as beagles are prone to it as they age. One morning she looked very slightly uncomfortable and her left eye was tearing. I took her down to the local small animal emergency clinic right away, but by the time we saw a vet Hallie was already blind in her left eye. She got started on medications and we made an appointment for her to be seen at The Animal Eye clinic in Seattle with the same Dr. O'Meara who had cared for Sump when he went blind. I had no idea how we were going to pay for it; the emergency visit was bad enough. I had to put it on my credit card. Thank God I *had* a credit card.

It was a one-two-three sucker punch----and I was down for the count. I slept late. I didn't ride anybody. Thank God I didn't have very many lessons to teach. For three days I was totally worthless. On the fourth day I began to resurrect a little bit. All could do was hold my shredded heart before Abba and cling to him.

Chapter Ninety-seven

I FINALLY RECOVERED ENOUGH TO think about riding, but I only wanted to go on a trail ride, alone, up at Lord's Hill Park. I just wanted to become absorbed in the quiet, calm green of the woods. I just wanted to hide in Abba's big bosom. I always found that easy to do in the woods. I thought about who I should ride.

So what did this girl do?

I chose Gus. *Gus?* Was I nuts? Head Bonked? Crazy? Last time I had taken him up there was when my friend Sissy was out visiting from North Carolina. She had been my bestest trail riding buddy when we were seniors in high school. She had fallen in love with Gandalf when she had come to visit in late winter and was excited to ride the trails on him.

By the time we pulled out of the drive that day with the horses in the trailer in was late afternoon. By the time we got to the park twenty minutes later it was the beginning of what I call "predator time," when carnivores living in the woods and hills start looking for their dinner. I should have known better. Actually I *did* know better. I had thought about it a little bit on the way over.

My lovely horse child Gus reminded me in a very graphic way why you don't ride horses in the woods at dusk. He stood quietly while I got on, which was really good for Gus, and then Sissy, Gandalf, Gus and I headed out of the parking lot. Gus walked a few steps with his ears pricked toward the woods, then he reared sky-high and kept walking. I leaned forward and gave him plenty of rein. Then he put his front feet on the ground and sent his back feet skyward. I was already very forward with no rein contact so it didn't take much to deposit me on the hard gravel parking lot. Thankfully, on my ample booty.

I had a lovely view from the ground looking up at Gandalf, who looked embarrassed for the horse species, and Sissy, who sat sobbing on his back. I got to my feet, caught Gus who hadn't gone far and gave him a whack with my dressage whip. Sissy had jumped off to help and picked the gravel out of my lower back. She was thinking we'd put the horses back in the trailer and head on home, but I said, "Oh no. We are gonna *do* this."

I knew I was headed for a major stove-up. I was *so* mad at Gus. I told Sissy to ride ahead of me and I would walk Gus on foot with my "stick of leadership" in hand. If Gus made one wrong move I was gonna let him have it; I was gonna make him rue the day he was born. Off we went; I made Gus stay two steps behind me like some poor old Chinese woman. We walked three-fourths of the way around the main trail. Gus behaved quite nicely and the walk up and down the hills was good for my back and hips. I mounted Gus from a park bench and rode him the rest of the way back. We even cantered a little up the last hill on the trail.

You would think I would have chosen a different horse for *this* ride, huh? But I had asked my Abba, and Gus was the one I think He recommended. With childlike trust and an aching heart this time instead of an aching backside I loaded up Gus in the *middle* of the day and headed for the park. I had such a lovely, healing, restorative ride. Gus was perfect. I think he knew he needed to be good. I was so thankful for Abba's protection and tender care.

I was very well acquainted with heartbreak and setback over the years, but this time felt different. I was closer to Abba than ever before. I had such a better perspective on death now thanks to my train ride and reading *Conversations With God.* Though my heart was full of grief for that moms' two daughters, I knew she was home and whole. I also knew Abba would take care of Hallie and the glaucoma. I believed God would see Caleb and I through buying a farm, even if it wasn't the one I had my heart set on.

Now we were old married duffers, not "young dumb single people". We had 40 years of training under our belts. I thought we were ready to wear the Harness of the Lord. Caleb and I both felt that we should stand so very still that not even the bells on our harness would tinkle. We did not want to step on our Lord who was underneath the carriage making repairs.

Caleb kept working, and I got back to riding and teaching my handful of students, now even smaller because of those two dear girls losing their mom. We looked half-heartedly at other properties on the internet, but nothing moved us. I really felt like we should stand firm in our belief that we had found THE farm. Lots of well-meaning folks said, "Maybe God will give you something better!" I knew that might be true, but I didn't want it to be. I couldn't imagine what would be a better place. We once again visited the equestrian property in north Lake Stevens because I was still infatuated with it. It had amazing horse facilities but not as much land or housing as the Granite Falls farm. It still needed thousands of dollars of plumbing and electrical repairs. It was still mired down in red tape and available for cash only. The Granite Falls farm had something for me, something for Len and something for the Buddies. It had the potential to fulfill *all* our dreams. I hoped all our dreams were inspired by Abba, and not just our selfish desires.

One of the dreams that I felt came from Abba was planted fifteen years ago when Gwen Johnston took her pony to the Evergreen Classic. I had fallen in love with the Hispanic children I saw with their dads, who were grooming the show horses. Someday I swore I would have a place where those kids could ride. Kids who wanted to ride but their parents couldn't afford it. Somehow I would make it happen. Their lessons would be free, but they would work their little bottoms off like their parents did, like I did, like my kids were doing. I would teach them to *ride like stink*. I would make sure they had good horses to ride. I would make sure they had the right clothes and stuff for a fancy show like the Evergreen Classic. We would go. We would show. We would *win*. No one would know us, but they *would* know they'd had their bottoms kicked thoroughly when the show was over. We would be entirely gracious about it though. We wouldn't act like the spoiled brats I saw at the show.

The name of my farm and program?

Kicking Angels Ranch.

At Woodland Farm after the show, my kids, Meredith, her mom Cayanna and I made up lots of jokes and stories about it. We used a different word starting with an A. One of us, pretending to be a grandma, would ask as her young granddaughter burst through her door, "My darling Susie, what have you been up to today?" Susie would breathlessly reply, "Oh *Grandma!* Today I went to Kicking Donkey's Bottom Ranch!!" Whoever was playing Grandma would contort her face into surprised dismay at her precious granddaughter's potty language. *WHAT* ranch? What kind of place is that?!?" We had great fun playing with that.

I arranged a pilot program through the school guidance counselor at Monroe Middle School, but it flopped. Some of the girls with prior horse experience who participated in the pilot program reported back to their counselor that our horses were ill-mannered and dangerous to handle. I don't know what kind of horses they were acquainted with, but ours were just acting like the young spirited thoroughbreds they were. They were not much different than the girls who were complaining. I was so disappointed. It just wasn't time. But it *is* now.

Chapter Ninety-eight

HALLIE WAS SCHEDULED TO GET a prosthetic eye at the Animal Eye Clinic in the University District with a Dr. Sanderson because I couldn't get her scheduled with Dr. O'Meara. But this was so very interesting: I got the time for the surgery wrong and even though I blew it, I was able to get her in with Dr. O'Meara who just happened to have an opening in his schedule. I was able to talk to Dr. O'Meara about Sump and my guilty feelings about him going blind. Dr. O'Meara reassured me I was not at fault at all, at all. That lifted a huge burden from my shoulders.

A month later we went back for a follow up visit. Hallie had gotten a little scratch on the lens of her prosthetic left eye, but other than that things were great. I told Dr. O'Meara how free I felt after he released me from guilt over Sump. He crossed himself like a good Catholic boy and laughed. Then he asked, "What are you guys up to these days?" I told him all about our farm trials and tribulations. He said, "Sounds like you might need an estate lawyer. My brother Raymond is a good one. He's expensive but he won't rip you off." He gave me his brother's phone number. I thanked him, made another follow-up appointment for Hallie my little Amazon Princess Beagle and I headed home.

I talked to Caleb about Raymond O'Meara. He had me call him, and Owen called *his* estate lawyer. Raymond O'Meara was quite accessible and very gracious; another good Irish Catholic boy like his brother Killian. He talked to me quite a while and gave me lots of advice. I passed it on to Caleb who passed it on to Owen and my In-laws. Before long it seemed clear that we should hire Raymond. We didn't know how we were going to pay him, but by that time it seemed like God was clearly managing our finances. My students had dwindled to almost nothing, but we always had money when we needed it. I made sure to give some away, too, as an exercise in faith.

Caleb drove down to Seattle to meet Raymond and take him some paperwork. Raymond and Owen's lawyer started working together as a team. An April 6th court date was set to decide if we could purchase the farm. That would make a very nice birthday present for Caleb, who was turning 62 three days before the hearing. The two brothers who owned all the Arby's stores Caleb supervised asked him to *please* retire on April 15th. so they could save money in the recession. Caleb had planned on working for two more years so that we would have money to pay the mortgage and build up the organic gardening and livestock production plan Caleb had in mind. Now we didn't know how we were going to pay for either, but I hoped *Abba* did.

Chapter Ninety-nine

ONE LATE AFTERNOON I LOADED Gus and Memphis in the trailer to take them to work up at Mission. I was pretty tired and could have bailed in favor of a nap, but they needed exercise and schooling, so I willed myself to go. I love fooling with the horses so much and I love riding, but it's so tiring. I am not a spring chicken. I sure hate to admit it.

The sweet stable girl I knew at Trinity was just finishing up with evening chores and soon said goodbye. The Punk Boys and I had the place to ourselves. John and Lisa's trailer was gone. The weather was lousy and threatening to get worse, so no boarders were out visiting their horses.

I tacked up Gus in a stall. He was cheeky and ornery, which meant I was in for a challenging ride. Usually I longe him first, but because the arena was empty, I chose to work him at liberty. He casually checked things out while I brought in poles and standards to make a vertical jump with placing rails that was helping improve his canter departs. He hated the pressure of my seat and leg aids when I asked for canter and constantly resisted all my aids. Jumping made it easier for him *and* me. He's gotten to the point where he broke into a canter a few strides before the jump. He was a smart cookie but a stubborn and willful cookie, too! I would give him a bit of carrot as soon as he did the smallest thing that I asked. After that he worked hard for those tasty little bits of orange crunch.

After I set up the little vertical I asked him to go forward away from me, which for him meant a sauntering walk, then a 180 back to me to see if I had any *more* carrots, or if I would play horse games with him. Basically his horse games are tests to see if he can dominate me by nipping, rearing, or pushing into my space so I back off. I have to be very assertive to get *him* to back off. Usually I have to thunk him hard with a whip handle or whatever is handy. This time it was the lash of my longe whip.

Soon he was lazily trotting and cantering around the arena, occasionally choosing to jump the little vertical on his own. Soon he would stop and face me, but he wouldn't join up, even if I made my body language very inviting. I would slowly count to ten and send him off again.

Gus enjoyed this game for awhile, then he started to tire. I knew that *he* knew he should come to me, but he surely didn't want to, for that meant I had won, and *Gus* wanted to win! After all, I am just a frail little human, and a *girl* human at that. I started to send him off more vigorously and more frequently, then at sustained speeds faster than he wanted to go. It didn't take long before he stopped and came right up and touched his muzzle to my outstretched hand. "I'm *toast*, Mom! Okay, you win, at least *this* time!"

Gus was very polite when I brought him to the mounting block and got on. He was superb under saddle that evening. I trotted a little, jumped a few times, got great canter departs with several strides added, and then we were done. He got lots of *Good Boys!* and carrots from me as I untacked and brushed him. Then I brought out Memphis.

I rarely have to longe Memphis. I just usually climb right on his back. He may be ¾ Thoroughbred, but the ¼ Percheron has done wonders for his mind. He is gentle, loving, and kind. Sometimes he is not sure of himself or of his environment, but he aims to please. When I have to use my whip to make him more responsive, it hurts his feelings. Being young, he doesn't understand why he should get a little spank when *he* thinks he is giving me his best. But the draft blood makes him just a tad insensitive; if he was all Tb, he would have launched me to the rafters by now. The Percheron blood also makes him sturdy and tough. That's hybrid vigor!

Memphis wasn't at all sure why he was fully tacked, yet loose in the arena. He wanted to join up right away. His feelings were crushed when

I sent him away. He simply did not get it. After a few seconds he would stop at a polite distance, ears pricked, and stare at me, trying to puzzle it out. I would invite him in, but he wouldn't budge. I would count to ten and send him off, adding insult to injury. We did this quite a few times, with the same results. I went to different spots in the arena. I got closer. I was very inviting. No dice, even though I could tell he really wanted to join up.

Finally things got the best of Memphis. He threw a hissy fit. He galloped off, bucking and kicking. He nailed the round pen bars with his heels a few times which made them ring. It took a couple more stops and send offs, then me walking a semi-circle around Memphis before he finally gave in and joined up. I rewarded him profusely. Then I swung up and we had a short but lovely ride.

I jumped off and pulled off his tack. I put it on the floor in the hall, got Memphis' cooler, and turned out Gus with Memphis. "You guys can visit and play while I put the jump stuff away," I told the boys. Soon Gus was playing the same nipping and pushing games he tries to play with me. Memphis responded with somewhat bored indulgence. After all he's Gus's pal and a big fellow to boot. What Gus did to Memphis would have injured me, but it barely made an impression on Memphis. Plus Memphis can bite and push back!

Soon Gus came to see what I was doing, which was stacking the poles by the sliding door before I opened it to take the poles outside. As soon as he saw I was defenseless, he gleefully started in on me. I could swear he wore a jeering look on that impish, childlike face of his. My feeble attempts to back him off with a wave of my hand fed the flames of his desire for dominance. I finally had to yell, scream, and attack him furiously with claws outstretched to get him to stop, which he finally did.

I explained things to Gus; "Bud. *Look* at me. I'm scrawny compared to you. I'm weak! I'm a different species altogether! I'm *human*. I'm a *girl*. I can't play those Punk Boy games with you." Gus seemed to understand, and he returned to his Punk Boy *horse* bud, Memphis, who was happy to entertain Gus. I finished putting the jumps away and loaded up the boys for home. I was as happy as can be and full of wonder at what I had learned.

Longeing is extremely useful, especially when a round pen or an empty arena isn't handy, but the work at liberty really opened my eyes. When you longe a horse, he's under your control (more or less) especially if he's in the tack and side reins, or a bitting rig. The only way he can assert his will is to throw a big enough hissy fit to yank the line out of your hands and take off (Gus has done that *many* times). At liberty, a horse can chose or refuse to join up. He can run away bucking and squealing as much as he likes, as long as he likes. Or he can choose to connect with his human partner. Choosing the latter is an act of submission. It's a choice. It's exercising *free will*.

Gus and Memphis were very different personalities, yet both struggled with joining up with me. Gus was somewhat of a juvenile delinquent. He just wanted to have fun, often at others' expense. Since he was very low on our herd pecking order, he was always trying to climb the social ladder. That is why he picked on Sump, the old blind guy. That's why he picked on me, or any other human because we are comparatively flimsy. But Gus was not mean at all, at all. He was actually very sweet and loving if you could be with him at the right moment, before he grabbed your sleeve in his teeth, or your arm, if you weren't careful. Gus was not selective about what went in his mouth, but he *was* learning to be more polite.

Memphis on the other hand is second in command behind Jazz. I guess that makes him Vice-Jazz! He challenged Jazz unsuccessfully once. Memphis reared at Jazz. Jazz reared back. They locked front legs, then Jazz very slowly and carefully walked forward on his hind legs until Memphis lost his balance and fell over. And that was that.

Even though Memphis is a *Big Love*, he has on rare occasion gotten assertive with me in the form of striking out at the air with a front hoof. But he never nips or kicks. I could sure tell that he sure didn't want to submit his free horsey will to a dumb *girl* last night. What if *Jazz* found out? Would it be a sign of weakness? Would I hurt him when we joined up? After all, I had sent him away for no good reason, and I had a really big whip. When he finally did come to me, I assured him all was well. For both punk Boys, it was a lesson in giving up self, and learning to trust.

When I was taking Jazz to the Parelli trainer a few years ago, she never really did get to the bottom of him. He thought he was *Number One.* Even though he's a very polite horse to handle, that's where he drew the line. To join up meant *giving* up. Giving up his Numero Uno position. He just couldn't do it.

As soon as we got our own farm and I had my very own indoor arena, it was going to be Jazz's turn for liberty work. I wondered how long it would take him to join up. It wasn't long, but it was in Jazz's own little Appaloosa way.

Chapter One Hundred

I TOOK ONE OF MY awesome students on a trail ride up on Lord's Hill Park. Nellie rode Shadow and I rode Jazz. Nellie was a great little rider and loved to ride most of the horses, but needed a *Steady Eddie,* or in this case *Steady Edie,* on the trail. Gandalf was side-lined with a bad hoof abscess, so I thought Shadow would be best, especially along with Jazz.

As we rode along the main loop I asked Nellie if she would like to try a different trail. She had been on the most popular trail a couple of times, and I had been riding it a lot lately. Nellie said yes, she was game for an adventure so we took a right turn off the main trail. I *thought* I knew where we were going. We rode that trail for a few minutes then went left on a different path. It looked well traveled and we passed several hikers with dogs and kids. We didn't see any *No Horses signs* as were posted at many intersections in the park.

The trail got steeper, narrower and rocky. Pretty soon it became doubtful altogether. We dismounted. It sort of looked like we could lead the horses to the top of the short ascent to the top of a hill. Turning around would be very difficult so I decided to keep going. Nellie squeaked as Shadow stepped on her foot. Before anything worse happened I told Nellie to put one rein behind a stirrup and let Shadow go ahead. I knew she would follow Jazz. I said a prayer that Jazz would not trample me or lose his cool. Two days earlier he had knocked me flat in the muck while shoving through a paddock gate that I had opened to let Gus and Memphis in after taking them out of the trailer. I don't know why Jazz did that, but he then proceeded to go flying off down to the cow's field. Shadow started to push past me to follow Jazz but thought better of it. Soon Jazz came roaring back and let me catch him. Wet and muddy, I yelled at Jazz and disciplined him with some natural horsemanship maneuvers. His behavior had been so unexpectedly random, but he does that sometimes. Jazz seemed genuinely repentant. Now on the trail was his chance to redeem himself.

Jazz was a perfect gentleman on the way up. Shadow came close on his heels, followed by Nellie. When we got to the top of the hill, there was a breathtaking view of the Snohomish River valley below. We stopped to admire it, decided it was well worth the effort, then set about finding an easier way down.

There wasn't one. We got a little ways down a trail on the other side of the vista, but soon it became impassable for a horse. I had to leave Jazz and get Shadow turned around. Jazz stood quietly by himself. By this time Nellie was really scared and I don't blame her. Shadow had to turn around on a steep, slippery rock surface. It was quite hard, but she was a surefooted superstar. I handed her to Nellie and went back for Jazz. As I turned him around his hindquarters slipped off the trail and he had to scramble hard to regain his footing. I held tight to his reins and prayed. Even though Jazz went to his knees and lost control of his hindquarters twice, he stayed calm and out of my way. We made it back to the top and decided to go back down the way we came up. Poor Nellie! It was not exactly a fun ride.

I led the way with Jazz. It was hard enough to walk down yourself, much less with a horse, so I let Nellie send Shadow along without her. Shadow stayed right behind Jazz. If he had made one wrong move I would have tripped, fallen and been stepped on by both horses. I asked Abba for help with my balance and boldly stepped down the slope, grabbing tree trunks for support as went along to the bottom. Jazz was perfect. So was Shadow. Nellie was brave, or at least she faked it superbly.

We finally got to the bottom of the hill. All four of us were sweating and breathing hard. We got a little more exercise than we planned that day. I gave Nellie a leg-up on Shadow, then we walked back to the main trail where I found a park bench to use as a mounting block. We had a very calm and uneventful ride around the main loop back to the trailers. I joked with Nellie that she would probably decline all offers for future trail rides.

When we got the horses home we thoroughly checked them out. Shadow was fine; Jazz had three tiny scrapes on his legs. I cleaned them thoroughly and sprayed them with an antiseptic. I told Nellie it was a blessing indeed that we had chosen the two sturdy, sure-footed Appaloosas for our ride that day. They had lived up to their breeding and heritage.

Before Nellie's Dad arrived to pick her up, this is what I told her: "Here is the lesson of your *lesson* today: whenever you are in a hairy, scary situation, you have two choices: get your *FREAK* on, or stay calm and visualize a happy outcome. Which one do you think would serve you best?" Nellie said that was a "no-brainer." I hope that lesson stays with her all her life. I might edit my favorite C.S. Lewis plaque to read: "No one can teach *life skills* better than a horse."

I needed to take my own advice, too, except maybe it is Shadow's and Jazz's advice. Jazz definitely showed his true colors that day and redeemed himself. I fell in love with him all over again.

Chapter One Hundred and One

TOMORROW A COURT COMMISSIONER WOULD decide whether or not we could close on the Granite Falls estate. Our offer was just enough to pay off the estate's debts, pay the estate lawyers and give Elaine a small sum of money as the executrix. Our lawyer's take is: "Go ahead and let the Greens buy it. If they don't, it will end up taking so long to get things wrapped up it will cost even *more* money and NO ONE will get paid in a timely way." We wondered if the estate lawyers think that if they can just get the commissioner to let the estate go to probate court, at least they and Elaine will get paid. If it does, Owen will counter-sue for his commission, and we will most likely sue for our expenses incurred to date. All of the sudden this simple farm girl is playing with the big boys; at least the medium-sized boys in Everett and Bellingham, Washington.

It certainly had been a couple of years of rigorous learning. When life became routine at the last barn I worked out of I used to tell the Lord I was bored and I missed learning new things. Oh *Boy.* I bet that made Him rub His holy hands together in delight!

We usually paid our rent on the 5th of each month. At first Caleb and I were in complete agreement that we should pay rent and give notice on the 5th, even though court was not until the next day. Then we took turns vacillating. He or I would talk to someone who thought it was a stupid or dangerous idea. We would think it over and change our minds a little. Then we would collide over it. It was pretty funny, really, because when Len wavered *I* gave him a hard time, and vice-versa. Then something happened that put us back on the same page.

Gandalf had been lame for about three weeks. His wonderful shoer Stacy accidentally hot-nailed Gandalf which meant driving a horseshoe nail too close to the sensitive part of his hoof wall. It was really hard *not* to hot-nail Gandalf, whose hoof wall layers are incredibly thin. I certainly didn't hold it against her.

It was possible for an abscess to brew from that, so we looked out for it. Gandalf looked great for a couple of weeks and then became very lame. His hoof did not test positive for an abscess, so we thought his stifle (a horse's kneecap) was bothering him. I took him up to my vet's clinic and she injected it with an anti-inflammatory. It didn't help as much as we hoped, but we thought being that sore had cause him to go lame all over from compensation. I nursed him and hand walked him as best as I could until it was time for him to be re-shod. I was very sad that he was lame. I was keeping a tiny flame of hope going that it would indeed turn out to be an abscess, because one of those is better than an unresponsive stifle or whatever else was bothering him.

When I took him up to Trinity for new shoes, Stacy did indeed uncover an abscess about the size of Lake Ontario. I was thrilled! She cleaned it all up. Doing so required her to take off a lot of Gandalf's sole. That left the bottom of his foot very tender and sensitive. She also decided to remove the pads on his other three feet so they could air out and be stronger in the long run. That meant no riding or turn out for Gandalf till the pads were put back on in eight weeks. I really had to protect those fragile thoroughbred tootsies in the meantime.

Stacy gave me some special pads to put on Gandalf so I could walk him around the farm, as I couldn't stand the thought of him being confined for eight weeks. I also fixed up the end of the barn hall so he and Sump could go in and out of their stalls into the sunshine at will. It was hard grooved concrete, but safe and *not* muddy.

One really cold and rainy week I briefly longed four horses in two separate out of the way places on the farm. I was working hard on finishing this book and the weather was gnarly. I didn't feel like hitching up the trailer and taking them to Trinity. They tore the grass up a little where I longed and I wondered if I would hear about it. I did. I also taught a new student on Shadow at the farm, so she could have a ride outside of an arena and I could save money. I heard about that too, even though all we did was walk around on the driveways, over by the pond and up the fence line. I didn't longe the horses anymore, but I needed to walk Sump and Gandalf. I mostly kept them on the concrete or the gravel driveways. I let them graze a tiny bit, but I made sure they didn't tear up the grassy area with their hooves.

I was told to cease all horse walking outside of the pasture. I kept asking "*Why?*" Finally it came out that our landlord's son just didn't like horses and just didn't like to see them walked around the property. A few more things were rather heatedly discussed. When the conversation was over I *knew* we had to give notice. Caleb came home a short time later and I told him what happened. It definitely put us back on the same page.

The next morning we gave a check and a letter giving notice to our landlord. He said, "Oh! A present for me!" I said, "Y-e-e-e-a-h, well, *kinda*". They were probably glad to see us go. We didn't have anywhere else to live, but it was spring and lush grass was growing everywhere. Our horses would have enough to eat. The rest of us could beg like our homeless friends, and we could catch fish in the many rivers around here.

We had *both* jumped off the cliff just like Much Afraid in *Hind's Feet on High* places. It won't be the first time, but it's definitely the highest cliff. So, as I told Nellie on that scary trail ride, I will *not* put my "FREAK" on. I will envision a very positive outcome. Caleb and I are tough and agile Appaloosas; we have the best Master and the finest training. We were trained on the Trail of Tears. It is also a very good thing Abba is at the bottom of the cliff; vast, soft and squishy, just like Mamma in *The Shack* by William Paul Young.

I told Caleb that every book we'd ever read, every movie we'd ever seen, every song we'd ever sung, every message we ever heard preached has prepared us for this time. For *tomorrow*. Caleb said, "Good! Then we're ready." "Yes, we *are* ready." I replied, as I dissolved into a puddle of Magical Mystery Tour bubble and squeaking.

We *were* ready. *People get ready* ...

Chapter One Hundred and Two

COURT DAY. APRIL 6TH, 2012. Good Friday. I did not think it a coincidence that it was Easter weekend. I got up at 3:30 and ran straight to Abba's arms. I even skipped making coffee. I didn't run because I was anxious or afraid of the outcome of today. I was *excited!*

As I sat quietly with Abba I imagined the courtroom proceedings. I imagined the judge with long gray hair, a pleated muslin gown and Captain Kangaroo bangs. I saw the glory of God fill that courtroom. I saw his Kingdom come there. That's what I prayed for. I knew that no matter the outcome, we'd be safe in Abba's arms. I just wanted His perfect will to be done.

It was wonderful to be so free.

This has been a special song for me for many years:

Simple Gifts

Tis a gift to be simple,
Tis to be free,
Tis a gift to come down where we ought to be.

And when we find ourselves in a place just right,
It will be in the valley of love and delight.

When true simplicity is gained,
Then to bow and to bend we shan't be ashamed,
To turn, turn will be our delight,

Till by turning, turning, we come round right.
Old Shaker Hymn

When I went down to feed the horses I told them what was going to take place that morning. I got dressed in my fabulous new "go to court" duds; the ones Caleb put on his credit card because our checking account was currently wiped out. All I owned was riding breeches and worn out jeans. My middle had slid south and thickened since the *change* occurred along with my head bonk, so none of my nice pants fit. I had one summer dress, not a single blouse, and certainly not a jacket. That is, except for my beautiful new dressage jacket that I hoped to wear at shows before too long. I put on a little make up, styling gel in my hair and ran a brush through it a few times. I wiped the barn dirt off my clogs. I was ready.

We met up with Evie, Rafe, Owen, and Owen's lawyer in the courthouse. We couldn't find our lawyer for the longest time, but that's because he had been waiting in another area for us. I had drunk my usual 20 oz. extra hot dilettante mocha which was good for three potty stops. After the last trip it was time to go in to the courtroom. As I sat down beside Caleb he whispered that Elaine was sitting right behind me. I really wanted to turn around to say, "Nice to meet you, finally!" but I was too shy. I sat still, breathed deeply, and repeated to Abba in my mind, "*Thy kingdom come. Thy will be done,*" all the while tightly squeezing Len's hand. We were One; Caleb, Abba, and me. That alone was an Easter Weekend miracle.

The court commissioner came in. Pleated gown, yes, but it was dark blue. Captain Kangaroo bangs, yes. Well … it was a stretch. But hmmm … short brown hair … and a *woman.*

God does enjoy changing characters.

We all stood. We all sat. Our lawyer, Owen's lawyer, the estate lawyer and the hospice company's lawyer went up to the bench. The commissioner heard our motion. It didn't take long for her to make a decision. "Let the sale close." And that was that.

All systems go! I remembered the train with all the green lights. I bubbled and squeaked a little in a *most* dignified manner. We turned to leave the room and I caught Elaine out of the corner of my eye. She looked devastated. Our eyes did not make contact. She looked *angry*.

Caleb and I waited in the hall outside the courtroom with Evie and Rafe for Owen and the lawyers to join us. We shook hands all around, but I hugged Owen. In a little bit we said goodbye to our lawyers and headed down to Chicago Title to sign the papers on our new farm.

Elaine was there, as she had to sign closing papers as well. We let her go first, as our deal would take a lot longer. When she was done, Elaine left the room, stomped past us and snarled, "I hope Owen has a quadruple cheeseburger for lunch and chokes on it!" "Wow, that's not very nice!" I blurted. I don't know if she heard me as she hustled out the doors. I was hoping to give her a hug. Someday maybe I will hug *all* the people I have ever hurt, or have hurt me, and it will flow outward like ripples on a pond. Thinking back as I have written this book, the people who caused me the greatest pain have also given me the greatest gifts.

Thank you all, for *both*.

After we put our *John Henry's* on everything all of us went back to Snohomish for lunch. Maeve joined us there. Sissy had given Caleb a *Collector's Choice* restaurant gift certificate for his birthday. I sent a text to Sissy early that morning, saying that we would be going there after court to either celebrate our victory or drown our sorrows. We *celebrated*, all right.

Free at last!
Free at last!
THANK GOD ALMIGHTY,
WE'RE FREE AT LAST! *Martin Luther King*

In Conclusion

ON EASTER SUNDAY I EMAILED, sent texts, and called everyone I could think of that would appreciate our good news. Maybe I should have sent smoke signals too, in case modern technology failed as it so often does. We got an automated response from one of our old Church at Raleigh friends saying, *"May you realize the power of His resurrection in your own personal way.* I guess so!

It's been four years since the Lord resurrected me from The Great Head Bonk. I was doing everything I've always done, only … *better*. I was happy. I was joyful. I was at peace. I was becoming *One* with my horses, my husband, my family, and my friends. Certainly with my Creator; the author and finisher of my faith. My feet were no longer stuck in concrete blocks. One quiet morning with Abba, he let me see how I've returned to the vibrant little girl, still glowing with the sunrise at dawn, that I was so very long ago. Full of wonder. Full of hope. Full of curiosity. Full of joy. There's been 50 years of trudging into the West, feeling the glory of heaven fade as life's struggles bore down on me and wore me out.

> *Our birth is but a sleep and a forgetting,*
> *Our life's Star*
> *Has elsewhere it's setting, and cometh from afar.*
> *Not in utter nakedness, and not in entire forgetfulness we come,*
> *From God, who is our home.*
>
> *Heaven lies about us in our infancy!*

Shades of the prison house began to close
Upon the growing Boy,
But he beholds the light and whence it flows,
He sees it in his joy.

The Youth, who daily from the east must travel,
Still is Nature's Priest.
And by the vision splendid
Is on his way attended.

At length, the Man perceives it die away,
And fade into the light of common day.
by *William Wordsworth*

Remember that I became *Chatty Cathy* a few days after I woke up out of the coma?" I talked to whoever would listen. I told my train story. I talked gibberish. I talked trash. I talked about what I felt God was showing me about the patients and the hospital staff. I talked and I talked and talked. Remember, I used to *walk and walk,* and there I was, non-ambulatory in Intensive Care. I guess that energy had to come out in a different form.

I've had a lot to say for as long as I can remember, but in high school I learned there wasn't much point in talking. There was so much competition between groups of girls to even be *heard.* Most girls were a lot more interested in talking than listening, so I learned to keep my mouth shut and my ears open. Not a bad thing, really; my animals communicate quite well without speaking a word of English. Of course, you have to take the time to listen to them with your eyes and your heart. I remained a watcher and a listener the rest of my life. Watching good riders ride and good trainers train were the best riding lessons I ever had. Watching God's children move and act in love were the best *love* lessons I ever had.

That dressage lesson with Sonja was pivotal when I told all those competing voices in my head to SHUT UP!!!

It must be time to say *my* piece.

That greatest thing of all is that I've learned to be still and wait for Abba to say *His* piece. Sometimes He can be *Chatty Cathy* too! He can talk to me as much as He wants.

Printed in the United States
By Bookmasters